ACCIDENTAL GRAVITY

T0345074

# Accidental
# GRAVITY

*Residents, Travelers, and the Landscape of Memory*

Bernard Quetchenbach

Oregon State University Press     Corvallis

Library of Congress Cataloging-in-Publication Data

Names: Quetchenbach, Bernard W., 1955- author.
Title: Accidental gravity : residents, travelers, and the landscape of memory / Bernard Quetchenbach.
Description: Corvallis : Oregon State University Press, 2017. | Includes bibliographical references.
Identifiers: LCCN 2016056185 (print) | LCCN 2017003351 (ebook) | ISBN 9780870718878 (paperback) | ISBN 9780870718885
Subjects: | BISAC: LITERARY COLLECTIONS / Essays. | BIOGRAPHY & AUTOBIOGRAPHY / Personal Memoirs. | NATURE / Essays.
Classification: LCC PS3617.U49 A6 2017 (print) | LCC PS3617.U49 (ebook) | DDC 814/.6—dc23
LC record available at https://lccn.loc.gov/2016056185

⊗ This paper meets the requirements of ANSI/NISO Z39.48-1992 (Permanence of Paper).

© 2017 Bernard Quetchenbach
All rights reserved.
First published in 2017 by Oregon State University Press
Printed in the United States of America

Oregon State University Press
121 The Valley Library
Corvallis OR 97331-4501
541-737-3166 • fax 541-737-3170
www.osupress.oregonstate.edu

*For my parents, Harold B. Quetchenbach and Norma A. Predmore Quetchenbach, and for Finn, whom they would have loved to meet.*

# Contents

## Acknowledgments

Grateful acknowledgments are made to the following publications: *Ascent* ("Canadas," "Thing in the Woods," "Travelers," "The Woods are Burning"); *EarthLines Review* ("A Good Bear"); *ISLE* ("Confluence"); *Isotope* ("Summertime"); *The Montreal Review* ("You Can't Always Want What You Want," "In Wonderland," "Red Summer"); *Newport Review* ("Ferry Crossing"); *Organization and Environment* ("Peregrines"); *Orion* online ("Billings, Montana"); *Stone's Throw* ("Invaders"); *Wild Thoughts* ("Black-Throated Blue"). "Canadas" is included in *Trash Animals: How We Live with Nature's Filthy, Feral, Invasive, and Unwanted Species*, edited by Kelsi Nagy and Phillip Johnson, published by the University of Minnesota Press. The original poems quoted in "Canadas" are from *In the Distance*, a chapbook from MAMMOTH press. I would also like to express my gratitude to Cara Chamberlain, who read every word of the manuscript—including thousands that are no longer there—multiple times, for her patience and support; to Tom Quetchenbach, for being along for so much of this journey; to Burt Bradley, Randall Gloege, Tami Haaland, Tom Leskiw, Patrick Lowery, W. Scott Olsen, Sydney Landon Plum, and Thomas Scarsella, who offered conversation and advice on individual essays, publication, and, in a couple of cases, birds; to Scott McMillion and the Yellowstone Association Institute; to the 2014 Jackson Hole Writing Festival faculty, especially Mark Hummel, Julene Bair, and Jon Mooallem; and to the editors and readers at Oregon State University Press.

## Introduction: The Music of Circumstance

I grew up surrounded by familiar neighborhood children and new tract homes in Greece, New York, a working-class suburb of Rochester. Enrolling in a Catholic high school brought me for the first time, excepting cousins, into regular contact with peers from other bedroom towns, even from the city itself. For a kid who lived close enough to walk to school, it was downright cosmopolitan. After classes ended, I sometimes lingered for a while, hanging out with companions who, delayed by team or drama practice, student newspaper meetings, or maybe detention, were waiting for the irregular arrival of the "late bus" that would take them to far-flung destinations. Eventually, I'd saunter home.

One of the usual bus-stop loiterers was Ann. I think she might have been in the orchestra. She was a senior when I was in tenth grade; mingling with upperclassmen was another kind of after-school cosmopolitanism. I knew her well enough to be startled when she sent my parents an invitation to her graduation. It turned out that she was none other than "Little Ann"—so called to distinguish her from Big Anne, my already established older sister—whom my parents had fostered a decade earlier. The next day, the school year's last, I walked up to the bus stop, pointed a finger in her direction and proclaimed, "You used to be my sister!" She smiled noncommittally, said something like "Yeah, I guess I was," boarded her bus, and was gone. I never saw her again.

Midcentury American suburbia was constructed as a refuge for a generation drained of its taste for surprises by the Depression and World War II. Houses and yards were not quite interchangeable, but they aspired to an ideal of safe homogeneity. When my former sister reappeared, and when it turned out that she was someone I had known without knowing who she was, I awoke to a world far stranger than I had thought, where unpredictable but resonant coincidence was inherent in the very way of things.

I knew, of course, that the larger patterns encompassing our neighborhood were guided by planetary and seasonal departures and returns, the ordinary pulses of robins and falling leaves. But nature, too, was given to unexpected portents—the deer momentarily stymied by a neighbor's fence, the screech owl peering from a garage corner. Like my own personal surprises, these were somehow allowed by, or incorporated into, the rhythms that animate all life. Routine balanced against chance, everyday reality punctuated by miracle.

Even then, there were darker, more inexorable, relentlessly linear processes underway. When the vacant lot across the street, "the weeds," where my friends and I played "guns"—no euphemisms for us—succumbed to new houses, I knew that this untamed pocket, along with its pheasants, was never to return. New construction was finding its way even into larger childhood wildernesses: the aptly named Toadland, the daredevil dirt-bike hollows of Hidden Valley.

Those processes and their consequences loom over every Toadland, every Hidden Valley, today. Sometimes it seems as if my whole life has been a gradual accretion of things that we can't have anymore. Some, like youth, are temporary by definition. Other losses occur in what passes for the general order: A *For Sale* sign appears on a best friend's lawn, the landmark tree is cut down to widen a road. "Life," says Arthur Miller's Linda Loman, "is a casting off. It's always that way." But then there are the victims of a peculiar less-is-more logic of our time. I grew up with new parks, art and music classes at school, manned space exploration, safely maintained bridges, a cultural panoply which, we're told, we can no longer afford. Sometimes it seems as though we can no longer afford even to like each other very much. I don't mean to ennoble my childhood beyond what it can bear. Greece was beset by unattractive sprawl and infused with a paranoid mania for conformity; almost all our neighbors, even exotic newcomers drawn by Kodak jobs from Pennsylvania or Michigan, were white. No surprises. Some things, then, are best cast off.

At odds with the underlying rhythms of the planet, the postwar experiment in life control was ultimately doomed to fail. Trees buckled sidewalks, messy Canada geese and garden-chomping deer ranged out from borrow pits and subdivision seams. The new shopping plaza, greeted as a virtual wonder of the world, was soon overshadowed by a bigger mall in some newer neighborhood. Mobility itself, that siren of the New World, played its hand: you could lead the kids to the cul-de-sac, but you couldn't make them stay, especially with no Hidden Valley where they could do things their parents disapproved of.

My own life has spun me to the interior West, some eighteen hundred miles from my hometown; like me, my son has found himself far from his parents, landing somewhere we passed along the way, where, in fact, he happened to be born. That cosmic irony is something you can't, you shouldn't, fight, a necessary trickster component to the natural rhythms of life on Earth and the cultural cadences that shape so much of our everyday experience. Taken together, those rhythms and their bolt-out-of-the-blue counterpoints form the basis for both understanding and awe.

A hypothesis, then: the interplay between routine and accident in our own individual experience reflects a parallel dynamic in the big picture, in our nature and the nature that surrounds us. If I have any essential spiritual belief, that sort of correspondence must be at the heart of it. When we lose sight of those larger patterns, we surrender our lives either to a going-through-the-motions Mr. Jones conventionality or, alternatively, to a desolate grasping at the straws of religious, sociopolitical, or technological fundamentalism. Or maybe to a forlorn cynicism.

A central concern of this book is the integrity of touchstone "Earth navel" places on an unraveling planet. Lake Ontario and Yellowstone are the twin natural centers of my universe, the ground on which I construct what I think and how I feel about my life, and the orienting lodestones of sections I and II, respectively, of *Accidental Gravity*. They are where my own rhythms and those larger ones meet. I don't know how I would understand anything without them. The great lake and the great park are where I best remember who I am.

The intersection of place and memory: a nexus where suburb and wilderness, routine and miracle, individual life and the big picture, merge. It is, as might be guessed, an unwieldy junction, always under construction. You make your way past obstacles—an ambulance, a deer in the road, a rockslide. Waiting at a one-lane bridge, you might or might not recognize in the car behind you someone you thought you'd never see again. And what is that almost-familiar sound you've been hearing? A nightbird? A car stereo? No, it has the unexpected shifts, the occasional missed notes, the open possibilities of a live performance. You're not sure, but you think the source could be the oldest, most important street band in the world, a Pythagorean jazz combo, and each of us, human and nonhuman alike, is in it. What we play is the music of circumstance, a ragged, delicate hymn, the soulsong of our shared and lonely lives.

I

## Peregrines

*A sudden opening of landscape, atmosphere, circumstance. What it must be like to encounter a ghost. But that's not right. Not otherworldly or ethereal, but solid, pushing air out of the way like water stripped of resistance. A moving center, coasting along a vertical plane with a wild echoing shout, then rising effortlessly until just a speck, not even a speck, in the wide sky.*

～

The peregrine falcon "has long been considered the embodiment of speed and power," notes bird guide author and artist David Allen Sibley. But it was the bird's wide-ranging travels that gave it its name. Peregrines are cosmopolitan in distribution and generalist in habitat. I've encountered them in haunts as diverse as the arid sandstone cliffs of Utah's Fin Canyon and the lush grasslands of Yellowstone's Hayden Valley, where I watched a falcon playfully half-stooping at swallows one summer evening. Peregrines often follow seacoasts, and I've met them along the Atlantic on Maine's Mount Desert Island, the Pacific in Northern California, and the Gulf of Mexico in Florida.

～

1999. I am in Boston's Logan International Airport. During the four years that I've lived in Maine, I've been through Boston many times—several times each year—but only here in and around the Logan concourses, niched between city and sea. The view from an airplane window is my only experience of landmarks like the Old North Church. Usually, though, the commuter from the Northern Maine Regional Airport in Presque Isle comes in low over the harbor, finding the airport, seemingly, at the last possible moment. I can imagine a peregrine, blessed with much better vision than my own, following the same route down the coast from Maine or Atlantic Canada, buzzing the airport's ducks and sparrows, cruising into the pigeon fields downtown. In fact, at least one peregrine from Acadia National Park has settled in Boston.

I wander out toward the grim, formidable fretwork of highway welding the airport to the city. Eventually, after squeezing between concrete walls and single-minded traffic, I do reach a place where airport walkways become city sidewalks, but Boston and the harbor are both inaccessible, cut off on one side by the freeway and on the other by the airport itself. I return to the terminal. An hour later, my next plane takes off over the long piers and frothy rocks of the harbor. As the jet banks, I get a distant view of Cape Cod, but I leave Boston, once more, without having been to Boston.

Westbound, I know the route. If I'm on the south side of the plane, in about forty-five minutes I'll see the long clefts of the Finger Lakes and the central trunk of the Genesee River, the river of my childhood. On a rare clear day, if the plane tracks far enough south, the abrupt gorge of Letchworth Park might be visible. If my seat is on the north side, the view will be even more familiar, the river channel inconspicuous between its more obvious pre-Pleistocene mouth at Irondequoit Bay and the lagoon ponds along the Lake Ontario shore. From the air, the northeastern United States, defined by natural boundaries, looks as distant and two-dimensional as a paper map.

～

Four years earlier, the summer of 1995. I've flown in from northwestern Wyoming—Yellowstone country—for my annual visit to my parents, still settled in a suburb on the north side, the lake side, of Rochester. I'm with an old friend at McGinity's Waterfront Tavern. McGinity's has been here for so long that my father—who has not frequented bars for, well, as long as I've been aware of such things—knows its history. At McGinity's the special is the Genesee River. After shouldering through the bar crowd, you can take your drink outside and sit on the massive riprap of the harbor, watching pleasure boats sidle in from a day on Lake Ontario.

I haven't lived in Rochester for decades, but, since I'm the one with the nomadic career, I still see my Rochester friends regularly, if infrequently. Our conversations are largely topical—"What have you been doing?" "Are you still . . .?" It's okay—we talk rarely, and when we do we make stories of experience for ourselves as well as for each other. But my companion tonight likes his talk more meaty and substantial. He asks what it feels like to live the perpetually unsettled life of a college professor, working for a few years here and a few years there, in a kind of parody of the military life (we even have ranks and dress uniforms, after all). I tell him the place I'm most uncomfortable is here. It's true. For years whenever I've boarded the bus, train, or, more recently, the plane after a visit home, I've felt a sense of relief, a "made it again."

~

It's inevitable, I suppose. But this sense—not exactly of alienation but of background tension—didn't sit well just the same, especially since my reading had taken me repeatedly to "place-based" writers, from Thoreau to Kathleen Norris, whose work reflects a deep long-standing loyalty to a particular landscape and neighborhood. And when it came time to leave Wyoming, a place I loved but where I found my tenuous economic toehold loosening, I looked east along with west (much to the chagrin of my westerner wife). Ironically, as it turns out, my decision to look homeward may have led to the loss of our best chance at sticking in a place that could have been home to my whole family.

We landed in Aroostook County, Maine, which proved farther, both physically and spiritually, from Upstate New York than I had imagined, and which turned out to be another temporary stop rather than a place to dig in. But our Rochester-bound drives in summer were through familiar, resonant, important country, the mountains of New England, the Champlain Valley, and best, the Adirondacks, my first wilderness. I showed off my favorite places—the High Peaks, Blue Mountain Lake, Moody Marsh. At a rainy pulloff in Wilmington Notch, we were surprised, happily, to find a sign warning rock climbers about nesting peregrines. There were no peregrines there, or anywhere else in New York, when I was a child from Rochester engaged in the midcentury ritual of going on vacation in the mountains.

~

Above the gorge, the Genesee is dangerous, pooling and dragging itself forward, heavy with runoff, pollution, and silt. It inches under Ballantine Bridge, hiding the force of its deep current. Just north of downtown, it dives through a series of waterfalls into the shadow of its past, entering a hidden world of rock, brick, and concrete.

The deepest ravine of its type bisecting a major American city, the Rochester gorge is a misty, forbidding two-hundred-foot sedimentary gash, home to extinct brachiopods and industrial pumping facilities. For much of the twentieth century, the upstream waterfall was encased in gradually disintegrating mills and warehouses, and the inner gorge was revealed mostly to emergency responders, utility employees, and students on officially sanctioned fossil-gathering field trips. I saw the High Falls, where Sam Patch, who had survived a tumble over Niagara, met his death in 1829, once in high school when a popular charity fundraising walk spanned the usually avoided, perennially closed-for-repairs bridge at Platt Street. During the 1980s, though, a renewed riverfront emerged, the falls revealed as the focal point of the Brown's Race Historic District, an urban park transforming the shells of Flour City mills into a modern archeological site, its brick proletarian bastions metamorphosed into grottoes decked with hanging gardens of ivy and wild grape.

My preteen son Tom and I wander through the ruins, reading interpretative signs stationed along the walkways. The centerpiece is a water turbine, unearthed whole by the surprised excavators. Analytically inclined Tom carefully considers the explanations of different kinds of wheels before we turn to face the river. The spray can be smelled and felt before we reach the falls, tucked into a fold of stone capped by another industrial cliff dwelling.

As we walk the Pont de Rennes, where Platt Street once crossed the river, High Falls finally centers beneath a web of clanging, oblivious railroad and highway bridges, a traffic network I've been part of on countless occasions. We stand high above the water in the middle of the footbridge named somewhat extravagantly to honor a French sister city. The falls are yellow-brown and dive ninety-six feet into the opening gorge, green with sumac and edge-defying maples. Just to our left is the old Genesee Brewery, looking top secret with its high fence and forbidding yellow walls. Over the falls' shoulder loom local landmarks: the burned-out shell of Saint Joseph's Church and the Xerox and Chase/Lincoln First office towers. Across the river, the alien spacecraft of the short-lived revolving restaurant (called, of course, the Changing Scene) squats atop First Federal Plaza. To the right, mostly concealed by the historic warehouses, is the new baseball stadium. Farther right, the Kodak tower lifts the huge block letters of the company name in serene isolation from the rest of the downtown skyline. It is here that peregrines have nested.

A flurry at the caprock draws us back to the river. The falcon, which must have been resting at the falls' edge, now lifts rapidly and easily up into the supporting thermal currents above the gorge. Its circles expand until it is revealed as a creature of the open air, the pattern of its flight encompassing falls and gorge, warehouses and skyscrapers.

~

Like most urban peregrines, the Rochester birds are local celebrities, closely monitored by scientists, schoolchildren, and the general public. They even have their own website. This summer has been particularly good for Mariah and Cabot-Sirocco (the "Cabot" part was given to him during an earlier stay in Toronto), who have successfully fledged no less than four young. Their presence is an indirect result of the Peregrine Fund's attempts to rebuild the DDT-decimated falcon population. The pesticide is now banned, at least in the United States (American companies continued to produce DDT for overseas markets until 1981; it is still made, and used, in India), and the characteristic predatory species it endangered—the osprey, the bald eagle, the brown pelican, the peregrine—are once again familiar sights over much of their former range. Reduced beyond recovery, the peregrine's eastern population had to be rebuilt artificially with birds introduced from the western United States, the Arctic, even South America and Europe.

Though formidable birds, peregrines are vulnerable when nesting, and any attempt to reestablish them would have to overcome the danger of predation in a depressed population of isolated nests. Falcon parents are impressive defenders, but because of the "hacking" method most often used in reintroduction, the young, fed and tended by disguised humans, frequently did not have the benefit of full-time parental protection. Under these circumstances, nocturnal predators like raccoons and great horned owls were a serious barrier to the reestablishment of peregrines in wild or rural places. Part of the solution was to take advantage of the falcons' occasional practice of living in pigeon-rich urban environments. Late in the 1970s, The Peregrine Fund began planting chicks on predator-unfriendly bridges and skyscraper ledges. By the turn of the millennium, peregrines nested coast-to-coast in American and Canadian cities, including Harrisburg, Pennsylvania, where the birds settled, appropriately, on the Rachel Carson office building. Especially in the Northeast, the birds became established in places where nesting sites had been rare or absent before.

City residents take pride in their new neighbors. In Rochester, where Dennis Money's Rochester Peregrine Falcon Project began in 1994, the falcons frequent the ballpark sky, and patrons who bring binoculars to the games sometimes split their attention between the Triple-A Red Wings and the actual birds. Rochester's falcon habitat is near ideal, the gorge complementing the city buildings, providing a relatively safe place for young birds to become adept at flying. Predators may be less common in urban areas, but one danger for city peregrines, particularly the young, is plate glass office towers, which inexperienced birds have difficulty seeing directly in front of them. Even in Rochester, where skyscrapers are few and widely spaced in a mostly open sky, a youthful flyer was killed crashing into a building. After the young are fledged, a migrating or dispersing falcon can choose between the river to the south and the gull- and shorebird-hunting grounds along Lake Ontario, leading, eventually, to the rest of the Great Lakes or the Saint Lawrence River.

⁓

We elect to follow the river north to the waterfront neighborhood of Charlotte (pronounced *Sha-LOT*) and the Genesee lighthouse, now a museum chronicling the history of Rochester's lakeshore and river harbor. The port long closed to commercial shipping, the waterfront is still a place of interest and rustbelt romance. I came to the lake as a toddler and as a teenager, and I return whenever I visit my hometown; a few hours at the shore soon became part of Tom's expected Rochester routine.

At the turn of the twentieth century, an interurban rail system brought Rochesterians down Lake Avenue to Charlotte picnics, boardwalk promenades, and dazzling entertainments including daredevil tightrope walkers, a "Japanese village," and even staged fires, using an elaborate setup of asbestos buildings and natural gas. Now, the restored 1905 carousel is the most prominent reminder of times out of the reach of almost everyone's memory. The lighthouse itself, a tapering fieldstone octagon, has retreated a considerable ways upriver, as beach fill and jetty silt distanced the lakeshore. Obsolete and as early as 1881 too far inland to serve its original purpose, the lighthouse still provides a home for waterfront memorabilia and an elevated view of the old port. The climb to the top is dark and claustrophobic, a rapidly narrowing utilitarian spiral; to maneuver through the last tight whorl back into sunlight requires a rope. The replica platform surrounds an unmatched lamp, strictly for looks as the interpretive brochures ethically confess. There's McGinity's across the river, which from up here is a ragged bloom of brown silt vased between Charlotte pier and the jetty of the Summerville Coast Guard station on the Irondequoit side.

We can't see it from the lighthouse, but seven miles to the west is the Braddock Bay hawk watch site. Each spring, thousands of raptors of various species migrate along the lake. When wind and weather conditions are favorable, an observer might see hundreds in a single afternoon. According to Braddock Bay Raptor Research, 69,118 birds were reported during the previous season. Of those, the total number of peregrines was eleven. This reflects both the peregrines' relative rarity and their solitary ways. By contrast, broad-winged hawks, which accounted for over half of the total number of birds, migrate en masse, riding the thermals in kettles that circle above the shore like enormous wheels. But eleven peregrines represents a distinct improvement from just a few decades earlier.

～

In 1982, just as the renaissance of the high falls was beginning, I left home for Louisiana. I had enrolled in a graduate program in creative writing. Though I did not know the extent of the peregrinations that this move would lead to, I was aware that I was rejecting what was shaping itself as a typical Rochester life in favor of the world "out there." After Louisiana, I spent a year in Denver, a year in Northern California, a year in Salt Lake City, five years working toward a PhD at Purdue University, then stints teaching at colleges in Wyoming, Maine, and Florida. This is typical for academics and problematic for those of us who see the need for wholesale changes in our culture, for valuing places and the quality of life over the siren call of career and the subtler urges of wanderlust. But where is home? I once asked one of the most eloquent "stickers," Scott Russell Sanders, how home identifies itself. His response was something to the effect that it can and will but you can't force it.

The Boston airport, gateway from New England to the rest of the world, eventually led me to a new home in Central Florida, an hour's drive from a picnic pavilion absurdly stranded in the shadow of the Big Bend Power Plant, on Tampa Bay. We had come to the facility to see manatees gathered in the provisional winter shelter of the artificial spring run created by the plant's heated discharge. A score or so of the mammals lazed and sported in the shallow inlet, along with mullet, snook, maybe a tarpon or two, under the gaze of the ubiquitous Florida crowd leaning over the railing of a platform constructed by the power company. In half a year I had learned some things about my new surroundings, but much was still mystery. How did the manatees come to gather at the power plant? Is it a good place for them? Where would they go if the plant closed?

~

*Parking lots glare in the subtropical sun. A manatee rises with an audible snuffle, scattering a few fish. A quick laugh from the platform. Gulls and pigeons wheel around the towers, along with tree swallows. But now another bird, there, swinging around the highest pinnacle, a peregrine. The falcon spirals higher, higher, out of sight. The wanderer, threading the wind across the world, tracing a pattern of tentative, necessary answers.*

## You Can't Always Want What You Want

After the late local news, I click aimlessly through channels, settling on one of those music specials that seem to universally signal pledgedrive, as if audiences, the PBS folks believe, can't possibly see and hear too many times the black-and-white Roy Orbison show, the Springsteen concert, the Johnny Cash tribute, the pudgy and all-but-forgotten stars of sixties pop, fifties doowop, Motown, or wherever. This one is new to me though, a made-for-the-BBC stage show hosted by the Rolling Stones, originally recorded, I've since found out, in December 1968. Guests include many of the usual suspects—Eric Clapton, The Who, John and Yoko, Marianne Faithful, Taj Mahal, Jethro Tull, and, of course, the Rolling Stones themselves.

The appearance of John Lennon's supergroup featuring Yoko Ono's diagnostic performance-art keening, is a sure sign that the lordly Beatles were already just about gone, never to reward the fading hopes for their restoration. Marianne Faithful was picking up a hint of the voice-of-the-already-damned edge she would achieve on *Broken English*. Mick Jagger looked, if not handsome, at least young, as did Keith Richard—his name would have been without the terminal *s* at the time. Brian Jones was there, though the *Rock and Roll Circus* proved to be his last public performance. The Stones played numbers like "No Expectations" and "You Can't Always Get What You Want," though not quite well enough, legend has it, to make them want to release the film at the time it was made. They had reason to be particular. *Beggar's Banquet* had already been released; *Let It Bleed* and their masterpiece, *Exile on Main Street*, would be their next studio albums. They were entering the period of their greatest glory, when they took on their own version of the abdicated Beatles' crown. But the Stones were not the Beatles. Their evocation of American rhythm-and-blues was paradoxically both more deeply felt and more studied. They brought a tough, weedy quality to the flower power generation. In all likelihood, they weren't especially nice, but they had a depth of soul that enabled them to flourish through times of disappointment. Or maybe they simply lacked the Bobby Kennedy imagination required to see the world as anything but what it was. If love, as it turns out, is not all we need, then we all surely need someone we can bleed on. Though they would never match the boys from Liverpool in breadth of appeal or originality, they were soon to be acclaimed "The World's Greatest Rock-and-Roll Band."

I saw the Stones three times in the late seventies and early eighties, during the height of my own rock-and-roll age. Sometimes I still play that music, though it's an indulgence I don't always want. I have no desire to become a creature of the past. I've got no expectations, after all, to pass through there again. I still have vinyl copies of *Beggar's Banquet* and *Exile* but the only Stones music I have on CD—let alone MP3—is a greatest hits compilation my son Tom gave me. I'm listening to it now. Recently an undergraduate at a student art exhibit, assuming I would know, asked me what it was like to live with disillusionment over what happened to the sixties. So it goes.

By the time I got to the sixties, it was already the seventies. Like Boone Caudill in A. B. Guthrie's *The Big Sky*, who arrived at Fort Union, according to his Uncle Zeb, "ten year too late anyhow," I got there when it was all over. I was a sheltered kid from the suburbs. My sister Anne had hit Beatlemania head on, but as she was four years older than me, her high school life was her own; until the end of the decade, I was still at Saint John the Evangelist parish school, sporting my official school tie with the SJS logo in the middle. I had fallen, as it were, out of the loop. I remember hearing "Get Back" on a transistor radio and thinking *so that's what they sound like now.* Of course, like everyone else, I had seen television images of medics crouching, holding their helmets, hauling bloody stretchers toward helicopters angled just off the ground, and of long-haired youths Anne's age, bedraggled but smiling, holding flowers and flashing peace signs. It wasn't hard to tell which image represented the better way to live, and, it seemed, the inevitably dawning future. But all that happened far away from the Rochester suburbs, where I was busy playing neighborhood pickup baseball and, later, worrying if my hair was too long to get by without rebuke at my

Catholic high school. Still, I guess I bought into what amounted to the core values of my childhood—creativity, response to nature, tolerance—things that seem so naïve today, that were already naïve in the seventies when Elvis Costello was singing Nick Lowe's "What's So Funny About Peace, Love, and Understanding."

~

I came to Brockport, some fourteen miles west of my parents' house, right out of high school in the fall of 1973. Unlike the amorphous sprawl where I grew up, Brockport prided itself on being a "real" place, a village on the Erie Canal, the fabled waterway that was just then escaping into anachronistic romance by scrapping the prosaic New York State Barge Canal moniker. Brockport was in some ways typical of such canalside villages. It had a corniced Victorian downtown, lift bridges, lots of shade trees, even a property that had grandfathered in the right to keep a couple of horses. But it also had people like me, a demographic associated either directly or indirectly with the state college.

Brockport, probably along with lots of similar college towns, served more-or-less unintentionally as a kind of wildlife refuge for sixties people, whose cultural habitat was, ironically, being lost as quickly as the hated Vietnam War. My arrival in Brockport was several years after the *Rock-and-Roll Circus* was recorded. After Woodstock, after Altamont. The heady atmosphere of that decade, full of positive transformation in the face of disaster, was soon to just about disappear, the Aquarian Age's less adaptable denizens fleeing underground into hippie enclaves, leaving behind a zeitgeist aura fossilized to informalities of language and attire; self-absorbed forms of faux spirituality and community; and, I suppose, the ghostly persistence of "classic rock" icons like Jimi Hendrix, Jim Morrison, eventually John Lennon. The landmarks of this descent are now clear, culminating perhaps in the development of the compact disk, which left black vinyl and cardboard jackets obsolete, the music translated, remastered, deluged in outtakes, sometimes reordered into "best of" compilations, with album cover art and liner notes reduced in size and scope or eliminated altogether. The dawn of the CD might not comprise the day the music died, but it does mark the point when the music became middle-aged. And it goes without saying that the sixties generation was inseparable from its music. The Stones powered on, and still do, their faces growing nearly as lithic as their name. But they were selected as a safe choice for the Super Bowl halftime show two years after the Jackson-Timberlake affair (following, perhaps inevitably, Paul McCartney), which must mean something I don't think I want to know. Other sixties groups, in the tradition of country singer Jim Reeves, built extended if somewhat ghoulish careers out of their endings. The Band, for example, made its own death the subject of a Martin Scorsese movie and a triple LP that eventually swelled into a four-CD set. And, of course, until 1980 the four Beatles had only to be in the same country to fuel rumors of a Phoenix-like rise from the ashes. Death itself proved no barrier for those anticipating the return of Jim Morrison.

I couldn't have known much of this when I started school at Brockport, ready to take my place in the uninhibited, creative life that seemed solidly in place as the legacy of the sixties revolution. I had no idea what my place would be, but finding out—personal development, if you will—was what education was all about. At first I commuted to school, or at least to the student union, moving to campus a couple of years later. I was an indifferent student, cutting classes, experimenting in dilettante fashion with various majors. But in spite of my lack of dedication, I learned a few things I remember to this day, and found friendships I still value. What I now see as my quintessential college experience, however, was squeezed into the few years between my return to Brockport in 1978 after a year in Rochester and my departure—for good—from Upstate New York in 1982. Since I was still in my twenties, those years seemed like, still seem like, a long time indeed.

All told, I had eight or nine successive Brockport addresses, the last and most definitive of which was a blue two-story village house on Adams Street, a place that came to be known among a fair number of Brockporters as "the Dada Hotel." The original Dada cast formed when my friend Keith, a wry, soft-spoken New York City transplant with an undergraduate degree from Saint John's University, and I were looking for a place one August, our respective summer arrangements coming to a close. I don't recall exactly what I was doing that summer, but it seems in retrospect that I was mostly sitting on my porch waiting for visitors; Keith, on the other hand, appeared to be perpetually walking the village streets, headed to or from irregular shifts at the sub shop where he worked. It was, I'd guess, on the porch of my summer rental that we decided to look for an apartment for the school year, eventually throwing in with two other students: Pat—athletic, spiritually minded, a bit mercurial—and Kenny, who had been rooming with Brockport's only genuine communist, their floor littered wall to wall with papers ranging from half-finished songs to drafts of flyers advertising political rallies. It all came together when an anthropology professor agreed to rent us her house, or at least most of it. When she had tenants, Marjorie lived in an apartment in the back, sometimes with a son and/or a beautiful exotic-looking daughter, each of whom spent a few weeks with their mother from time to time. The apartment was also home to a blind, superannuated rabbit who sat in his litter box all day but hopped out to deposit pellets on the surrounding floor. The family seemed to live in vague apprehension that the missing father, rumored to be hiding out Jim Morrison–style in Africa, would emerge from wherever he was and repossess the furniture. Perhaps the prospect of additional eyes around the place made trusting the house to college students more palatable. For whatever reason, Marjorie was willing to put up with the late night rock-and-roll carousing of the Dada with only an occasional complaint about noise, after which we'd try sincerely but mostly ineffectually to lower the volume of our late-night gatherings. The son did take exception when our nomadic friend Matt started getting mail at the house without being an official renter, but we could hardly blame the young man, close to our own age, for looking out for his mother's interests. We fed the rabbit when the family was away, and our relations remained generally good.

I don't remember how, but I managed to snag the best digs in the house, a spacious upstairs bedroom at the front end of a stairtop hallway. I had three windows, and best of all, a small nook suitable for a writing desk. (Evidently I wasn't the only one who found my secluded quarters desirable. During one kitchen conversation, a question somehow arose concerning who had experienced sex in my room. I was surprised, though only momentarily, to see hands shoot up from every one of the six or seven people present). Keith's quarters were near the top of the stairs. A door to Marjorie's apartment was at the back end of the hall. Downstairs, Pat had a bedroom off the kitchen. Kenny's room was the "sunporch," hard by the front door, separated only by a suspended blanket from an entryway that led to the living room. He maintained his cheerful disposition with virtually no privacy and no shelter from the stereo, often blasting to the best of its ability the dulcet tones of, say, Bob Dylan singing "Queen Jane Approximately." In fact, Kenny was known to come dancing out of his room when the music woke him up, wearing the torn black pajamas that doubled as the stage clothes he donned to sing with the Party Dogs. But more on that later.

One of the power nodes of the Dada was the living room, furnished only with our poor excuse for a stereo, records leaned against a wall, a lamp or two, a small-screen portable television, and the obligatory sofa. I don't remember much about the sofa, probably because all Brockport living rooms were equipped with such a couch. I couldn't tell you what color it was—maybe a faded gray-green—but it was almost certainly a swayback affair, with a hollow in the middle reflecting years of service in the cause of student housing. Long enough to accommodate three, sometimes four, people, the couch slumped against the far wall from the front door, where a recessed fireplace created a kind of alcove. When you walked through the entryway, past the sun porch and into the living room, the sofa was the first visual indicator of the energy the house was sponsoring at that moment. Sometimes the couch would be empty, a bit forlorn but also restful, a reminder that the house predated us; with luck, it would outlast its stint as the Dada Hotel. On a Saturday afternoon, one or two of us might sprawl listlessly before the black-and-white TV coaxed by a coat hanger or a makeshift bow-tie antenna into providing an old movie or Big East basketball game. If it was late at night, a small party was likely to be grouped around the couch, leaning into the music, which we were really trying, after all, to keep at a reasonable volume. We might be listening to the Stones, or maybe *The Basement Tapes*, or maybe even the Party Dogs demo.

The real center of house energy was the kitchen table, a high island affair surrounded by standard wood-finish cabinets, linoleum counters, and the requisite appliances. In the morning there would be coffee, later beer, maybe a nickel bag of marijuana, and always cigarettes. It was quite possible to spend an entire day, continuing well into the evening, around that table. Occasionally, our "pet" mouse would emerge from a stove burner and circuit the counters, disappearing at another convenient mouse portal. Once we even set up an obstacle course with a reward at the end. During the latter Dada days, the mouse was trapped by Tim, who had replaced Kenny in the sunporch. Bewildered by our lack of enthusiasm for his fastidiousness, Tim soon moved on to, one hopes, more compatible circumstances.

◯

All four of the original Dada residents were writers. The college had a respectable creative writing program—through the MA level—that we thought didn't get the credit it deserved. This, of course, provided an outsider frisson that made it even better. Not that the program had gone completely without notice. An endorsement by Archibald MacLeish proliferated ubiquitously throughout college publicity materials, an excerpt appearing even today as an epigraph for the village website's portrait of Brockport life in 1979. But with New York City at the other end of the state, Rochester, much less Brockport, was at a distinct disadvantage as a cultural center, a situation reflected in the patronizing attitudes of Long Islanders who found their way to the college because it was both in-state and far away from home. There's always some background tension between Upstate and Downstate New Yorkers; colorful New York City mayor Ed Koch's 1982 bid for governor derailed when he made derogatory comments about Upstate farmers. In Brockport, such intrastate rivalries merged with a mild but persistent chaffing between college people and "townies," the predictable result of subjecting a dependent local population to a transient, careless student body. Neither townie nor Gothamite, I occupied something like a neutral no-man's-land. I had both local and Downstater friends, and visited New York City myself several times during those years, to this day my only first-hand experience of the city aside from airport layovers. A fair chunk of what I know about life in New York, I suppose, was gathered in conversations that took place in Brockport.

Poetry—Deep Image poetry specifically—was coin of the realm. We were surrealistic pastoralists by day, rock-and-roll partiers by night. This may seem strange in retrospect, but we were basking in what was left of the penumbra of the sixties, before the Reagan revolution succeeded in branding as hokey any notion that nature had a spiritual energy vital to human creativity and happiness. Our tastes and aesthetic backgrounds weren't identical. Kenny, for example, brought to Brockport a sensibility forged by the Beats and by other counterculture movements with which he had had some measure of first-hand experience, and Keith was more thoroughly versed in the work of canonical European literary influences ranging from Aesop to Chekhov. But if you leaf through a copy of *The Brockport Review*, our student literary magazine, it's pretty obvious that there was a "Brockport style" shaped in the image of Robert Bly and James Wright.

Those Brockport years were my one and only experience being part of a "scene." Life was vivid. We borrowed typewriters, edited magazines, talked far into the night, even occasionally gathered in candlelit rooms to read and listen to each other's poems. Kenny and a friend created a tabloid, receiving the obligatory submissions from Lyn Lifshin—then the most published poet in America—almost before the periodical got beyond the sitting-on-the-couch planning phase. My friend Tony enlisted me in the formation of a small press. We published several poetry chapbooks and broadsides (the broadsides were my department). The press, in fact, is still in operation, without me, as Mammoth Books, a gag name for a tiny concern, but inspired by a hair from a thawed woolly mammoth exchanged as a gift between the college and Russian poet Andrei Voznesenski, though I'm not certain who gave it to whom. I vaguely remember it being presented to Voznesenski, though it seems more logical that it would be the other way around, as freeze-dried mammoths are more likely to emerge from the snows of Siberia than the New York countryside (both mammoth and mastodon bones, on the other hand, are Upstate specialties).

As young people in a basically undemanding college environment, we wasted lots of time, with more thinking about books, talking about books, than actually reading them. But there was creativity. Poems and songs were written. Kenny came up with a novel. We did enough work to maintain something like the hopes of our professors, most of whom trailed their own long histories of accomplishment and disappointment. We believed in our teachers for the most part, considered them mentors, though we knew some of them to be at times petty, sexist, judgmental. Kenny, particularly, was often singled out, even feared, for his protechnology, antipastoral sensibility. And female students were expected to "prove themselves" in a patriarchal culture punctuated by stereotypes—one faculty member told me that he thought most women, necessarily more conscious of their socioeconomic status, had yet to reach the higher stages of mystical awareness that characterized the greatest poetry—and of a male-oriented social milieu of poker nights and smoky bars. What strikes me now as remarkable is that the women among us were generous enough to put up with it all and perceptive enough to see that our mentors, despite their faults, had much to offer young writers regardless of gender.

Although neither we nor our teachers would have appreciated or understood the comparison, like the Stones the Brockport faculty had something that we vaguely understood we needed, a measure of worldliness reflecting life experience that far exceeded our own. Most had even met with at least some degree of recognition beyond backwater Brockport. There was Bill Heyen, whose book jackets proclaimed him one of the major young poets of his generation. A Long Islander by birth who had been a soccer star as a Brockport undergraduate, he was a commanding reader who could electrify a classroom through sheer force of personality. Tony Piccione, not to be confused with the Tony of Mammoth Books, was gruff but infinitely patient, and taught all of us a way into poetry. He lived in a farmhouse outside of town, and was, despite his girth, a formidable racquetball player. His was the first doctoral dissertation on Robert Bly. While he methodically built a reputation as a poet, publisher, anthologist, and translator, Al Poulin's cynical wit kept the romanticism of the others in check. Versatile, open-minded, hard-working, self-assured yet genuinely humble, Stan Rubin, the story went, had turned down a chair at Columbia to be with us. He had so many admirable qualities that one of my friends used to say that if he ever had kids, he wanted them to be just like Stan Rubin. The four of them divvied up most of the poetry workshops. Fiction was handled by Stan and by Gregory Fitz Gerald, who walked with a limp, wore ascot ties, and endowed a cash-award student fiction contest that Kenny won one year after agreeing in advance to split the prize with myself, Keith, and someone else—Tony maybe—a gesture reflecting solidarity and our confidence that one of us was likely to win. In 1967, Fitz Gerald had founded the Brockport Writers' Forum, a reading series that spawned a library of videotaped interviews frequently shown in our classes and still considered a major resource of its kind today. The most ubiquitous influence on any of us students, I suppose, was each other. The sense of generational community at Brockport was deeper and more sincere than in any other academic environment I've been a part of. We may have been distracted, lazy, immature, a shade arrogant, but we knew that we belonged.

Except for me, the Dadas were also musicians. Eventually, there was a band, the Party Dogs—named for a cheap brand of frankfurter—which pretty much was Brockport's Punk/New Wave scene, and which eventually evolved into the Bulus, a respectable component of the bigger and considerably more urban, if just as complacent, live music community in Rochester. The *Rochester BandWEB*, chronicling the history of the city's rock groups since the seventies, calls the Bulus a "seminal Brockport NY band."

The Party Dogs had an easier time getting gigs in bars than they did finding a place to practice in the residential village, so each performance was an adventure. And the equipment was—well, not exactly what the Rolling Stones would use. The Dogs played original material—songs with titles like "Romping through the Jungle" and "Glad Handed"—mixed with the occasional cover. Pat was the drummer, the "human metronome" as a poster proclaimed him for his ability to maintain a relentless beat. Matt, a homegrown punker from the lake plain countryside northwest of town, played lead guitar and sang versions of "Wild Thing" and Lou Reed's "Vicious," though he never sang and played at the same time. Hughie, whose musical sensibility was quite different but whom everyone liked, played bass. Except for Matt's trademark covers, Kenny was the lead singer, stalking ungracefully about in his black pajamas, all scruffy, spontaneous energy laced with irreverent wit. At one show, after Kenny introduced the band members someone in the audience shouted, "Who are you?" Kenny's response was a too-good-natured-to-be-called-a-sneer smile, and one word: "Hinckley!"—the name of the would-be Reagan assassin. At the end of each gig, everyone exchanged instruments for a version of Sinatra's "Strangers in the Night" culminating in "to do is to be / to be is to do / dooby dooby dooby dooby dooby dooby do / Jean Paul Sartre is dead." Of course, you had to be there.

Sometimes the Dogs were joined onstage by friends. Keith played harmonica and sang, allowing the group to incorporate a more traditional bluesy sound, and even occasionally to evoke the spirit of the legendary Grateful Dead, Brockport's favorite sixties band. Quashi was a professional Nigerian percussionist who, it was said, had played with the likes of B. B. King and Stevie Wonder, but who was stranded in Brockport after falling out with a mentor he had followed there; he had a set of congas with him, and a purported roomful of instruments he couldn't get to somewhere in Germany. He had adopted an English name—Geoffrey Chaucer—and sat in with the Dogs. I sometimes acted as manager, which gave me something to do even though I possessed none of the background or business savvy required by the position. I put up posters, worked the door, and parceled out what little money was in the kitty, occasionally slipping a few extra dollars to Quashi to keep him reasonably happy, considering.

~

Brockport was a walking town, at least for us, since none of the Dadas and few of our village friends had cars. Hughie had a VW Beetle. Alone among Party Dogs, he also had a genuine dog, a skinny lab mix named Evelyn—after the dog in the Frank Zappa song—he had inherited from a former girlfriend. I knew Evelyn before I met Hughie. Since I grew up with pets and felt their absence in my daily life, I could never say which of them I was happier to see, and I made sure that Evelyn got a bowl of water as quickly as Hughie got a beer. Along with the VW, Evelyn usually showed up during the day. Most nights, unless we had visitors from Rochester, if we wanted to go somewhere (which we almost certainly did), we, including Hughie, walked, and walked home later in whatever state we happened to be in.

Typically, early evenings at the Dada were quiet. Except for occasional days when we stayed at the kitchen table through dinner, it was rare for all or even most of us to be home. After eleven, heading off from wherever we were, we hit the myriad bars in town, returning at two a.m. with a six-pack, maybe several, of the cheapest brew and whatever eclectic mix of friends, stragglers, hangers-on, overnight visitors from out-of-town, etc., we happened to find ourselves among. The Dada would spring to life, quietly we hoped, with music; smoky blazes in the fireplace fed only by newspaper and six-pack cartons; more conversation, albeit somewhat disjointed and confused.

Imagine a typical night between 1978 and 1982. Let's make it a Wednesday in 1981, right around eleven (except for Pat, who pulls bent spoons out of garbage disposals for an apartment super, most mornings we can afford to sleep in). A left at the sidewalk leads us toward downtown. We might be with Keith, or maybe Matt, who spends almost as much time at the Dada as those of us who live there. Just as likely though, it's only me, along with the fictional you in this case. It's a scene, after all, and we'll find each other. The journey of a few blocks follows a familiar route, but that doesn't mean that it's without a tingle of anticipation. We might first look in at the Rox—the

Roxbury Inn, that is—a dank, sticky cavern quarried out of a house that had once belonged to a United States ambassador. Vaguely suggesting the grand diplomatic hallways of the past, the entry is lined with stately columns, looking almost passable in the murky darkness. Directly ahead is a claustrophobic corridor leading to a cramped poolroom and chronically neglected bathrooms. The bar is to the right, to the left a large high-ceilinged hall partially divided into front and back sections. One winter night in that room, at a heavy, round, graffiti-etched wooden table, probably that one over there in the front corner, I was sitting with a fellow student, a woman with whom I was spending a prodigious amount of time—mostly sitting at tables—when it occurred to us that the music had shifted to a long unbroken set of Beatles songs. Then Kenny was there, a stunned look on his face. That was December 8, 1980, the night John Lennon was killed in New York.

But this is a different night, and it's the Rox itself that's dead, so we head downtown, passing the Brockport Diner where we might have eaten supper a few hours earlier. Every so often, we brush by a small group of students wandering, as we are, from nightspot to nightspot. Perhaps we should try—we usually do—Jim Higgins' taproom, newly renamed Priority One in a half-hearted attempt at hipness. The Dogs play here, at the stage end of an undecorated hall furnished with two widely spaced rows of cafeteria-style tables and separated from the bar by a paneled wall with window cutouts. Tonight stage and tables are empty, leaving a few barstool patrons and the barkeep, a bald argumentative fellow with a withered arm. He owns the place, but he isn't Jim Higgins. I don't remember his name.

Two or three doors down from Higgins' is Barber's—on the corner, everyday lighting, tin roof. With its greasy pancake-like burgers, it might be a quiet neighborhood after-work pub, and it probably was at one time. But now, patrons pack the aisle between stools and booths, and jockey for the attention of a couple of harried bartenders stationed behind glass-decanter taps placed soda-fountain style at the front of the bar. There, across the aisle on a booth table, sit a pitcher of beer and a scatter of cigarette packs open for everyone, surrounded already by earnest talk about classes, poets, music, dance, occasionally politics or sports. The night has begun.

Still maintaining the illusion that it's 1981, let's take the same walk downtown in daytime to get a better sense of the lay of the village as it was in the days of the Dada. If it happens to be spring, our walk will be punctuated by the sound of passing geese. If it's June, exuberant cardinals and, maybe, a wood thrush fluting from somewhere in the deep light-transmuting green of northeastern hardwoods. If it's autumn, the same shade trees will be in high color, mostly an explosive yellow. If we are walking at noon on a clear January day, the sidewalk will be icy, the yards bright with snow. Most likely, though, it's between seasons, the sky an even gray, the air cool with a hint of rain.

As we did last night, we turn left from the Dada, walk up Adams, then turn left again on Main—Route 19. We're heading north, with the here-gentle rise of the Niagara Escarpment behind us. Lake Ontario is about a dozen flat, apple-orchard miles ahead. We walk under the railroad bridge; if you look back, you can see "Lionel" painted in convincing white model-train-set stencil letters. Then past the convenience store, then the Rox. No point in stopping there. The door's just open to air the place out so it won't smell quite so much like stale beer tonight, at least at first.

The traffic signal at Main and Erie (which changes to State Street east of Main) marks the beginning of the two-block downtown, with the Brockport Diner on the left and the art deco movie theatre kitty-corner across the intersection. This is one of few junctions in town where the roads on either side of Main line up without a jag, the local legend explaining that Brockway and Seymour, the village founders, didn't get along. Seymour's mansion on State is still in good shape, but the Brockway house a block or two to the west is semi-abandoned, many of its windows boarded up.

The light happens to be green, so we might as well cross here, our destination of the moment the Lift Bridge Bookstore. The Lift Bridge's bread and butter is its role as an alternate textbook supplier, but there's also a splendid poetry section with books by all our profs and guest writers, lots of limited editions, even Mammoth productions. After checking for anything new in stock—maybe a small-press chapbook of Lucien Stryk's Issa translations or a new release from Poulin's fledgling BOA editions—and inevitably pausing to compare notes with whoever else is browsing the poetry section, we continue our walk, glancing across the street at Higgins' and Barber's, until we pass the ice cream shop and reach the north end of downtown, just before the bridge. There's not much of interest on the other side, so, following an iron railing, we descend a few stairs to a kind of sidewalk by the canal, really just a landing for the building's fire escape. That's where, sitting on a concrete wall close against the green water one summer afternoon, the two Tonys and I hatched a scheme to drive down to Juarez, snag a letter press, and bring it back north. Tony Piccione knew where presses could be had cheap, at least when he was an undergraduate in El Paso. Of course, we'd have had to get to Juarez, which is probably why we never did it.

~

The Erie Canal at Brockport was mostly abandoned, and for half the year sat empty, reduced to a muddy ditch. The municipal government saw the hollow channel as a convenient place to dump truckloads of snow after winter storms. But each spring the canal would spend a day or two refilling in preparation for the occasional stray boatload of tourists reenacting the historic journey from Albany to Buffalo. In addition to the lift bridge on Main, there was another a block away on Park Avenue. When a motorboat or cabin cruiser did show up, an attendant perched in an elevated control room would raise one bridge, then jump in his car and drive over to raise the other before the boat arrived, reversing the trip to lower the bridges after it passed.

The old towpath was a pleasant place to walk, its buffer of thickets and shrubby trees providing something like a village park, home to cottontails and cedar waxwings. Going west from downtown, the path led to a lawn in front of the college dormitories that was used for sunbathing and frisbee games. There, a guard gate protected the village from unruly pulses in the narrow channel during times of flood or when the canal was being filled or drained. If the gate was raised, you could climb an iron ladder and catwalk across to the other side, though the top of the gate was exposed and sometimes windy. The high walkway was the best place in town to watch the stars. One autumn night, I sat with my back against the metal frame for as long as I could stand the cold while northern lights played across the sky.

Between semesters and especially during summer, Brockport, being a college town, emptied out, and those of us who stayed all year thought we had a special claim on the place, as if fidelity made us honorary townies. During one of these quiet periods, my friend Charlie, who read Carlos Castaneda and was much given to "adventures," and I got into the habit of climbing fire escapes to the flattop downtown roofs to peer over the cornices at the nighttime panorama of empty sidewalks and closed shops. This gave us a perspective that, we thought, even few real townies had experienced. Eventually, we found a well-like opening into abandoned sections of the upper stories. Inside were decades-old newspapers, shriveled apples, a bedspring—a veritable hobo jungle. Then one night I opened a sliding door and found myself inside a shoe-store storage room. After that, we stayed away from the rooftops. When perspective was wanted, I would settle instead for the view from a downtown corner apartment rented by one of our friends, the editor of *The Brockport Review.* That's where two distinguished, elderly Chinese writers visiting campus ended up spending the night after finding themselves accidentally locked out of their motel room with no desk clerk on duty; not to worry, they explained, during the Cultural Revolution they had had to sleep "in a dung hill."

Somewhere on those flat roofs, nighthawks nested; on early summer evenings they coursed the canal, their Tuvan calls filling hollow spaces in the solstice twilight. For mysterious reasons, their population had plummeted across the Northeast. Mary Oliver, conducting a summer poetry workshop with Stan Rubin one year, happily noted their presence. Maybe they had vanished from around her home in Provincetown. Maybe she sensed that they, like us, belonged to a more sustaining set of circumstances that was in the process of unraveling elsewhere.

It's hard for even me to believe, but I can still recall Mary Oliver's comment about nighthawks, made in passing one summer afternoon thirty-odd years ago. Other Brockport conversations, including a few that went, well, not where I would have chosen, are still so vivid in memory that I can replay them in their entirety—almost—even if they no longer seem especially momentous. But memory finds them, always, in their own time. If something was left hanging, it's still unfinished, like a figure on a flawed urn a Greek potter tossed in his dustbin before it could be beheld by Keats. The unresolved relationships, the intense, ephemeral friendships that slipped away, were and remain an ineluctable part of the scene.

Every so often, Bill Heyen would bring out his collection of what he called "the real rock 'n roll" recordings—songs like "She Cried" by Jay and the Americans—from the pre-Beatles sixties, from, I suppose, his own Brockport student days. At such times, he'd listen with an odd blend of ecstasy, melancholy, and ironic humor. He had taken a job at his undergraduate college, and had brought Tony Piccione, whom he'd met in graduate school at Ohio University, with him. As far as I know he still lives in

Brockport, a place that must by now be haunted by geological layers of loose ends. If you can deal with it, says a Party Dogs song, you can live forever. "Never forget," says Issa, we stand suspended between the ephemeral and the eternal.

~

Those of us who called the Dada home were not consciously anachronistic. We were too young to adopt the "halcyon sixties" attitude portrayed ambivalently a few years later in *The Big Chill*. We weren't displaced hippies, though there certainly were such people among our acquaintances. But we might spend a whole week listening to a rediscovered copy of *The Basement Tapes*, and a new release by a long-standing talent like the Stones was a cause for celebration. Kenny played David Bowie's *Scary Monsters* over and over for days, focusing on each song until he was satisfied it had become part of him. Though an old hand, Bowie was always changing, and such open-minded movement was an important component of our understanding of intellectual and spiritual life. Rochester was close enough to New York City to occasionally attract bands—the Cramps, the Ramones—more typically found at CBGBs or the Mud Club. We caught concerts when we could afford to, and not uncommonly an LP by the Clash or the Talking Heads made its way onto the Dada turntable. For someone who grew up with the music of the Beatles and the Stones, the Punk and New Wave acts were traditionalists, trying to recapture the creativity and excitement of the British Invasion. If the Fab Four couldn't be reunited, perhaps they could be reinvented. Welcome the Party Dogs.

In a way, we were like less self-conscious, less monumental versions of World War I Modernists; aware on some level that we were at the tail end of what we took to be the normal state of human civilization, we lived among the fragments, making them new as best we could. Even Brockport's favorite poets—Galway Kinnell, James Wright—had gained their greatest acclaim in the late sixties and early seventies. Kenny once told me he had trouble reading anything written before 1990—it was 1980 at the time—but Ginsberg, Burroughs, and Timothy Leary held places in his pantheon, and he would later write glowingly about life in the "shadow" of the sixties counterculture. Things look different from today's vantage point: futuristic optimism isn't what it used to be. In retrospect, Kenny's faith in the progressive evolution of the human intellect seems a bit quaint—perhaps even to him—like a more profound, brainier version of *Star Trek* utopianism. I can't remember the last time I heard anyone who wasn't selling something talk about how great the future looks.

And what did happen to the sixties? The generally accepted answer, of course, is the seventies, when sixties people grew up, had children, gradually morphed, like Jerry Rubin, into responsible adults, giving up their shallow ideals and recognizing that the pursuit of wealth and status constituted an acknowledgment of reality. But for me, since so much of my sixties happened during the seventies, a better answer would be the eighties, which saw the repudiation of much that I had taken for granted. In 1986, I started teaching composition classes as a graduate student at Purdue after having been away from the academic environment for several years. It was when I saw how eagerly and proudly my students decked themselves in corporate logos on their way to their future cubicles that I realized that the world, my world anyway, had changed.

I'd like to think that American social history naturally swings between liberal and conservative poles, each correcting the excesses of the other, but with the general direction revealing a progressive tilt when measured across decades or centuries. I can picture a sixties conservative—let's say my eighth-grade teacher, a thoughtful, genuinely decent man with sincerely held beliefs—waiting for the country to come to its senses, and I can accept that it's now my turn to do the same. This morning, walking to my office, I passed a truck with a bumper sticker proclaiming the owner a "proud member of the vast right-wing conspiracy." I can see that as a gesture not essentially different from the flower power slogans that popped up everywhere during the Vietnam War. It means that the bearer of such a message is with the flow, or, as the expression went, "where it's at." And if time waits for no one, then it also follows that time is on my side, that the pendulum is bound to swing back one of these days.

But the current rightward tilt has lasted for more than a quarter century, and, despite the art student's question, I really haven't been spending all those years lamenting the societal failures of politics past. Frankly, I'm more worried about the present. As for the future, its saving grace is that no one really knows; even the most educated guess is likely to be wrong. What does seem safe to say is that each of our lives is moving toward something we might as well call completion, in which case if I have things to do I'd better find out what they are and do them. Outside it's spring in Billings, Montana, a late snowfall melting in the bright sunshine, and the first thing I have to do is turn off the CD player and take my dog for a walk.

~

It is, after all, pointless to regret the false steps and missed opportunities of one's youth. Keith and I agreed on that, a few years ago, sitting at a patio table outside the community college writing lab where he works, watching Orlando traffic back up on the interstate in the distance. We hadn't seen each other for over two decades. Until he told me in an email that he lived just an hour away from my then-home in Lakeland, I thought he was teaching English someplace in Asia. I had kept in regular touch with Pat, who had moved to Rochester after leaving the Dada. I knew that Kenny had become something like famous in California under a nom de plume, or alter ego as the case may be.

Pat's marriage, as it turned out, was the beginning of the end of the Dada days. Kenny left about then too, Keith shortly after. I guess I must have been the last of the originals to move on. My Rochester friend Glenn took Pat's old room, beginning a succession of others—fussy Tim in place of messy Kenny; a couple of nice enough Long Islanders; Jamie, who suffered from what his Party Dog brother Matt called a "bad brain," sending him sometimes to jail, sometimes to the Abbey of the Genesee, sometimes just into a haze of marijuana smoke and Marty Robbins records, eventually to suicide. A couple of years after our Florida reunion, Keith and I saw Kenny read from his recently released *Counterculture Through the Ages* at a New Age store—"your headquarters for occult gifts"—in Tampa's Ybor City, the closest we've come to a Beatlesesque reunion. He signed my copy of the book "All hail Party Dogs!"

Kenny has, for the most part, stayed on the West Coast, where he helped usher in the "cyberculture" of the nineties, editing a magazine that bears an obscure but generally acknowledged relationship to *Wired*. He appeared on *Donahue* and *Nightline*, discussing, I think, virtual reality, and has even run for President. He wasn't on the ballot in my state—or any other, for that matter—but, all things being equal, he'd have had my vote. Pat made a career teaching in Rochester schools, starting by substituting at the city's toughest buildings. Over the years, he has earned a reputation as, according to *BandWEB*, "a stalwart of the Rochester scene." The demo he put together around 1990 to showcase his lyrics features a cross-section of area talent appropriate to the range—from country blues to pop to rock—of the songs themselves. Keith is still in Orlando, having returned stateside from Saipan so his son and daughter could experience the world beyond the island. After a spring training baseball game, he fired off some impromptu observations to an old friend who writes a sports column for the New York *Daily News*, and became a kind of informal on-the-scene correspondent whose annual observations are, no doubt, enjoyed by millions of readers. I haven't seen him since I moved again, from Florida to Montana; I've lived in ten states all told, looking for that home I hoped I'd find. And I've moved closer to some things with older and more resonant claims on my soul than any scene, spending long days outdoors in the open air for one. Though I can't claim to be a systematic scholar, I've even gotten around to reading at least a few of those books we used to mostly talk about. Not enough, though, never enough. Lost time is not found again.

The house on Adams Street in Brockport has been repainted a somber deep brown. My guess is that no one currently associated with it has any inkling that it was once the Dada Hotel. The village has become something of a historic site, the canal having caught on as at least a minor tourist attraction. With sidewalk tables where we planned our letterpress raid on Juarez and a new dockside visitors' center, a spruced-up Brockport, proclaiming itself "the Victorian Village on the Erie Canal," caters to pleasure boaters as well as college students.

Retired with emeritus status, Bill Heyen has been feted with an honorary Brockport doctorate and a gig as commencement speaker. He's still a respected poet. The never-healthy Al Poulin died young, and Tony Piccione wasn't much older when he too passed away. Stan Rubin left Brockport to direct a low-residency MFA program in Washington State. Despite the inevitable changes, Brockport's creative writing program, staffed by new and undoubtedly capable people, is still a going concern. I suppose today's students must have a kind of condescending familiarity with Poulin, Piccione, and the others—*look at their hair, the way they dress!*—from watching Writers' Forum interviews now and again in their classes.

∽

Like I say, I don't dwell on the past. Or maybe I do. I've written about growing up in Rochester, about leaving Upstate New York. I know that the Brockport years were as important, formative even, as anything that came before or since. But Brockport claws at an edge; reliving those years is vaguely painful in ways that I'm just beginning to understand. It's a familiar enough story, something to do with being young, with struggling to come to grips with who I was, and maybe who I was not. I don't know how anyone could live through their twenties without garnering a complicated collection of losses, not the least of which is that one is no longer there. If I think of my past as a series of boxes, the Brockport box is the hardest to open, even though, for one brief shining moment, I was part of a scene. And that really meant something then. Or maybe it didn't, and maybe I wasn't, and maybe the part of me that still lives in that box is eternally regretting that the Age of Aquarius pulled away like a bus named Furthur with my younger self a commuter running futilely behind and my older self waiting like a character in *Ghost World* for its return. Or maybe that me is still wishing I had had the guts to ask so-and-so to come back to the Dada Hotel, or that I had or hadn't said or done this or that on one of those nights I can still so clearly envision. You can't always get what you want, especially when it's already gone.

The third time I saw the Rolling Stones was at the Carrier Dome in Syracuse, a couple of hours east of Brockport on the New York State thruway. I was with Pat, his brother-in-law Jack, and someone else. Maybe two someones. We ate at a Lebanese fast-food restaurant that played Middle Eastern muzak versions of Beatles songs. We were, I remember, strangely disconcerted by the city, perhaps because Brockport had become so much our world. I went to Rochester fairly often to spend time with my family and older friends, but somehow Syracuse, which really isn't all that different from Rochester, seemed cold, impersonal, artificial, that day. As individuals, we functioned in various environments, but as the Dadas, we belonged, it seemed, in Brockport.

At the concert we had to roam the grandstands to find a spot where Pat could see Charlie Watts; I think we ended up in a stairway, at least until someone made us move. By that point in their lives the Stones were unassailably themselves, ranging across a suitably outrageous stage set, replete with oversized, suggestively angled, unapologetically adolescent phallic guitars. The Glimmer Twins were newly wireless, and relished the freedom with cherry pickers and runways. But more than that, they were comfortable enough to wander freely through the band's history, even playing "Satisfaction," which Jagger had famously said he hoped not to be singing when he was middle-aged. That night the Stones played like the World's Greatest Rock-and-Roll Band, and I was confident at the time that I could say that, having seen a pretty fair sampling of the best.

I play other music, read newer (and sometimes older) poems. My son in California tells me he's been listening to *The Basement Tapes*, and I have too. I still buy each new Dylan album, maybe because he has allowed growing old to be as important as being young. Alternatively, the Band, like the Beatles, found a paradoxical immortality set in time, unlike the less fortunate performers doomed to the eternal twilight of the PBS special. The Rolling Stones, though, will never be a maudlin nostalgia act. They'll play "Satisfaction," "You Can't Always Get What You Want," "Jumpin' Jack Flash." They'll play them all, new songs too, because that's what they do, because in rehearsal someone will say "let's do that one," and someone else will say "yeah, let's." Determination and perseverance, which they must have swallowed whole along with the vocal stylings and instrumental licks of people like Muddy Waters and John Lee Hooker, are their greatest gifts. And even if I usually let their records rest on the shelf, it's nice to know that the Stones are still out there. In fact, I might say, quoting a Party Dogs lyric, it's a groove.

## Canadas

> The wild gander leads his flock through the cool night,
> *Ya-honk* he says, and sounds it down to me like an invitation;
> —Walt Whitman, *Song of Myself*

A June morning in Boston. A quiet tributary greenbelts its way toward the Charles River. Two large Canada geese balance forward across the path as I walk by, preserving their dignity through a kind of aloof disdain. Geese appear at intervals in pairs and groups of three or four. Some don't lift their heads from under their wings when I pass.

Two old men converse on a bench, tossing breadcrumbs in the general direction of several Canadas. They seem hardly to notice the geese, which, for their part, approach the men slantwise, not out of wariness but as if they find their benefactors uninteresting. They are simply going about their business, including, in this case, sampling the bread that has appeared in the grass.

I'm in New England's capital for an academic conference. According to urban historian Sam Bass Warner, the meeting's keynote speaker, the Charles, where Bostonians go for a green reprieve, is in fact distinctly artificial, the original watercourse altered beyond recognition by the designs of municipalities, landscape architects, even rowing clubs. The geese, then, aren't much different from other city dwellers. Not looking too closely at the source of their well-being, they integrate benches and bread, reservoirs and the Olmstead philosophy of city planning, into their "natural" habitat. Like the landscape that surrounds them, they have become civilized.

Boston is not alone in hosting a resident population of Canada geese. The big goose with the black neck and white chinstrap has become a fixture in city parks and suburban neighborhoods throughout much of temperate

North America. Introduced populations thrive as far from their namesake country as New Zealand. But Canadas have not always been welcomed with the easy equanimity of the men on the Boston bench, especially in suburban towns where fatalistic urban expectations are replaced by a quixotic belief that, in the midst of rapid unregulated growth, a homogenous neatness is both attainable and desirable.

The appearance of wildlife in cities and suburbs anchors us to the earth, but also shows that our control over these environments is tentative, illusory, maybe a little dangerous. There's something vaguely disconcerting about Canadas sauntering through city parks in June. Obvious changes in the behavior of neighborhood animals undermine a deep if unspoken faith that the actions of our elaborate human communities have little connection to the world at large and no consequences beyond those desirable, even mandatory, results claimed by advertisers: convenience, green lawns, a dependable flow of summer jobs and cheap consumer goods. We call the shots within the gates, but the world goes on around us as it always has. God's in his heaven, all's right with the subdivision.

The year-round presence of the once almost exclusively migratory Canada goose testifies that our actions can result in unintended, apparently permanent disruptions in what we like to think of as serene, dependable nature. One consequence of the growth of the resident flocks is that our view of Canadas has changed as the geese have adapted to us. Might we forget, might *they* forget, that the migration of Canada geese has been one of North America's most vivid and universal reminders that the everyday demands and dramas of our lives are set in and surrounded by grand and resonant natural cycles and rhythms by which we all, geese and humans alike, really live?

~

The line, a temporary skyform long enough to link horizons, at least as the village allows for horizons, extends across the clouds, both ends lost in trees. It ripples softly like a curtain of northern lights, puts forward broad points, breaks off trailers only to absorb them elsewhere.

It is early morning and I am twenty-one, walking across a Brockport parking lot, perhaps on my way to class or home from a long night full of the vague angst and ecstasy of that period in my life. I'm looking up, of course, have been for perhaps a minute or two. Because the line snaking across the morning sky was not first a visual phenomenon. Its initial manifestation was an equally undulant laughter, or maybe a single bark ahead of the flock like a stray raindrop in the heavy April air.

Looking up. Such behavior, cocking the head spaniel-fashion, then standing transfixed waiting for the line to cover the sky, then slowly spinning under it as it passes, does not go unnoticed in even as eccentric a small town as Brockport. I wrote about Canadas often enough so that goose imagery became my trademark idiosyncrasy. But for me there was no question. One watched geese because—well, who wouldn't? They talked to me. They talked to everyone. Aldo Leopold calls the geese that migrate through Wisconsin "a wild poem dropped from the murky skies upon the muds of March." Poet Galway Kinnell says that poetry is a "paradigm of what people might wish to say in addressing the cosmos." It seemed pretty clear that something important was in those voices. I wasn't the only one looking up. At least for a moment, when the first *ya-honk* broke the horizon like a distant train whistle, it changed everything, carrying the garden back into the machine, affirming the breath of the continent. It was as if time itself were arching across the sky, hauling lilacs, fresh grass, and long days inexorably northward, and in the process of that journey opening the doors of perception closed by the quotidian blinders of habit. "Geese ring over the bell tower," I wrote in one of my undergraduate poems, words that strike me as overdramatic today. But at that time, with the experience of those great lines of geese fresh in mind, they seemed not quite strong enough.

For northerners like Leopold, the music of springtime geese has been the very embodiment of something beyond blank mechanism at work in or through the soul of the earth. By force of beauty and essential truth, the spectacle of migration justifies a moral imperative to do right by the planet; Leopold's hard-headed scientific realism runs on a parallel track with the transcendental link between truth, beauty, and the realm of ethics and morality. The necessary rightness of natural cycles shows the way to appropriate human conduct in Paul Annixter's 1950 young adult novel *Swiftwater*. In that story of a father's and son's efforts to provide a Northwoods sanctuary for migrating Canadas, a biologist encourages young Bucky Calloway by telling him that "it doesn't take long for geese to adapt themselves to man." Even so, the migrants remain themselves, visitors with their own appointments and priorities, Leopold's wild poem.

~

April, sometime in the mid-1960s. I would have been around nine or ten, searching with my family for the immediate source of those incredible all-across-the-sky lines that crossed our bland suburban horizon each spring. That source, we knew, was a staging area out in the ever-so-slightly undulating lowland woods and fields west of Rochester. Eagle Harbor was not much more than a steel-deck Erie Canal bridge and a few houses, just a dot on a map, but since the directions my father had found called for us to turn off "the Ridge"—Route 104—at Eagle Harbor Road, the wetlands complex known to local geographers as the Alabama Swamp and to wildlife managers as the Iroquois National Wildlife Refuge and its satellite state game management areas, Oak Orchard on the east and Tonawanda on the west, became known to my family as Eagle Harbor, though the refuge itself is about ten miles south of the hamlet.

Eagle Harbor was only about an hour from our home in Rochester, but anticipation and uncertainty had stretched the miles. Finally, after a couple of brief detours where our directions failed to warn of forks in the road, we rounded a gently curving rise and swung into a gravel parking lot overlooking a shallow bowl occupied by Stafford, or Goose, Pond. And there we looked out on—nothing. Just a quiet, unassuming, and evidently empty body of water lapsing into a narrow fringe of marsh with woods and fields beyond, all under the gray sky of early spring.

And so we discovered the importance of timing in what was, after all, a great demonstration of the life of time in the world. This was the first of many visits to the geese, but even later when we supposedly knew what we were doing, it was not uncommon for us to try the refuge a little too early or late. Local and continental weather systems could stall or advance the migration's course. Other, more ominous changes in climate and goose behavior were already underway, though we didn't know it at the time. We did find quickly enough that the swamp was a pretty interesting place even when the goose migration was short of its peak. There might be a few tundra (then-whistling) swans, the jaunty flash of a deer's tail, a "dead" opossum coming back to life in roadside undergrowth. The ride itself became a vernal ritual—the subtle contours of the muddy fields, the rich agrarian tang of Podunk Road and Johnny Cake Lane, the coots and wood ducks in the shallow swales.

We also found out soon enough that the geese had daily as well as seasonal routines. They would vacate Stafford Pond early in the morning to forage in fields subsidized for their benefit (and for the benefit of hunters) and return en masse late in the afternoon, around 4:00 p.m. to be just about exact.

Four o'clock, like magic. One spring day years later, some college friends and I were returning to Brockport from Niagara Falls, driving past fields of floodwater and last year's corn stubble. On impulse I said something to the effect that in five minutes, the sky would be full of geese. And just in time, the fields exploded with the flight of hitherto unseen presences, probably bound for Stafford Pond or elsewhere in the refuges. At 4:00 on an April afternoon, the time was ripe for geese.

～

The marshes, woods, and pools of the Alabama Swamp were the local wildlands of my youth. I have rarely been there since I left Upstate New York in the early 1980s, but the swamp inhabits my memory as a place too wild to be pastoral, overgrown to the point of escape—an image which is, in one sense, profoundly illusory. The Iroquois refuge was at best a compromise between bureaucratic order and the deeper resonance of primeval nature. The original glacial wetland had been cleared and drained, albeit imperfectly, generations of farmers earlier, and, like so many of our designated wildlife areas, Iroquois was a mosaic of second-growth hardwoods, impoundments flooded and dried in accordance with managerial schedules, grain dutifully planted by "sharecropping" farmers picking up a little extra cash from the government. The Oak Orchard section of the refuge complex was a site for New York's successful bald eagle hacking program—an eagle harbor in fact—and for a while a rickety-looking wooden structure loomed at the edge of Stafford Pond across from the gravel lot, looking not unlike the skeleton of a dilapidated farm outbuilding. Except, of course, for the eaglets that flopped about the enclosure, testing their wings. They too, were an artifact of the wildlife managers. Once I saw a fledgling careening through the trees at Swallow Hollow, where picnic tables and a boardwalk trail offered the nearest the refuge complex had to an official recreation area; the young bird had already launched from the treehouse-like flight platform a few miles away, but the experience hardly seemed like a real encounter with a wild eagle. For that matter, the name Swallow Hollow itself seemed invented from whole cloth by a public relations specialist, perhaps the same one responsible for the historically authentic Iroquois nation monikers applied to the recently constructed Seneca, Cayuga, Onondaga, Oneida, and Mohawk pools.

Sometimes, though, artificiality was easy to forget. One April evening, as a young man with fresh access to a car, I found myself more-or-less spontaneously racing nightfall to the Alabama Swamp. Stafford Pond had already exchanged the day's last sun for the rising moon. There was just enough light through the bare trees to make out where the Swallow Hollow boardwalk dipped into flooded woods. Somewhere close a barred owl called. There were rustlings of small creatures near the trail, the occasional crash of something bigger—fox? deer? And over it all, goose voices from out in the ponds, the nervous expressions of resting birds mingled with the announcement of new arrivals.

As with most birds, the migration of geese often occurs after dark, and their calls in the night are especially evocative. One evening, perhaps a decade earlier, a migrating V had passed low enough over my elementary school to catch the parking lot lights. It was probably the first time I saw birds flying at night, and the experience made the world bigger, stranger, and the movements across it by wild creatures somehow less predictable, more mysterious. Goose calls heard at night through a tent flap or open window took on an interrogative tone, posing a question that I could never begin to answer (though I tried, insufficiently, to phrase the question itself as "Canada? Canada?" in a poem written shortly after my evening run to the refuge). It was the same quality I heard when I stood on my grandparents' cobble beach and listened as disembodied voices drifted in over Lake Ontario, from, I thought, great rafts of geese beyond the horizon, though maybe they were really coming from smaller, closer gaggles tucked in valleys and pockets of the waves.

And that night on the moonlit Swallow Hollow boardwalk, goose calls were both intimately close and immersed in the incredible distances of the flyway.

~

Despite its location between Rochester, Batavia, and Buffalo, the Alabama Swamp really was remote, or at least neglected, a ragged loose end of American enterprise. Its few "towns" existed mostly on maps. Two farmhouses for one, three for another. None had a gas station or store. There were still some working farms, but they lacked both the mystique of the apple country north of Ridge Road and the calendar appeal of the tidy, bucolic landscape to the south, where the escarpments of the Allegheny Plateau folded into the pastoral sweep of ridges and valleys that Western New York is known for. In the Alabama Swamp, most of the farmers had given up long ago, leaving empty barns, old trucks peering from swayback garages, farmsteads owned by city cousins. I suppose the swamp was really no more depopulated than many other northeastern rural areas. What seemed unusual, though, was the sense of obscurity, houses perhaps occupied, maybe not, the shades always half drawn. One almost never encountered anyone on the refuge roads or trails. For a kid from the suburbs, it was *Deliverance* country. Iroquois had a headquarters, but there never seemed to be anyone there. The interpretive materials were few. Even the eagles seemed to have arrived on their own, as if they had built their treehouse themselves. It was better that way, of course, most visits innocent of refuge staff, birdwatching tourists, anyone, though there was evidence—an annual newspaper feature at the peak of migration and the occasional pickup leaned mysteriously into the grass along a refuge road—that the place was not really abandoned.

Though migration was for me a spring phenomenon, Iroquois and its satellites catered primarily to fall hunters. October migrants were purposefully withdrawing from advancing winter, rather than dallying behind the slowly retreating season. Flocks kept high in the sky, risking descent into shotgun range only when absolutely necessary. The geese were quieter during autumn, "their calls / dried to whispers" in yet another old poem. What was heard in fall was mostly shooting, a more fulfilling sound, no doubt, for (human) participants than for spectators. Spring or fall, the mere presence of the refuge complex, a cooperative venture between state and federal entities with enough modesty to stay mostly out of sight, was itself significant. The world was going about its business, and even its noisiest, most disruptive species could, at least sometimes, ply its meddlesome, manipulative ways in harmony with those larger planetary rhythms.

The Alabama wetland constituted a soggy backwater, a liminal space between better known, more appreciated places. And when I attended college at Brockport, just a half hour away, I went there as often as I could. Sometimes I slipped away when I should have been in class. Sometimes I went alone, sometimes with a friend or two, occasionally with a girlfriend who shared at least somewhat in my enthusiasm. Now and again, I would still go with my parents. On one of these occasions, on a late summer morning, I saw my first egrets. At other times, a close-range encounter with a redhead or a pair of blue-winged teal along the Feeder Canal might mark a visit. But it was usually geese we came to see.

Today, Iroquois highlights its eagle program, appealing to patriotism while hailing a genuine conservation victory. But the adoption of an alternative flagship species also shows that what the Canada goose means to people in temperate North America has changed. Obvious all year in cities and suburban towns, geese have become less viable as a sublime embodiment of planetary rhythms. In fact, they increasingly are lumped with raccoons and gulls in the category of "nuisance animals": ubiquitous, inconvenient, maybe downright unnatural. "It doesn't take long for geese to adapt themselves to man," says Annixter's biologist, innocent of his words' double edge. Today, that tendency to adapt has compromised the Canadas' image to the point that, even in the remote Yaak Valley of Montana, nowhere near, one might think, the nearest neighborhood goose, Rick Bass feels obliged to establish that the birds he's praising in an *Audubon* article are "not backyard, yearlong golf course geese, but the wild migrators."

～

The Atlantic population of Canada geese rides the flyway twice each year between northern Quebec's muskeg and Chesapeake Bay, some birds continuing farther south during hard winters. Even the most jaded suburbanite would probably admit that Canadas are handsome creatures, more swanlike in proportions than other North American wild geese, and for that matter, most geese elsewhere. The larger forms are the world's biggest wild geese. Canadas excel at a kind of avian triathlon—they swim like ducks, walk with an ambling but not undignified gait, and, with just a short runway, can lift their ten-pound weight, quite substantial by bird standards, and take clean, direct, powerful flight. And then there's the "falling leaf" maneuver. The slightly elevated Stafford Pond parking lot was an ideal place to watch geese break formation. As a great rippling line would reach the pond, a few birds at a time would simply drop, drifting this way and that like leaves caught in the wind. Then, somehow, when they were maybe a hundred feet above the water, they would right themselves, easing into a long glide that ended in a graceful wake-producing splashdown, wings poised for a few seconds in a folding arc above each now-swimming goose. Then they would be at rest, as if they had been there all day, and always—this was the part that was hard to believe—in a clear spot, no matter how many thousands had already gathered at the pond.

Maybe one reason neighborhood geese lack charisma is that they are not often seen in flight, and when they do take to the air, bustling to and fro like harried shoppers, the cramped glimpse between houses isn't much of a substitute for the wide-ranging freedom and uncanny wisdom of the flyways. How could they have given up such freedom, such a life in the great world? How could we? Resident Canadas face a kind of double bind. On the one hand, they are wild enough to constitute a nuisance; on the other, they remind suburbanites that, like the neighborhood geese, we too, or at least our grandparents, must once have lived more natural, more adventurous, maybe more genuine lives.

~

In the suburbs of Rochester, one year-round home to Canada geese is Mendon Ponds, a county park built around a series of glacial eskers and the namesake kettle ponds, one of which is a popular swimming hole. The summer when my son Tom was ten, he and I joined my friend Chris's family there on a hazy, humid, overheated afternoon.

Just past the beach was a gathering place for park waterfowl—white domestic ducks; half-mallard, half-something-else dabblers; a few Canada geese. After swimming, we took a sack of leftover bread, not the most nutritious fare but an enduring tradition with people and park flocks, to throw to the ducks. The Canadas, aloof but also more aggressive than the smaller birds, stalked along the perimeter of the waterfowl crowd, snaking their necks forward to chase the ducks away from choice bits of bread.

As we stood by the pond, one big Canada that had been resting peacefully—listlessly?—at the edge of the milling congregation of birds suddenly shook violently in a kind of seizure, flipped over, and died. That's all. Our small group of witnesses stood and shifted for a moment before parents began ushering children back toward the swimming beach. Chris, who had seen a similar occurrence at a golf course, guessed that the bird had suffered a heart attack.

We learn about death from our pets, the common wisdom goes. But these birds weren't pets. They were park waterfowl—part wildlife, part scenery, perhaps part surrogate barnyard stock for suburbanites indulging a kind of semiconscious nostalgia for the farming life. But in their own right, they were individual organisms who had found a place in the world that worked for them even if giving up all that wild sky and golden marsh lacked appeal for us. Their lineages, apparent in unnatural amalgamations of breed and species traits, suggested that each had traveled a different route to Mendon Ponds. The domestics, or their ancestors, were perhaps dropped off in the dark of night a few weeks after Easter. The half-mallards descended, maybe, from wild birds that found life among the domestics both cushy and satis-fying. The Canadas spent their days in a testy but largely workable associa-tion with their distant relatives, snapping up bits of stale bread in a place that must have seemed like a kind of miracle, goods and services provided without ever leaving the neighborhood. Paradise. Shelter from the vicis-situdes of life in the wild for them, a break from stress and heat for the human swimmers. And then, one of the geese we had been feeding met the fate of all living things, the only creature I ever saw die of natural causes. Right there, in front of the kids.

~

The cover of the 1949 edition of Leopold's *Sand County Almanac* features an image of Canada geese, heads tilted upward releasing those evocative calls that struck something atavistic and irresistible within, I like to think, most people. But those were not the Mendon birds, or the Boston birds, or any of those "sky carp" that have taken to decorating or infesting parks and golf courses. In fact, flyway and neighborhood geese really are not the same birds. Although all are genetically *Branta canadensis*, migrants and residents represent discrete populations that generally interact little and that interbreed hardly at all.

Biologists and birders are still grappling with Canada goose taxonomy, with some, mostly older, analyses positing as many as eleven genetically rec-ognizable races. In a 2004 taxonomic shake-up, the small Aleutian and cack-ling races were split into their own species; at the same time, the American

Ornithologists' Union recognized the once-endangered giant Canada as a distinct subspecies. Current sources typically list from six to nine Canada goose subspecies. Conspiracy-minded skeptics, including some shooters' groups and animal rights activists, hold that the taxonomic divisions are designed either to inhibit or promulgate hunting. But regardless of the biological and political technicalities, there is a general consensus that the resident and migratory or "wild" birds are clearly different in behavior and lifeways, and that the resident population is a relatively recent development.

How did these birds come to be ensconced in park lakes and mall drainage ponds? Apparently, the residents are descendants of more-or-less domesticated geese from decorative flocks and, especially, birds used as "live decoys" early in the twentieth century. This practice struck later generations of hunters and wildlife managers, their collective consciousness raised by Teddy Roosevelt, Aldo Leopold, and the like, as unsporting, and was outlawed in many places in the 1930s. As a result, birds that had been kept captive for this purpose were dropped off in local "wilds" to mingle with the motley assortment of Easter ducklings. Other Canadas were released at refuges to augment migratory flocks or to reestablish extirpated populations. Whether because they were raised in captivity or because relocation compromised their migratory instincts, the freed birds showed no inclination to join the flyway Vs, preferring the easy life of city parks and, especially, suburbs, where malls, office lawns, and subdivisions provided an attractive combination of amenities.

In New York, according to the state's Department of Environmental Conservation, the ancestors of today's resident geese were set loose at Long Island and lower Hudson Valley sites. The population increased further when the state added more birds "north and west of Albany." The White Game Farm in the Alabama Swamp was one place where geese were released into the wild (I distinctly remember seeing pens filled with Canadas while riding past the game farm during one of my childhood days at the refuge). It was generally assumed that the newcomers would blend with existing populations, creating bigger flocks for sportsmen up and down the Atlantic coast.

But that's not what happened. At least not exactly. Migratory geese—Atlantic Canadas to taxonomic splitters—continued their long-distance flights, while the released birds settled into local habitats where the living, often assisted by park-bench patrons carrying cracked corn or stale bread, was easy. Not only that, but since the 1980s, the residents, despite diets packed with human-generated junk food, have done considerably better than the migrants, constituting an ever-increasing percentage of the species's regional population.

According to the DEC, the number of resident geese rose from a "handful" at the beginning of the twentieth century to about 120,000 by the mid-1990s. But, while the residents prospered, it eventually became apparent that something was amiss with migration. Breeding Atlantic Canadas in Quebec declined to 29,000 pairs in 1995 from over 100,000 just seven years earlier. At Iroquois, numbers of migrants dwindled by 70 percent, forcing New York to suspend the traditional fall goose-hunting season in 1995. Since then, the DEC has tried to alter the timing of the hunt so that it occurs either before or after migration, when mostly resident birds are present. Even with these belated adjustments, the most common face of the species in its interactions with New Yorkers is now that of the residents, classed with landfill gulls as degenerate, lazy freeloaders that should be out "in the wild" earning an honest living. Goose calls may still be stirring riding a brisk wind above the bare trees of April, but the same sound coming from the fussy confines of a suburban neighborhood may instead call up decidedly prosaic images of soiled lawns and other hazards. A 1999 DEC brochure lists goose-related threats as "over-grazed lawns, accumulation of droppings and feathers on play areas and walkways, nutrient loading in ponds, public health concerns at beaches and drinking water supplies, aggressive behavior by nesting birds, and safety hazards near roads and airports." The state recommends strategies to "discourage" the birds, a far cry from Cam and Bucky Calloway's heroic efforts to entice them, which included, in Cam's case, taking a fatal shotgun blast intended for a flock of migrant Canadas.

Leopold's essay "Goose Music" compares golf and hunting, concluding that, while golf is "sophisticated exercise," the enjoyment of wildlife is fundamental to the human experience. "A man may not care for golf and still be human," he asserts, "but the man who does not like to see, hunt, photograph, or otherwise outwit birds or animals is hardly normal." Such a person, says Leopold, is "supercivilized." Ironically, what's sauce for the human may be sauce for the gander too. There seems to be a widespread sense that geese on the links are a different matter from geese in the marsh. And Leopold's conclusion about the supercivilized human, "I for one do not know how to deal with him," is echoed by suburbanites concerning the resident Canadas.

Why have the residents done so well while the migrants struggled? One reason is that the mid-1980s through the mid-1990s were bad years for breeding in Quebec; although Atlantic Canada numbers have rebounded some since, the drop in the migratory population, corresponding with a period of expansion for the residents, shifted demographic proportions significantly. And in general, all other things being equal, the migratory life is more demanding than, say, hanging around a golf course, especially as mild, open winters become increasingly frequent. But hunting is also implicated. After all, goose hunters, immersed in family tradition and Aldo Leopold, want the romance of the marsh, the music of migration. Beats popping out of a sand trap, camouflaged in golf shoes and a Nike visor, or aiming between park bench slats with one eye on the lookout for the local police. Also, the general abundance of the species may have led managers to forget about the cultural and the alleged taxonomic differences between populations, concluding, both rightly and wrongly, that the Canada goose is hardly declining.

~

The swimming pool, an above-ground attached to a nondescript yellow 1960s-era house, is still there. It's been almost twenty years since we—my friend Tom, who now lives in Texas, and myself—last visited the Alabama Swamp, but the landmark that we traditionally used to make the left off Route 31 west of Brockport is intact and, as near as we can tell, unchanged. I resist the two wrong forks, and there's the curve, the gravel lot. Stafford Pond is more marshy, less open than we remember, perhaps because of the mid-August season, perhaps due to a scheduled maintenance drawdown, maybe, probably, a little of both. There are other changes. Plant succession has turned open marsh into soggy woods, while managers have reversed the process elsewhere. Swallow Hollow boardwalk is gapped and overgrown, a sign proclaiming it "dangerously unsafe." Nearby, an eagle-viewing tower already shows considerable signs of wear, a chainlink barrier slung around the top platform bulging and loose.

We don't see any eagles from the tower. Other typical birds of the area do make appearances. In the sumac and wild grape near the tower's base are catbirds, song sparrows, yellow warblers, and a secretive brownish bird, perhaps a female yellowthroat, though it's hard to say from our elevated perch. Great blue herons stalk through cattails at the water's edge, far below the tilting turkey vultures. In the distance, blue-winged teal flash their powder-blue namesake patches against the Swallow Hollow trees. And there are geese, residents no doubt, adding the distinctive sound that, even out of season, makes this place in my mind. Fittingly, there are few people, though it is a fine breezy summer Sunday, a cold front having blown in the day before. There are, though, empty cars—mostly pickups and SUVs—by the roadside, suggesting that local people are off somewhere in the refuge, maybe fishing.

The brick visitor's center is appropriately empty, evidently closed for the weekend. Elsewhere on the refuge, there are a couple of new trails and overlooks heralded by rustic signs. Leopard frogs are everywhere. Near the Onondaga trailhead, turtles bask and Joe Pye Weed blooms. At the Cayuga Pool overlook on the west side of the refuge, several great egrets are hunting, heads and necks tensely waving among black willows; it might have been at this same impoundment that I saw my first egrets in 1982. Today they are accompanied by a couple of cormorants and the day's only eagle, a young bald hunched at the top of a snag undoubtedly flooded by the managers when the pond was expanded.

After leaving Iroquois we head north, toward Lake Ontario. We wait for a turkey hen and seven half-grown chicks to cross Griswold Road. We pay our respects to the lake, then finish the outing with an unplanned stop at a lake-plain farmhouse where a retired Brockport professor, the mother of two of our college friends, lives. She relates her daughter's adventure in the New York City subway during the previous week's power blackout and tells us about her dog's frisbee accident. When we say we have been at the refuge, she says that when she first moved to the farm large flocks of springtime geese used to feed in the fields across the road. In recent years, they have been absent, but there has been a family of residents on a nearby farm pond.

~

I spent the evening before my return visit to the refuge with Tom, Chris, and Dave, friends whom I have known since my Brockport days. We were at Dave's home in a prosperous, pleasant neighborhood of shade trees and gardens, streets with names like Red Fox Lane and Hunter's Run, at the far edge of Rochester's suburban sprawl. It was a reunion of sorts; it had been many years since the four of us had been in the same place at the same time. There were steaks sputtering on the grill, potatoes baking in foil, corn on the cob boiling in the kitchen. Shortly after sunset a voice in the distance, then several. Goose music. The two of us who live away stopped our conversation immediately to listen. As for Upstaters Chris—with whom I had watched the goose die at Mendon Ponds some years earlier—and Dave, the last thing they wanted to hear was those damned geese, not in August, not in town. The birds were residents, annoying their neighbors in prime suburban style, with the classic suburban weapons—noise, dirt, bad timing. Acting inappropriately, out of control, dangerously unsafe for all we could tell. "Aggressive behavior by nesting birds." Then again, wasn't that spontaneous vibrant flash what we used to like about the untamed presences living—and dying—at the edges of our towns—the deer that could, did, erupt into the highway, the potentially rabid raccoons and cat-eating owls. Well, yes, but—

It's tempting to think that mid-twentieth century Americans moved to the suburbs to recapture the agrarian world of their grandparents, as if the suburbanite were a kind of homesteader from the city. But this isn't the truth. At least not the whole truth. The fact is that the suburbs were populated by newly mobile urban families seeking refuge from the cities with their mixed races, their motley juxtapositions of presences—urban expats freed from, among other things, sharing parks with strangers. But, since the suburbs were built for city people on land that was recently rural, danger could also come from the hinterland, where wild animals and disreputable inbred persons abound. The Alabama Swamp. *Deliverance*. Encased in a paranoia of interchangeable streets and pedigreed shrubbery, suburban gentry engage in a constant low-intensity struggle to maintain an inherently unstable secured zone between the bad schools and crime of the city and the feral countryside. Whether they hail from an urban reservoir or from White Game Farm, resident geese have moved in on the 'burbs from the less desirable real estate, less desirable in part because there are folks like them there, folks who don't know how to act around people. Like cousins from farm or inner city, not quite supercivilized enough to appreciate the putting-green perfection of a subdivision lawn, they park on the grass. And they come to stay. Leopold's wild poem rings like Walt Whitman's barbaric yawp or Allen Ginsberg's "Howl" or like the neighbor kid's music through the windows and streets, parks and parking lots, of little worlds carefully constructed to keep everything in its place and everything else out.

Homesteaders with no more respect for preexisting claims than their human counterparts, Canada geese throw down stakes at malls and school-yards, insinuating themselves between the tame and the wild, the city and the country, moving in on turf marked and prepared by suburban development. Like the city hoods and rural hillbillies that haunt suburban dreams, they squeeze the subdivisions from both sides. Clambering up from green-ways or dropping from the sky without the permission of the Neighborhood Association, they represent the world outside the gate.

But that's not all. Resident geese remind us of newer, deeper, threats to the insular quality of contemporary American life. Year-round Canadas have, in effect, released the species from its seasonal cage, undermining our sense of the orderliness of nature, giving voice to the profoundly troubling sense that those natural rhythms that the geese embodied are themselves unraveling. The resident population is, after all, a result of human med-dling. Meddling with geese. Meddling with habitat. Meddling even with the climate. "It doesn't take long for geese to adapt themselves to man." An accusation? At least a reminder of the law of unintended consequences, an unpleasant law, that, in self-contained neighborhoods constructed for safety and control by a culture increasingly dedicated to the assumption that, at the "big picture" level, our daily actions don't much matter. Don't worry, the slogan says, just do it.

Better not get too close. Things'll go for you, sure.

~

At dusk, the old men pack up what's left of their picnic supplies and abandon their Boston park bench. Perhaps they fold a checker or back-gammon board under an arm. Several hundred miles inland to the west at Iroquois, fishermen are returning to their cars with stringers of bass and sunfish. In the far north, Atlantic Canadas are raising the future of the flyway. From where I stand by Lake Ontario, none of this is visible. But if

I listen I might hear distant goose music, a question on the night air, from across a pond, across a continent. I still can't claim to know much of what the song or poem is saying. But something I think it might mean, at least to me, is *we're still here, we're still alive. The world changes. It changes you. It changes us. We adapt, we abide. You can't live on the earth and fence yourself off from us. Listen. In this place, at this time, you are not alone.*

## Summertime

August in Rochester. Another day of haze, temperature in the nineties—the twelfth time already this year. The Ontario Beach Park pier stirs the smell of decaying algae into the calm, dark opacity of the lake. No shelf of dried scum like a few decades ago, just a gently pulsing green soup. Bulldozers prod seaweed into dripping heaps. Caspian terns wheel while ring-billed gulls plow the shallows, picking at zebra mussels. No sign yet of West Nile virus or the avian botulism working its way over from Lake Erie. The beach is even open for swimming, the bacteria count having dipped to acceptable levels. In short, summer as it is now, in the twenty-first century.

I walk back toward the car, cutting through the virtually abandoned Georgian-style bathhouse constructed in 1931. The county is showing movies on Saturday nights, a bright banner slung bravely across the park's main entrance announces (though a looming fiscal crisis threatens to close all county parks most of the week). Across Beach Avenue, an endless construction project has been reconstituting the beach parking lot as, apparently, a beach parking lot, but fancy enough to suit the hypothetical new waterfront, the centerpiece of which is the proposed ferry across the lake to Toronto.

There was a ferry at one time, reaching into my mother's memory, a "working boat" bringing both merchandise and passengers between a then-much-glitzier Charlotte waterfront and Cobourg, Ontario, sixty miles east of a then-much-smaller Toronto. Now a cosmopolitan metropolis complete with major league sports and several million people, Toronto is clean, modern yet interesting, pedestrian-dominated—"friendly, familiar, foreign, and near" as the Ontario tourism boosters used to have it. Rochester, on the other hand, is adrift in the long-term doldrums of the rustbelt, with a slightly upscale, light industry twist. Ah, then, there's the rub. Why would anyone but a desperado (and most of those would be going the other way) pay for a boatride from Toronto to Rochester?

When I was in college, my friend Charlie and I envisioned—purely for fun—a similar project. Because our ship was imaginary, we had considerable leeway in solving this problem. Still, the best plan we could come up with was to Shanghai unsuspecting Canadians and force them to visit our fair city, presumably charging to take them home. The current ferry godmother fantasy, along with the beachside movies and colossal parking lot are—what? A statement of faith in the resilience of the blighted world, in our ability to come to our senses? Or faith in a return to past glory, another round on the historic carousel packed with merrymakers, Canadians this time? Progress, grinding inexorably in its tired old snake-oiled track, taking on all comers with the same old answers. The devil we know.

I'm cruising in the big red 1989 Pontiac Bonneville bomb my parents bought used when their sensible Taurus, beset with ordinary rust and the not-so-ordinary mysterious disintegration that leaves rings of corruption like bedsores on the roofs and hoods of Rochester cars, could no longer be held together with duct tape. I'm working the radio, exploring the steering-wheel-mounted controls that the folks make a point never to use. But there's nothing worth listening to, the NPR station on pledge break and everywhere else a wasteland of repetitive local news (ah, yes, the county is still broke) and equally repetitive right-wing commentary. Finally, having rounded the dial more than once, I settle on an old song just interesting enough to listen to under the circumstances.

When the record ends, the station proudly announces itself as none other than WBBF, the hoary Top 40 (once Top 20) station from my youth, before I was sophisticated enough to move on to the "album rock" of WCMF in high school. WBBF was typical of its ilk, with loud DJs who marketed themselves as local celebrities (one, Jerry Fogel, later a TV sitcom actor, even styled himself an "emperor" and urged his many fans to send for a publicity package including an autographed photo of his majesty in vaguely Napoleonic pre-Sergeant Pepper getup). The music? Everything from bubble gum to British Invasion to Motown, a cross-section of mid-sixties popular tunes, each under four minutes long. And now, I confess that the song that has arrested my aimless radio scanning is the Strawberry

Alarm Clock's "Incense and Peppermints," undoubtedly introduced in the overblown frenetic style that must have marked its debut in 1967. At least right now, WBBF is playing the same songs it did when I was a kid, which strikes me as some sort of revelation. Of course, there is a difference: the station is no longer considered Top 40 but has matured into the Classic Oldies genre that has become as ubiquitous as country or right-wing talk all over America, zeroing in on that great baby-booming mass that still secretly wants it to be the sixties.

I don't mean the die-hard hippies who seem to think that, with a little luck, it might still *be* the sixties, at least in small isolated places or individual lives (though there were a few of them, complete with flowing gray David Crosby locks, ambling out the pier, as I was, on a Monday morning, but probably without the precautionary sunscreen). They, it seems to me, have long-since rejected an unrecognizable present. I'm talking about my fellow *hoi polloi*, the drivers of most of these other cars, conscious of their luck at having the day off, the mothers and fathers and grandmothers and grandfathers taking the children to swim in the overheated, bacteria-nurturing waters of Lake Ontario, just as we swam in the equally dangerous water of our youth. People who need the world, including its changes, to be the same world it's always been.

And that means, of course, everyone, or at least everyone who reaches what might be called the "age of nostalgia," which is probably currently somewhere in the forties. I suppose I'm on my way to assuming my place as a classic old grump, grumbling about the changes in the world and bemoaning all of the things that only people my age care about and remember, like, say, evergreen forests or New England autumn colors or the streets of New Orleans or—Well, this is a problem then, isn't it? These are not things like bellbottom jeans or even the Beatles, though we tend to mix them all together in our middle-aged muddles, these people listening to the Zombies or The 1910 Fruitgum Company or The Supremes on WBBF while driving to and from the beach with the air temperature at ninety-two and the lake temperature pushing eighty and the bulldozers carting loads of algae, slimy green wakes trailing after them.

～

We need the world to continue to be the world, whatever that means to each of us. Yet we also need to change the world. And this is not just an inspirational slogan aimed at boosting ourselves up the socioeconomic ladder or making incremental progress toward some admirable social goal. No one to save with the world in a grave. We need, it seems, to replace an entire culture and we can't even complete the renovation of a parking lot.

Later, in the relative cool of evening, I walk out from my parents' apartment complex, a haphazard scatter of institutional-looking brick buildings I used to imagine as a Soviet-bloc prison, now overpriced and growing slightly shabby, toward our old house, where I lived between the ages of four and twenty, where, therefore, I grew up. It feels a little like the scene near the end of *My Ántonia* when Jim Burden returns to Black Hawk and wanders around looking for a town that existed years before, finding new and vaguely hostile people in all his old haunts. Here, though, Jim Burden notwithstanding, not much has really changed. The neighborhood is pure 1950s–60s suburban-tract America. Most of the streets were laid out by a single builder, Alfonso DiNardo. Certain architectural features—the slightly jutting upper story, the recessed front doorway and underslung garage—repeat in various combinations all along Alfonso Drive, Laura (DiNardo) Drive, and Sharon (DiNardo) Drive. Our house, for some reason, was not a DiNardo house. Perhaps it predated DiNardo by a handful of years. This was always a source of pride. We were different. Our house was a very very very fine house. If it was really as cookie-cutter as the others, at least the cutter pattern was from a different set. In our own minds, our house provided the same kind of distinction as the fact that my father didn't work at Kodak.

I've spent the last five days walking suburban streets, listening to the neighborhood, its sounds and overheard conversations—talk of families, jobs, the weather. Does my voice have that flattened *a*, that occasional rasping rise? I don't think I'm the same as everyone else. But I am like my Rochester friends, who sound like, who are like, everyone else here. When I'm going to the lake, I say "downt the lake" like everyone else. My non-Rochesterian wife and son say they can tell when I'm talking on the phone to someone from Rochester. So this is me, then, reflected in the mirrored sunglasses of shirtless car washers and wading-pool supervisors and bike-riding adolescents. I think of my current home in a neighborhood about as much like this one as the differences in local culture and geography afford. I'm beginning to suspect that something in the life we grow up with—call it the tone or the atmosphere (*color* would be a good word if not for the unintended racial connotations that lurk inevitably in any mid-twentieth-century suburban context)—exerts an inexorable and mostly unconscious pull on those of us scattered across the country, enmeshed in the pointless diaspora of the post–World War II "mobile society." Three thousand miles I roam, Otis Redding whistles from across the continent, just to make this dock my home. Or this tentacled crossroads collection of chain stores, convenience gas stations, franchise restaurants. And there we are again, stuck to the velcro of the familiar in a world that desperately needs change.

Of course, things are not what they were. The world does turn, something that, in the sixties, was considered a wellspring of hope. There's a whole generation, with a new explanation, after all. Not much of an explanation, as it turns out. The wars and slithery corporations that seemed already to be falling before the dawning Age of Aquarius are still with us. The changes that are manifest are not the kind to put a mind at ease.

~

Cormorants hunch against the barkless snag that marks the mouth of Braddock's Bay. A new boardwalk leads through tall cattails to an observation deck, where if I perch on the railing I can peer over the reeds at a family of mute swans—European transplants, aggressive harassers of native waterfowl—with four cygnets, resting placid on a bar. Farther off, a less successful pair serenely lead a single cygnet against the backdrop wall of cattails. A quick resonant *plunkle* close at hand reveals a sizeable fish, likely a carp, another Old World transplant. A purple martin swings over. A green heron cuts the thick air. Still the haze, but here, in the cover of the deep green reeds, past the droughty yellow of Braddock (the *'s* everyone pronounces is apparently unofficial) Bay Park's picnic table grass, it seems cooler, bearable, normal.

Not that normal's necessarily good. Besides, the Great Lakes haven't been really normal in my lifetime, and in some ways, are as healthy now as they've been. In 1998, several deepwater sculpins were caught by scientists, the first on the American side since the 1940s. And there's even some room for optimism concerning lake trout, which seem to be breeding in the lake after years of failed reintroductions. Recently, I watched a fisherman catch smallmouth bass from the Ontario Beach Park pier, although bass may soon be threatened by the newly arrived round goby, an egg-eater. I remember the bass—black bass in the local parlance—but Lake Ontario's trout heyday was before my time.

Early in the twentieth century, double-crested cormorants colonized the Great Lakes from the Lake of the Woods, moving first to Lake Superior and then gradually but steadily working their way across to the lower lakes. But not long after the birds arrived on Lake Ontario in the 1930s, DDT and other chemical pollutants virtually wiped them out. So cormorants have little claim on the memory of my grandparents' generation, my parents' generation (lake dwellers all, at least seasonally) or my own. I still find them exotic, bringing to mind social studies textbook pictures of Chinese fishing birds. I remember as a near-eidetic image the first one I saw, in typical wing-drying posture on a buoy in the lower Penobscot River in Maine in 1968, when I was thirteen. Since the late seventies, responding to reduced DDT and PCB contamination, cormorants on the Great Lakes have recovered so dramatically that they are now sometimes seen as nuisances. Perhaps their immigrant status has contributed to their unpopularity on the lakes, where newcomers—zebra mussels, round gobies—are generally bad news. Cormorants are easy to blame when the fishing goes bad; in 1998 Lake Ontario's major breeding colony on Little Galloo Island was ransacked by xenophobic marauders who shot eight hundred adult and fledgling birds, leaving nestlings to starve.

I'm not one to pretend that everything's okay. Or was. The "good old days"?—eutrophication, DDT, suburbs spilling into the wetlands to the vapid strains of bubble-gum pop. There's still something important out in the lake, down in the secret passages through marshes where I paddled tagalong canoes. But I can't stay here. Here might not even be able to stay here.

~

Great Lakes water levels—at least in the upper lakes, which are less manipulated and thus better reflect the overall water supply in the basin—ended the century unusually low; lake levels have fluctuated since, rebounding some before plunging again to well below their historic averages. This is not necessarily a bad thing. Indeed, any attempt to force constant water levels onto the lakes' poorly understood hydrologic fluctuations leads to environmental disenfranchisement of one sort or another. Newly distanced from the beach, resorts may go broke while shorebirds enjoy banner seasons on extended mudflats. Bad is good. Unfortunately, good is also bad.

A combination of warmer temperatures and the easy pickings provided by all those millions of zebra mussels has brought unheard of numbers of scaup—greater and lesser—into Lakes Erie and Ontario in recent winters. But these ducks are experiencing an overall decline in numbers and, apparently, productivity. Why? A strong suspect is selenium and other pollutants that zebra mussels are especially adept at concentrating. As Earth continues to heat up, lake levels and ecosystems could be altered fundamentally, perhaps irrevocably; if that happens, all bets are off. Except of course, for those of high, dry beach hotels on the sands of Lake Michigan, where the odds are long and the results not hard to predict. The cause of the current low water level is a series of hot dry summers and mild dry winters, exactly what climate change is predicted to bring to the basin. Maybe we should believe we're on the eve of destruction.

A few winters back, Rochester enjoyed a year with virtually no snow cover. No shoveling, no boots, and little use for heavy parkas. For people for whom winter has traditionally been protracted and hard, there is a certain pleasure in such things. As long as they don't happen all the time, which, it seems, they might. On the phone, my parents and I recalled the blizzard of '66—snow blocking living room windows—and the year the lake froze. Without admitting it, maybe without knowing it, there were, I'm guessing, a lot of people harboring secret wishes that the next year would feature high drifts and a shelf of solid surface ice reaching far out toward Canada.

That climate change threatens winter is obvious. But summer also has something to lose. *Summertime. Long hot (but not so very hot) days by the lakeshore, the water not clean, but better than it was, sure, and always cool. Black terns skim the shore. Ospreys will return, with DDT banned. So much time. Out of school, lying back with the transistor radio, BBF tossing out "Day Tripper" and "The Kids Are Alright" along with harmless fluff like "Incense and Peppermints," as lampreys sail in on the Saint Lawrence Seaway, waterfront houses pop up faster than cattails around Long Pond, the war in Vietnam inches across the years toward my eighteenth birthday. But for now, sings Janis, the living is easy.*

Returning to the source offers a chance to "be whole again beyond confusion," Robert Frost says in "Directive." But it isn't the same. It can never be the same. Time passes, our children's world is not our own. We have what we've made, and not so much of what made us. We'll have to live with it. But let's not get too comfortable when we sink into our climate-controlled cars and bury ourselves in the "classics" on the way downt the lake, our trusty DEET in the glove compartment, for the beachfront showing of—what should it be—*To Sir With Love? Woodstock? The kids are alright?* Why would they be? Are we?

While we dust off the uniforms of Emperor Jerry Fogel's army, the kids are deliberately scratching the vinyl we guarded from stray fingernails and bad needles. One way or another, time, it would appear, is most definitely not on our side. At least the movie won't get rained out; not even the radio holds any hope for an evening storm to break the heat. We'll have to get ice cream at Abbott's, still the best; there'll be a long line. The temperature's rising and the jukebox is blowing a fuse. The Strawberry Alarm Clock is ringing.

# Ferry Crossing

I

In 1960, the year I turned five, my father had his first heart attack: at forty, serious enough for his doctors to resort to "it could go either way." They said he had to quit smoking. He did. Not good enough. Another attack came ten years later. A "two-time loser," he was one of the first in Rochester to undergo bypass surgery. The operation cleared three arteries. Today it would be five. As it was, the remaining two plagued him the rest of his life, along with cumulative scar tissue, residual pain in the leg from which vein grafts were taken, and generally weakened circulation. It probably didn't help that the prevailing wisdom recommended rest and warned against exertion, as if his body were a small boat in open water, with no rescuers in sight except Charon, the underworld ferryman of Greek mythology, who was always there to pick him up should it capsize.

Still, he made do, enduring a gradual decline that culminated in bouts of heart failure, each one cutting a little deeper into his already-deficient circulation. During the autumn of 2003, about two years before his death, a particularly catastrophic episode resulted in intermittent hospitalization for a period of several months. He emerged—much to the surprise of his long-time general practitioner—but weakened to the point that his contin-ued ability to live at home with my octogenarian mother, reasonably robust but a bit worn herself by the demands of nursing care, was in doubt. On the phone, his voice often crackled like an amateur radio signal from a galaxy far away (though he had little use for science fiction, which he dismissed as "those crazy things"). Or maybe from "the other side"? That would be the traditional view from Charon to Kübler-Ross, so familiar that it swirls into the fog of cliché. Perhaps it's best to focus on what we know, though that, too, is convention. Asked if he could see anything of the other side, the dying Thoreau replied, "One world at a time."

~

One world at a time. My father's early life is a mystery to me, held in a time and place that is, and must always be, beyond my experience. I find some perspective when I imagine my son envisioning his parents' world before his birth; the landmarks and icons—*Dr. Strangelove, Sgt. Pepper*, Watergate—are there, but the texture of individual days, entire weeks and months, has vanished. What do I know about the lives of men and women shaped by forces and events—like World War II—that I can apprehend only indirectly? Even if it might help me understand my parents, I can't free FDR, Tojo, Hitler from the grainy retrospective of the recent past. There's *der Führer* just over the horizon, stiffarm saluting from the back seat of his car or prancing on stage before cheering crowds, orchestrating the deaths of millions. But it's no use. The veil of a decade or two may be thin, but it is a barrier nonetheless. And who would want to relive the nightmares of the past? My father was part of that, and he appreciated his place in it. He kept his army pictures, maintained at least one lifelong friendship with a service buddy, and visited his name on the local veterans' monument. But he was not ready to declare himself a hero. He found politicians boasting of their battle conquests unseemly, even disgusting, though his own "greatest generation" journey was the most obviously significant adventure of his life.

In his pictures from the war, my father leans casually in exotic doorways or against sandbagged bunkers; one staged photo shows him—in a fez no less—riding a camel beneath the pyramids and Sphinx, as nonchalant as if he'd been traveling by camel his whole life. And there were stories: the jackals that crept into Indian tents at night, the Chinese youth who wanted, and was duly promised, a "dogger." Some of these stories, the Army Air Corps equivalent of urban legends, I suppose, weren't all that nice, reflecting the easy Euroamerican bigotry that dismisses everyone other than ourselves as inexplicable and wild. Chinese crewmen accompanied their allies on "over the Hump" cargo flights between India and China; unaware of the sanctity of human life, one story went, they gambled, with losers being pushed from the plane, resulting in mysterious personnel shortages on the other side. The C-47 may have been traversing Earth's highest mountains, but the missing men had made an even longer crossing on their own, without parachute or plane.

Though he was no flag-waver, my father didn't downplay the importance of the big war. How could he, since that "struggle between good and evil" became the virtual definition of significant action? But he knew his own role was modest and seemed to prefer it that way. He was discharged as a private first class, an honorable but unassuming rank. I saw the pictures and heard the stories, and for a while in high school wore his Flying Tigers patch on my red plaid jacket. But he never talked much about what it felt like to go to war, see the world, and return to his old life in Rochester. He wasn't exactly evasive, but in personal matters he kept his counsel.

In his own way he reflected the values of his generation. For the most part, he respected the authority represented by the government, the medical profession, higher education, and reliable brand names. Though he saw through the rhetoric rigged up in support of the Vietnam War, he could not have been completely comfortable with the anti-establishment, "let it all hang out" sixties. Maybe he never lost the soldier's resigned determination; no matter what happened in the larger spheres of politics and culture, he approached his chosen or destined life role—maintaining his house, raising his children, providing for his family—as a job that needed to be done. If he did his job well, everything was likely to work out, at least for himself and his own. Play it close to the vest. Just live your way through confusion and doubt, moving forward bravely with your head down.

A significant portion of my father's inner life, down to his small idiosyncrasies, was cloaked in a durable, self-perpetuating armor composed of roughly equal parts hope and fear. He could be outspoken and frank at times, allowing himself a carefully constrained measure of cynicism. But there was always an inaccessible center, a place guarded, perhaps, even from his own close examination, where doubts, impulses, and unruly desires were quarantined. One trivial example: in his final years he grew very concerned about his appearance. From a husky 200-plus pounds, he dwindled to about 115. In need of new clothes, he took to his catalogs with a sartorial eye that left the family flabbergasted. This newfound enthusiasm made it easier to shop for him; his used to be the hardest Christmas present. Like most of his peers, he preferred things neat and trim; he had his sparse hair cut every two weeks, "whether it needed it or not." But when he echoed his father in labeling the longhaired youths of the late sixties and early seventies "apes," I knew he did so mostly from amusement at my grandfather's caricature and the way it could easily be applied to me. By the standards of midcentury suburban America, his neatness was not excessive, and he was no dandy. His tastes had always been conventional—he wore leisure suits in the seventies—but not overly trendy. He chose the products of trusted, even stodgy, companies noted for workmanship over the offerings of the latest purveyors of style. Moreover, his condition at the end of his life prevented him from going out much anyway. What, then, was the source of his late plunge into fashion? Perhaps it was a symptom of some long-suppressed desire or anxiety endemic to the midcentury suburbs, where appearances were everything and strict, arbitrary neighborhood standards measured both competence and worth. Whatever the underlying cause, he left a closetful of carefully chosen but unworn shirts and pants, a dresser bulging with socks. A selection of those unworn clothes made their way to my own dresser and closet; some are still there.

~

Like my father, my paternal grandfather suffered through a protracted illness with remarkable resilience and a frazzled but enduring good humor. He too was in and out of hospitals, his old-fashioned family doctor shaking his head, somberly asserting that each time would be the last. His problem was pulmonary: chronic asthma, aggravated by a lifetime of pipe and cigar smoking. Like my father, he was subject to fluid in the lungs. One difference between them was my grandfather's contrary ambition. He never admitted he was sick, and continued to embark on major home improvements—knocking out walls was a specialty—until he was in his seventies. Even after his health forced him to give up his house at Wautoma Beach and move in with us, he would inch his walker toward some destination across the neighborhood, his flannel shirt sagging from his shrunken arms, a wry, determined smile on his face. He kept himself young, or at least in motion, but was a constant source of worry to his sons. My father opted, perhaps partly unconsciously, to accommodate reality. He pushed back a little: he had a hard time resisting the snow shovel. But he protected what health he had. He said he never wanted to be a "burden," a pledge he took seriously, although his decline ultimately resulted in an understandable weariness overtaking my sister Anne and her husband Al, who spent so much of their time running to the store, the doctor, the hospital.

The word that best characterizes my father's later years is *calm*. He was always inclined toward mildness. Oh, I remember arguments, vigorous but brief, sometimes with me. My grades weren't as good as they could have been or the grass wasn't cut often enough—the usual subjects of minor family disputes. Not very appreciative of the aesthetics of the suburban yard, I was an indifferent edger, a flaw he found particularly unbecoming. But he never held a grudge, and as he aged and his health unraveled, his calmness, part steadiness, part stress avoidance, maybe part apathy, grew until he seemed incapable of anything more like anger than a passing in-dignation at the war-hero posturing of some presidential candidate or the goading of a noisy neighbor or inconsiderate relative.

How does one find such calm in what must have been a typically stress-ful, hectic life? It didn't, in his case, come from a deeply ingrained spiritual practice. At least I know of no such thing, unless the years of sitting be-fore the television, which ran each day from mid-afternoon till after the *Tonight Show* monologue, opened in him a kind of Zen space that he him-self was unaware of. Deep bitterness seems just as unlikely as deep fulfill-ment. People have told me that I show a similar if less profound calmness, something that, if true, I must have inherited along with a playful sense of humor I've long recognized as his.

He found delight in verbal mannerisms, including his own, and would sometimes repeat a phrase he'd just said or heard on television, empha-sizing and exaggerating inflections as if perplexed that such things were said in quite that way. One night at an Adirondack motel—I was, I think, twelve or thirteen—we laughed so long and hard over the quaint message on an antique post card that my mother took me aside and told me to stop, that he might have a heart attack, and literally die laughing over nothing more than a young girl named Eulalia's 1906 enumeration of her Christmas presents: a basket for handkerchiefs, a "large picture of the ocean in a lovely frame."

At some point long before I was born, my parents lived near a shared household consisting of three young couples, the "Jolly Six." They must have had parties, I suppose, or at least been a bit boisterous. At any rate, for years my parents and other relatives would chuckle when they recalled the Jolly Six. I have no idea who they were, and I suppose I never will—maybe no one ever will now—but I'd be surprised if it wasn't my father who gave them that moniker. It didn't take him long to tag neighborhood newcomers he'd see through his window with odd but appropriate nicknames—the Sidewinder, Mr. and Mrs. Yellowcar, Eggthrower. Never mean-spirited, his wit emerged as a natural expression of the understated astonishment with which he viewed the people and circumstances defining his everyday existence.

Perhaps his guarded ease was innate, brought out by fear for his delicate state of health and the postwar suburban reticence to confront anything very private and important. Whatever the source, the result was a quiet approach to life he cultivated in order to stay in this one world for a time, which, as Thoreau implies, was enough.

## 2

My grandparents on my father's side owned a year-round house across quiet, dead-end Wautoma Beach Road from a shore of glacier-scarred, wave-rounded limestone, sandstone, and granite cobbles. The light gray one-story converted cottage had been backed up from the rising Lake Ontario—twice—during long-ago periods of high water. As early as I can remember, the house was far enough from the beach to be safe from storms, but close enough to have its own lakefront. Each Saturday morning, we'd drive the thinly traveled Lake Ontario State Parkway to Wautoma, skirting the inland edges of the lake's lagoon ponds—iceboats in winter, great blue herons in the summer marshes. Weather permitting, after dinner while Anne and the adults were washing dishes or gossiping about neighbors and relatives, I was free to go over to the lake, where I practiced skipping stones, bombed driftwood ships with larger rocks, watched seaway-bound "big boats" in the hazy distance, and hunted around for things washed up on shore.

My parents met at Wautoma Beach, where both their families owned cottages. It must have seemed almost unnerving after a gray winter in the vertical spaces of the city to have all that expanse spread out in front of them, all the way to some over-the-horizon Canada. Though far and foreign, the other side was not inaccessible. You could go there, as my parents did now and again, on the Cobourg ferry, which carried coal mostly, but made a good show, with dinner, dancing, and live bands, for joyriding guests. Not much in Cobourg, but who cared? A day on the water was its own reward.

Today, with shore linked to city by a network of highways, most waterfront residents stay year round, but when my parents were young, the beaches were a little ways out of town, and it was common even for people of ordinary means to have a summer place somewhere like Wautoma Beach and a winter home in the city. When my father's parents purchased the cottage soon to be their permanent residence, my mother's family were already long-established as summer people. They would head for the lake around Memorial Day and return to town for school after the Labor Day weekend. Their winter home was on Birr Street, in the city's Tenth Ward, a typical northeastern urban neighborhood of houses that, to me, still always look much larger than they are, their height and closeness to each other creating the impression that each one is trying to break free from its miniscule lot. You could hardly look out a side window without feeling that you were in the next-door dining room with the legendary Mrs. Penn or Mrs. Shea. Oddly, considering the claustrophobic proximity of the houses, I don't remember ever seeing either woman, though they, especially Mrs. Penn, were great friends of my grandmother. Eventually, after my mother's father died at fifty-three and the children grew up, my grandmother reluctantly gave up the cottage to live full time on Birr Street.

My father's family discovered Wautoma just as their two living boys—a third had died young of diphtheria—were going off to war. So when my mother returned to the beach the summer after V-E Day, the older couple busily winterizing the place next door suddenly appeared to have sprouted sons, Fran and Harold, close to her own age. A few years later, when my grandfather retired from the electric company, they moved to the lake for good, so precipitously, the family legend goes, that my grandmother hardly had time to pack. I don't know what prompted the move, but I suppose it had something to do with their West Side neighborhood "turning," becoming home to dark-skinned people. This is, after all, a mid-twentieth century American story. Whatever the reason, they were year-round residents of Wautoma by the time I was born; until they moved in with us, their lakeside home was the only one I ever associated with them.

∾

My mother swam. Her father built his own boats. When her younger brother—my Uncle Gene—grew up, he bought a cabin cruiser, which became his refuge and weekend home. Though my paternal grandfather was a good casual fisherman, I don't think I ever saw him in his aluminum outboard motorboat, which was never formally suspended from its metal frame boathouse but simply tipped hull-up in the grass a safe distance from the water. So it isn't surprising that my father, content to stroll around the shallows with a bar of soap, was no swimmer. One of my mother's enduring disappointments was that he was never interested enough to get a pool, despite several others, mostly above-grounds, in our neighborhood. His lack of enthusiasm may have had something to do with "backwashing" the pool at Arcadia High School, where he was head building custodian. I remember going with him Saturday mornings, but I don't recall exactly what backwashing entailed, except that it was an unpleasant duty, if only because it added an extra day to the work week. Arcadia was his last building before he was promoted to department head of "central stores," a position balanced uneasily between the blue-collar world he had always inhabited and the accountability, if not the social status, of management. He ran the school district's warehouse until he retired, an early exit resulting from the second heart attack and ensuing surgery.

While he was working he brought home animated discussions of characters he dealt with—that Burton, that Mike—and of unreasonable school principals who expected instant delivery of everything from paper to desks, even when they hadn't requisitioned them beforehand. Officially, he was parallel in rank to other educational administrators, but he was not equal in either salary or prestige, and the limitations of his own high-school education must have exacerbated his discomfort among glib white-collar colleagues. Just the same, my memory has him close to universally liked and respected by his co-workers. I can't imagine him as anything but a conscientious, reliable employee. He believed in work and in the potential for self-betterment, and his experience seems to justify that faith. His salary remained working-class, but that was enough in those prosperous days for him to move his family into an almost-new house in a neighborhood still under construction. Our home was eventually furnished with most of the obligatory accoutrements—window-mounted air conditioner, color TV—that defined a modest but solid level of suburban success. The driveway sported a sensible Falcon for errands in town and a full-size Galaxy 500 for visits to the lake, country rambles, and summer vacations.

Vacation was practically an American ritual. With my father behind the wheel, I'd play navigator, pressing for the smallest roads, the ones in light gray on the map. I considered him a cautious ally in route negotiations. Knowing the condition of the tires, the price of gas, his own physical state, he might not turn off the main thoroughfare, but he wanted to, and once in a while he did. Whether on highways or secondary roads, we'd cruise from destination to destination till late afternoon, when my parents' attention would turn casually at first but with increasing and sometimes anxious concentration to finding, at my mother's insistence, a self-contained motor court or "housekeeping cottage" unit for the night. Though my mother had a license and often drove in Rochester, on the open road my father did all the driving; his sport shirt untucked, unbuttoned at the neck over a white T-shirt, he looked a little weary at day's end, especially when we had trouble finding an acceptable, affordable place to stay. One evening in Vermont my father and sister, stretching their legs after a long day in the car, happened on some corner spot where he sat down and had a beer, so out of character that Anne reported the scandal with considerable glee.

Of all the rural New York and New England locales we'd explore, "the mountains" were my father's favorite. Just across the Adirondack Blue Line, he embraced the smell of pine and the lift of the road with a characteristic "we're climbing!" He must have gone to the Adirondacks when he was young, because every year he'd say that the sadness he felt on leaving the mountains, and that he saw in me also, was something from his childhood, a time of his life obscure even to my mother, another other side, too far, perhaps, for Charon himself.

~

Retirement magnified my father's calm. Whatever satisfaction he received from his job was not sufficient to prevent him from easily letting go. And once started, the letting go inevitably took its course. Anne married. I went to college. The house gradually became "too much," and my parents moved first to a mobile home close to Anne's family, and then to an apartment in their old neighborhood. When the stairs came to be more trouble than they were worth to his circulation-challenged legs, my parents exchanged their third-floor place for a gloomy, flood-prone basement apartment in the same complex, where they stayed for the last twenty years of his life. Losses easily absorbed and accepted, it seemed at the time, and still does, at least from my vantage point.

Not that it was all melancholy. Both Harold and Norma had always loved children, and they found sincere, enthusiastic joy in grandparenthood's little league games, birthday parties, and, eventually, graduations and weddings. They took to eating out regularly, and came to be on a first-name basis with waitresses all over town, a few of whom invited them to first communions or brought their kids for trick-or-treat on Halloween.

There were even journeys. My parents drove to Indiana to visit my family and meet their youngest grandchild when my wife Cara and I were graduate students at Purdue. When Tom and I visited Rochester each summer (our family's limited finances dictated that it was usually just the two of us), my parents always planned a day trip to Niagara Falls, making an obligatory stop at the small aquarium on the New York side before crossing the Rainbow Bridge into Canada. They rested in the Queen Victoria Park gardens while I took Tom on the *Maid of the Mist* or farther along the river walk above the falls. For a while, Harold and Norma joined my uncle and aunt—Fran and Fran—on mysterious overnighters to Clarence, a nondescript factory outlet town east of Buffalo. I don't think any of them could have explained the appeal of Clarence, but it became something of a tradition nonetheless. Later, somewhat surprisingly given my father's ambivalence toward military glory, they attended a series of army reunions. He maintained his characteristic reserve about the present but perhaps made his peace with the processes of history, as if his past were finally far enough away to be safe from adulation and abuse. He even successfully enlisted his congresswoman in reclaiming some missing service medals. But after a few years the reunions shifted from Niagara to a Sunbelt location beyond the horizon of my parents' lives.

That horizon closed so gently that you could easily forget it was happening. If you weren't them, that is. I have no way of knowing how gradual or abrupt it seemed to my father. The long-impaired legs went first. Walking grew more and more difficult, less and less rewarding. But walking was never something he relished, and so its loss too was taken, an unfortunate expression, in stride. The other side became the other room, and a passage from one part of the apartment to another a journey requiring planning and care. The mountains were relegated to memory and the glossy photographs in *Adirondack Life*. Out of sight but faithful in its way, Lake Ontario remained, its presence seen and felt as a quality of light and sky through basement windows.

## 3

My adult life has happened far from Rochester and my relatives. The space between us has not been the transparent span defined by water, but is best measured in the twin nemeses of modern life: time and circumstance. I'm a college teacher and the Christmas vacation is busy with grading; then the holidays themselves, which, with relatives far away and scattered in different directions, we've usually celebrated in our own nuclear family; then gearing up for the next semester. I haven't lived in New York since I left in 1982, and haven't had the means or opportunity for frequent or protracted visits—once a year for a week or two during July or August, for the most part, except for special occasions like my parents' fiftieth wedding anniversary. But summer, my mother told me, finding a time to call when he wasn't listening, might be too late. Better come now during the holiday break.

Christmas week in Rochester was enveloped in the daily gray of the Upstate winter. Much of the time my father spent slumped in the corner of a couch, sometimes watching television, but just as often faced away, toward the wall, as if finally achieving an armistice with the machine that had held the greatest generation captive since the big war's end. Most days he didn't get dressed unless company was expected. He dutifully endured the obligatory parade of cousins and Christmas presents, tinged with the awareness that, for him, this would be the last—the Last Christmas, maybe the last visit. As it was in my case.

One afternoon that December, with my father and mother dozing on their respective couch and recliner, I drove to the Charlotte pier, at the mouth of the Genesee River, a significant roistering spot for generations of young Rochesterians, my parents' and my own in a sequence extending deeper into both past and future. On the corresponding structure across the river in Summerville, a snowy owl had been terrorizing the gulls, according to the *Democrat and Chronicle*'s weekly bird column. He looked innocent enough from the Charlotte side, a bit grumpy perhaps, the source of his apparent discomfiture unclear. Snowies migrate to the Great Lakes most winters, sometimes driven south in significant numbers by lack of Arctic prey. During these "invasion years," my father encountered them regularly in Arcadia High School's sports fields, just a short flight from the lake; once or twice he picked his way across the frozen ground in an uncharacteristically athletic effort to see how close he could get. Though he was not a birdwatcher or amateur naturalist, he had encouraged my childhood fascination with birds and other animals, and he was quietly attuned to the presence of wildness in the Adirondacks and the New England woods. In his own understated manner he maintained an active curiosity about his surroundings, at least until his cardiac battles progressed from sharp engagements with angina to the siege of congestive heart failure.

The pier was treacherous, with fantastic ice draperies gilding the handrails and a wicked sheeting making for a slow, slippery trek out to the foghorn. Distant flocks of ducks—probably mergansers—skimmed the waves. It was not snowing or overly cold, but I encountered few people. The adjacent *Spirit of Ontario* terminal was not much more populated than the pier, though with its big central Christmas tree it put on a brave face. After surviving typhoon winds and accidents on its way from a shipyard in Perth, Australia, a port my father's transport called at in 1945, the huge, expensive "fast ferry" had arrived in Rochester amid controversy—there were doubters—and fanfare. With cruise ship amenities evoking the carefree festive atmosphere of the Cobourg days, the *Spirit of Ontario* was touted as the centerpiece of lakefront economic renewal. But the time, it seems, had passed. The ferry was soon plagued by a series of financial and mechanical failures, once even stranding a load of paying customers in the middle of the lake. By the conclusion of the first year of service, the company that operated the ferry had already gone belly-up, and the city was mounting a game but futile effort to redeem the venture as a public enterprise. In the optimistically grandiose terminal, little tourist shops—refrigerator magnets, postcards, various gewgaws touting Canadian-American friendship—forlornly surrounded the cordoned off main tenant. The ship itself was broken down again, drydocked at a considerably less ostentatious berth across the lake in Toronto.

My always-helpful brother-in-law took me back to the airport on the kind of deep blue winter afternoon that promises lake-effect snow. When we left the apartment, my father was curled into his usual corner of the sofa. Though I had already said goodbye, I went back inside pretending I had forgotten something. I thought I should attempt another, more private, farewell, which, after making a cursory inspection of a few randomly chosen surfaces, I did. Truth is, it wasn't much different from the previous leave-taking. He was, he had told me before, glad I had come. So was I. There wasn't much more to offer. Besides, the car was running, and my mother was waiting with Al in the cold. Still, given the chance, I'd do the same thing again, no doubt with the same vaguely unsatisfactory result. Who can say what such a gesture meant to someone already waiting on Charon's dock?

~

The next time I found myself in Rochester was at the beginning of April; the memorial service, delayed to skirt the worst of winter, took place in a bitterly cold rain as my Catholic family awaited inevitable news from Rome about the failing Pope John Paul II, whose age made him an exact contemporary of my father.

Both brothers, Harold first and then Fran, died within two months of each other that winter, each a victim of years of cardiac disease, perhaps the definitive ailment for men of their generation. They weren't alone. World War II's survivors are being lost at an alarming if not surprising rate, taking with them the last black-and-white wedding pictures, the last summers without beach closures, the last unquestioned assumptions that people like us must, by definition, be the good guys, and that, somehow, things would all work out for the better. The war, the flight to the suburbs, the summer vacations, the heart attacks: all traces of passage through the complex landscape of the American century. And what's left at the end of that lifetime, that century? My father's disdain for fictional space utopias has turned out to be prescient: we really don't seem to be bound, at least anytime soon, for a glorious evolutionary future on the Starship *Enterprise*. Maybe we aren't bound anywhere at all.

At this point of impasse, the temptation is to take refuge in the obvious. Clichés. Life goes on. It's better this way. If you're a literary sort, you can add others. Charon. Thoreau. It all adds up to one more journey. At least that's the way we inevitably think of it, the dead ferrying off, the after-image of their presence gradually precipitating as a collection of remnant facts, analyses, images. There they go, the ferryman in a pressed white shirt with gold-trimmed epaulets, my father waving cheerfully from the railing, a full company of his peers leaning casually against Packards and Hudsons, Impalas and Galaxies, growing smaller in the distance. Ultimately, there's little left to say. But of course, that's not true. There's always more to say. That's what clichés are for, to carry us across those impossible gaps between what we know, or almost know, and what we can express, when you can't get there from here. But that's not right either. You always get there from here. You can't not get there from here. Unlike the *Spirit of Ontario*, Charon can be trusted.

## Black-Throated Blue

> We grieve only for what we know.
> — Aldo Leopold

I was playing three-corner catch with two friends at Lakeside Beach, one of a chain of state parks providing public camping along Lake Ontario's shore. When the ball skipped past me into brushy woods, it was my duty to find it (a baseball can stay hidden in undergrowth for a very long time). As I scratched my way through wild grape and mayapple—carefully avoiding that most ubiquitous of New York groundcover plants, poison ivy—I glanced up into the low branches of a small beech, warped nearly horizontal by the play of forces in the young woods' developing understory, and there I saw a "different" bird, oddly patterned with a black mask separating an indigo back from white underparts. I knew at once that it was a warbler, the first I'd seen except for the yellows that appeared from time to time in my suburban yard. The next week, when I looked the bird up in a Lift Bridge Bookstore copy of Roger Tory Peterson's *Field Guide to the Birds of Eastern North America*, I was able to identify it as a black-throated blue, called by another guide the least common of the common species.

I've been alert to the presence of birds ever since my family and I discovered the cardinal. These southern finches were new as a common songbird in Upstate New York, and we noted the difference between the red male and the subtly green-gray female. Soon we found another bird, superficially similar to the female cardinal, but smaller and given to barreling through my grandparents' lakeshore neighborhood in gangs, calling in thin high voices while ransacking berry bushes and hawking insects, then disappearing again a week or so later. So the new bird in town introduced us to the cedar waxwing, which had been there all along. Now it's hard for me to imagine not knowing waxwings as garrulous, impulsive neighbors. With birds, one discovery leads to another. We first recognized the yellow warbler as a small bird that almost, but not quite, looked like a goldfinch.

Despite their bright colors and distinctive patterns, warblers can be challenging to spot, much less identify. They are tiny, smaller than a sparrow, and move through the trees like windblown leaves, with which it can be surprisingly easy to confuse them. They are common and famous in aggregate, yet obscure as individual species, the black-throated blue reduced to sharing a page with two other kinds in the old Herbert Zim *Golden Guide* that everyone starts with, the one with robins on the cover.

A few years after that camping trip at Lakeside Beach, I saw my second black-throated blue. I was at a cottage on Wellesley Island, one of the largest of the Thousand Islands, a long-time resort area where the Frontenac Arch bridges the Saint Lawrence River at its source, where the Adirondack Mountains swim the river from the Canadian Shield to form their outpost in the northeastern bulge of New York State. The black-throated blue was creeping along one of the great arms of an enormous oak, almost at eye-level from my lookout on the unfinished upstairs porch; my companions (not the ones from the camping trip) were below, on the main floor.

Both of these encounters owe some of their charm, and perhaps some of the clarity with which I remember them decades later, to their intimacy. Despite the presence of other people nearby, the warbler appeared to me and me alone, at least as far as I knew. Encounters with warblers are generally fleeting, and I made no attempt to point the birds out to anyone else. Perhaps I should have.

~

The black-throated blue belongs to a diverse group of small New World passerine birds, with half a hundred species in several genera spending at least part of each year in the United States. Because they are essentially woodland birds, most—though by no means all—prefer the eastern half of the country. Many are among the most brightly colored springtime migrants, drifting through the woods in mixed flocks. On their breeding grounds, they gravitate to particular levels of the forest. Some, like the ovenbird, are found on or near the ground, while others, such as the cerulean, prefer the canopy. Redstarts and yellow warblers might be found at an intermediate level. A few, like the marsh- and thicket-loving yellowthroat, choose nonforested habitats. The black-throated blue is usually found in the lower reaches of the forest canopy or beneath a shrubby ceiling like the one at Lakeside Beach.

Each of my first two black-throated blues was quietly and deliberately working along a main branch, probably gleaning insects, their prime summer food source, from bark or leaf undersides in a way that makes the birds both inconspicuous and easy to watch. This behavior, though not unique to the black-throated blue, is characteristic; I've encountered black-throated blues occupied similarly several times since then. Both of my early sightings were of males; the female is a delicate olive-gray, sharing with the male a distinctive white patch on the primaries, visible in the folded wing.

Warblers and other passerines still migrate through the eastern United States in numbers sufficient to be detected by radar. There are still "warbler fallouts" in which an observer in Upstate New York might find as many as twenty species in one small woodlot or city park on a single day. A few species, such as the magnolia, appear to be profiting from recent land use changes. But the total number of warblers grows smaller year by year, with some species only half as plentiful as they were a few decades ago. The causes of the decline are complex and poorly understood, involving winter, summer, and migration habitat loss, and forest fragmentation that has made nests vulnerable to a variety of edge predators ranging from housecats to parasitic brown-headed cowbirds.

Black-throated blues are subject to pressure at both ends of their migration, as well as at points along the way. The birds breed in deciduous or mixed woodlands from the Maritime Provinces to Minnesota and West Virginia. They winter across Central and South America, the Bahamas, and the larger islands of the Caribbean. Though their preference for undergrowth makes them more resilient than some species, the black-throated blue has apparently always been less common than, say, the redstart or yellow-rumped warbler. The current population of black-throated blues appears to be stable or even slightly increasing, but, as with many warblers, pre-settlement populations were probably much higher, and their future remains murky.

The time may come when small woodlots like the one at Lakeside Beach and even more extensive forests such as those on Wellesley Island no longer support black-throated blue warblers. And, since I may be the only one among my friends who saw them, I could also be the only one to know they are gone. A world will have passed, and how many will not know that it was there in the first place?

~

As with the human population, no one is really sure how many warblers graced the American forests before Columbus. Because they are too small to constitute a major food source or millinery item, they had been, up until a few decades ago, taken for granted. Even birdwatchers turned their attention to rarer or more dramatic species, and conservationists have found only two compelling enough to devote much time to. One, the Kirtland's warbler, seems to be holding its own for now in the jack pine forests of Michigan. Bachman's warbler, on the other hand, has almost certainly been lost along with its southeastern canebrake habitat, its occasional alleged reappearances overshadowed by the famed cat-and-mouse-with-extinction game of the spectacular ivory-billed woodpecker. The general decline of the neotropical migrants became apparent in the early 1980s, a fitting harbinger of the large-scale environmental problems that are so dispiriting today.

All told, there are twenty-nine species of warbler among the neotropical migrants considered most vulnerable to deforestation in their wintering grounds. Others, like the black-throated blue, also head south in winter but do not require mature forest habitat. A few, such as the familiar yellow-rumped warbler, winter mostly in the United States. But all are affected when habitat is lost or fragmented in the breeding grounds and migration pathways. No one can yet determine the effects that climate change is having or will have on warbler populations, but it seems likely that some birds, especially those like the Kirtland's with restricted ranges, will find it difficult to adapt to disappearing or shifting habitat zones.

Right now, warblers are nesting in the trees around the house in northern Maine where I am writing this. Among the dozen or so species is the black-throated blue, whose ascending slightly buzzy notes I can hear as I walk about the back yard. Most people are, perhaps, less fortunate. But yellow warblers might breed in any garden or hedgerow, piling nests one on top of the other to combat the cowbirds, and yellowthroats, though they require patience to see, might be in any damp roadside thicket. Returning after a long absence to my old Rochester neighborhood, I was surprised to hear Tennessee warblers singing from trees that had grown so much bigger in the intervening years.

⁓

*It is the summer of 1975. I have been searching for a baseball among mayapples, and have just ducked into a thicket of berry bushes, grapevines, and small trees. The strikingly patterned bird appears in a young beech. I turn to my friends and gesture, urging them to approach quickly, silently. We all forget our game and watch the warbler gleaning insects, not one of us having ever seen a bird like that before.*

One of my friends went on to teach mathematics. The other, who was studying physics—I don't know where he is. I think he had a disappointing love affair along the way. Would it have mattered if they had stopped to watch a black-throated blue warbler at Lakeside Beach that long-ago summer morning? Or would the warbler have disappeared the minute I turned around to call them, or when they shouted their way forward to find out what I wanted? And what if they had seen the warbler, not spontaneously as I had but as a result of my own conscious effort to point it out to them? Would it have mattered to them? If they read somewhere that warblers are slowly fading into the past, would they be as quick to turn to the box scores or political news? I have no desire to make anyone suffer. People generally do that well enough without help. But it is also true that people tend, maybe even want, to be oblivious to much of the intensity of the world. Maybe if the black-throated blue warbler disappears, it will be easier for those who never knew it was there in the first place. But I'm going to the back yard again, to the upstairs porch, to the thicket at Lakeside Beach, and I want you to come with me and see and hear them—chestnut-sided, blackburnian, parula, black-throated blue—singing, chasing bugs, raising their young in the trees just beyond the cropped lawn. Will you join me?

# Thing in the Woods

I

Despite the spooky name, Shades State Park—short for Shades of Death, a reference to the deep gloom under the trees—is a welcoming place, a cool, picturesque beauty spot amid dusty agribusiness fields near Crawfordsville, Indiana. Bordering Sugar Creek, the park features picnic areas, "rally camping" sites, and short loop trails in a mature forest cut by steep ravines. These ravines, overhung by a canopy of beeches, walnuts, and hickories accented with the occasional sassafras or eastern hemlock, are all that has prevented the park from being converted into "fencerow to fencerow" corn and soybean fields like most of the surrounding countryside.

During the 1980s, when I was a graduate student at Purdue, my family and I often wandered through Shades and its sister state park Turkey Run. We'd string together trails to make a respectable hike, watching for deer and birds ranging from the small but colorful warblers to the dramatic pileated woodpecker. Since we had moved to Indiana after several years in the West, we relished any chance to get away from the strait-jacket squares of beans and corn. To this day, I've never seen a rural place so adulterated as that part of the Midwest. One tableau I noted in passing has become for me emblematic of the impoverishment of the natural world in northwestern Indiana: a man dressed in traditional autumn plaid hunting cap and jacket standing on a railroad grade overlooking the bleak panorama of stripped fields. In the middle of the particular field below him was a single hardwood, perhaps a walnut, and there he stood, gun in hand, waiting for whatever it was that must have been holed up somewhere in that solitary tree.

The wildest creature I can say with certainty that I encountered at Shades was a mink, one of only two I've seen, both, as it happened, during the same summer though at widely different locations. A fascinating creature, and certainly untamed, but small and inconspicuous. Mostly, Shades trails provided forest songbirds, squirrels, and, no small wonder in itself, happy humans enjoying the outdoors as we were. But despite the park's popularity and limited acreage, at sundown, with most of the day's shouting children safely tucked into carseats and barred owls bestirring themselves in the shadowy old growth, a walk along Sugar Creek really did offer a touch of the primeval.

Adjoining Shades was the somewhat wilder—at least less crowded— Pine Hills Nature Preserve, where, on a bare limestone spine known as Devil's Backbone, some settler artist had carved a "bas relief" of the name-sake personage himself, along with, according to the preserve brochure, likenesses of "birds thought to be passenger pigeons." On one particular evening, perhaps in late summer or early autumn, we had chosen a long-ish trail through a part of the park close to Pine Hills and some distance from the more frequented paths through the scenic ravines. Heading back toward the parking lot in the dark, we had to pick our way past encroaching roots and overhanging branches we hadn't noticed much before, me with a baby pack rocking on my back. Where the trail skirted a small hollow, something, somewhere close ahead, growled. We stopped and waited. But that was it, a single growl. After a few moments we moved on, reaching the car without incident. Of course, we knew we were in a place with nary a lion or tiger or bear. So what was it? A great horned owl? Maybe, but the growl sounded distinctly mammalian. Perhaps a coyote or feral dog. One thing I could tell, I thought, was that the sound emanated from a spot in the darkness more-or-less at my height, though the shallow depres-sion made it difficult to gauge the invisible growler's "tallness." If I were to speculate now, I'd guess that the thing in the woods was a raccoon in a tree, although the growl lacked the chirpy quality of most raccoon vocalizations. It was a pretty deep growl.

That growl has marked my memory of an otherwise pleasant but unre-markable walk ever since, a surprising persistence given that even at the time we knew there was nothing to be seriously afraid of. Rabies, I suppose, was a possibility, but the creature, whatever it was, didn't seem to be acting in an aberrant or erratic manner—at least it didn't sound sick. I once saw a skunk I believed was rabid; in broad daylight, it was running in circles in a freeway median. That night at Shades, there was nothing to suggest disease. We came close, something growled. That's all.

Aside from the usual rustlings and quick surges through underbrush, that growl was my one tangible encounter with the "unexplained" thing in the woods. Once or twice, I've had the familiar eerie sensation of being watched. Hiking at Yellowstone's Riddle Lake one summer, I drifted away from my family until I was caught by a vague but pronounced tingle, triggered, perhaps, by some unseen presence. In Yellowstone, that catalyst might be a mountain lion or grizzly bear, so caution in such matters isn't much different from wisdom. In Edward Hoagland's essay "Up the Black to Chalkyitsik," an Alaskan trapper posits that animals like grizzlies may have a telepathic connection to humans because, as Hoagland puts it, "an animal that large and formidable may be required to 'register'" while "the brain waves of slighter wildlife slip past." That may be. But as far as I know, there was nothing at Riddle Lake except a trumpeter swan and ourselves. Just a feeling. Whatever it was that we encountered at Shades, it was definitely present, and real.

~

For early American naturalists, the vast continental *terra incognita* supplied a bulwark against European snobbery. The prodigiousness of North American "productions" afforded Thomas Jefferson grounds for a vigorous rejection of French provincialism in *Notes on the State of Virginia*, and led to his hopes that mammoths or mastodons might still be wandering the interior. Audubon did him one better, identifying, shooting, and painting life-size a colossal eagle he grandiloquently dubbed the Bird of Washington. Audubon was a world-renowned expert, and major American museums soon listed specimens of the Washington eagle in their collections. Biographer William Souder points out that the artist painstakingly measured each bird he painted and that the proportions he recorded for the Washington eagle are consistent with each other and with his painting. But the most ardent boosters of American natural history were eventually forced to admit the implausibility that such a giant—Audubon claimed a wingspan of over ten feet—could have haunted the mid-American rivers Audubon frequented. No specimens are known to exist today, and neither ornithologists nor Audubon admirers can offer a conclusive explanation for the Bird of Washington.

Even without Audubon's eagle, North America harbors formidable fauna. One summer, bear reports circulated through the Rochester suburbs. In light of simultaneous but scattered ursine appearances, it was thought that multiple animals were involved. One Rochester *Democrat and Chronicle* article speculated that there might be as many as five. Though the bruin or bruins never caused any serious trouble, the mere presence of bear gave the community a case of the heebie-jeebies. At one point my sister received a "reverse 911" call warning that a bear had been sighted in her neighborhood. *Not to worry, ma'am. Don't try to apprehend the bear yourself. But you'd better bring in those birdfeeders.* Eventually, a young black bear was trapped and collared in a yard near Lake Ontario, confirming that at least one of the animals had been roaming the Rochester metropolitan area.

Not all "wild animal on the loose" rumors yield such unequivocal resolutions. When I was growing up, one of Rochester's tonier suburbs was haunted by the specter of the "Brighton Beast." Most often described as a "big cat," the creature would drop from a backyard tree or flick its long tail through a lilac hedge, startling the local authorities and precipitating a series of unskilled but enthusiastic "manhunts." Eventually the beast would vanish, only to reappear again a few years later like a zoological version of the phantom hitchhiker. What, if anything, was the Brighton Beast? The most popular explanation was that the creature was a mountain lion that had wandered down from Ontario or the Adirondacks, though cougars were not known to inhabit either place. That explanation seemed as good as any; some residents claimed to have found footprints or fur, but no one could capture, or even photograph, the Brighton Beast.

Every so often a mountain lion appears in Billings. Shortly after we moved here, an early morning newspaper carrier saw one crossing Grand Avenue, a major commercial street. Another turned up in Lockwood, a suburb with a penchant for disaster: refinery explosions, pedestrian accidents on unsidewalked roads, fires in the dry grass of new subdivisions. It's understandable that police patrolling such an apocalyptic beat might be a shade trigger-happy, but it did cause a short-lived controversy when an officer shot the lion out of a tree—at least there was a sense that it was an unfortunate conclusion to the story. It was not, however, the end of cougars in Billings. A recent high school science fair project turned up hair samples at a couple of locations, including one close to the airport.

With its rough rimrock environs, Billings is a much more likely locale for a wandering cougar than the woodlots and housing tracts of Upstate New York, but despite the admittedly shaky quality of its claim to big cats, Rochester is not without less anomalous but nevertheless startling apparitions of nature. Some years ago, my brother-in-law photographed a fork-tailed flycatcher from South America—later remembered by my mother as the "tropical bird"—landing on a barn at the edge of the city's sprawl zone. And each winter brings a snowy owl or two. During periodic irruption years when arctic prey is short, owls can be seen perched like incongruous snowmen not only on lakeside piers, but at golf courses and high school athletic fields, anywhere with an open vista reminiscent to owl eyes of their home on the tundra. Perhaps the lives of "ordinary" animals—the migration of songbirds, the cyclic visitations of owls, the generational outbursts of seventeen-year cicadas—are miraculous enough to justify poet William Stafford's decision to "place my feet / with care in such a world."

In such a world maybe the Brighton Beast really was a wandering cougar. At any rate, an encounter with such an apparition, whether follow-up investigations reveal anything or not, offers a momentary frisson in communities where life has grown generally predicable. A student in one of my research writing classes claimed that the ostensibly safe contemporary American lifestyle has fed the popularity of "extreme sports." But the occasional suburban bear or city lion provides something more than a simple adrenaline jolt. The thing in the woods, whatever or wherever it may be, cracks open the door to mystery, to an older, larger world that, tattered and fragmentary, still lurks just beyond the high-powered streetlights of American towns and subdivisions.

～

In addition to the occasional bear, our remaining woods, however circumscribed, are home to a variety of haunts—crazed hermits, inconsolable ghosts, escaped convicts and other human "predators." Or maybe even sub-human. One of my Brockport roommates told hunting stories, hearkening back to earlier autumns he'd spent in New York's pastoral Southern Tier with ex-marines who took to the woods to work out their frustrations on whatever "game" they could find. His own first victim, he said, was a porcupine. In one of his stories, his campfire was approached by the thing in the woods—running heavily, stopping, crashing again through the darkness, snapping branches and uttering the strangest screams he had ever heard. Because I know how to make a good story better, I asked if the footfalls indicated four legs or two. He paused, considered—I remember smoke rings; he may have been ruminating over a corncob pipe—then answered "two." Bigfoot, no doubt, in the backwoods of the Allegheny Plateau.

When I was a boy, I read Ivan T. Sanderson's *Abominable Snowmen: Legend Come to Life*, and thought, *why not?* I had a glossy coffee table book in which the same Sanderson detailed the biomes of North America, sans Bigfoot, so I knew him as a credible expert on the natural world. Ange, our family barber, subscribed to *Argosy*, a men's magazine—the adventurous, not the pornographic kind—and he let me take each old issue home when a new one arrived at the shop. In one of those magazines Sanderson announced his and Belgian "cryptozoologist" Bernard Heuvelmans's discovery of an "iceman" encased in a Minnesota carnival exhibitor's freezer. Given the limitations of such methods of refrigeration and considering the iceman's apparent gunshot wounds, they concluded that the apish fellow had quite recently been walking about, an in-the-flesh example of Sanderson's legends come to life. If such an authority as Sanderson, who modestly credited Heuvelmans as the real scientist, thought there were "wild hominids" in the woods, who was I to demur? And why, for that matter, would I want to? I pictured Sanderson as a nineteenth-century adventurer in puttees and pith helmet, scouring the last unexplored ends and overlooked corners of Earth, convinced there were still great mysteries to be unlocked. Who in their right mind would want to believe it wasn't so?

I found my roommate's tale engrossing, chilling even, an effect no doubt owing as much to my childhood reading and romantic inclinations as to his yarn-spinning talent. I suppose I believed the story only, or at least mostly, in the Coleridgean sense. I extended the willing suspension of disbelief because the situation seemed to call for it. I have another friend whose stories I am occasionally a part of. If my memory is accurate, these tales tend to be "stretchers," but they are good stories, full of a spirit of adventure in keeping with the tenor of the original experiences they recount. On the other hand, when writing nonfiction (like this essay, for instance), I take the *non* part seriously, though some selecting, maybe even shaping, of events is necessary and inevitable, beginning with the hidden hand of memory and ending with the writer's irrepressible duty to the work as such. Ultimately what's acceptable has to do with the implicit "contract" between storyteller and audience. When I asked my college pal about the number of legs, I think it was mutually understood that I was expanding that contract to let the tale grow. If not for that "raconteur's license," maybe I wouldn't remember the story at all after so many years.

~

Driving Interstate 15—"the 15" in Southern California parlance—on a June afternoon when the giant thermometer that marks the Mojave Desert town of Baker read a relatively modest 97 degrees, Cara and I followed an official brown BLM point-of-interest sign to the Calico Early Man Site. We expected a barely discernable Paleoindian encampment and an interesting roadside stop with, hopefully, a patch of mesquite shade. What we found was more ambitious, an archeological dig that Louis S. B. Leakey, of *National Geographic* Olduvai Gorge fame, believed was chock-full of artifacts created by hominid hands up to two hundred thousand years ago. If Leakey was right, creatures not unlike Sanderson's subhumans may at least at one time have inhabited the American West. Were these the ancestors of Bigfoot? As it turns out, probably not. Calico was controversial from the start. Louis's wife Mary, herself a noted and perhaps more discerning paleontologist, rejected her husband's optimistic appraisal of the site. More recently, critics armed with comprehensive technical analyses have concluded that the "Calico lithic industry" tools are actually the result of natural weathering processes. For one thing, they note, over sixty thousand of these "scrapers" have been unearthed in strata showing no clear evidence of human habitation.

Though the site is still called Camp Leakey, the glory days when the famous paleontologist directed the excavations are long gone. We passed no cars on the two-mile gravel road from the highway, and the semiabandoned look of the parking lot suggested that visitors of any kind were few and far between, at least during the searing Mojave summer. We were free to wander around with a self-guiding brochure explaining trenches and geological deposits. Tours may be conducted at times and dig weekends are scheduled during more temperate seasons, but there was no sign of anybody working as I climbed the barren knoll to the main pit. From the top, I looked out over dry Lake Manix and the busy interstate to the desert ranges beyond, and down to where Cara and Rita the dog sensibly huddled in the shade of the forlorn one-room museum, described by the California-based nonprofit Center for Land Use Interpretation as a "visitors center and gift shop, with stones and dessicated [*sic*] lizards."

Exhibiting British Empire–style chin-up pluck that would have made Louis Leakey proud, the museum bravely displays casts and samples of the finds and directs visitors' attention to new excavations, which are claimed to reveal a hearth, an interpretation already disputed by mainstream archeologists. The BLM maintains the site, and over the years professionals from nearby museums and colleges have been involved to varying degrees in research at Camp Leakey, but much of the recent work has been done by volunteers. If not completely isolated in their faith, Calico's adherents are clearly an embattled minority, and much of the site's interpretive material adopts a defensive tone; even a more-or-less official website highlights the controversy on its home page. One cannot easily avoid the impression that the Early Man Site has become something of a La Brea tarpit into which a handful of researchers—Louis Leakey among them—and a somewhat larger sampling of San Bernardino County boosters have foundered.

∾

All in all, I wasn't much convinced by the Calico Early Man Site, though it provided an even more interesting roadside stop than I'd anticipated. Undoubtedly my twelve-year-old self would have been more receptive to the Calico claims if presented with breathless astonishment by Ivan Sanderson in *Argosy*. These days, I have to admit, Sanderson and Heuvelmans strike me as first-rate crackpots. Leakey is not so easily dismissed. Though his conclusions sometimes outstripped his evidence, his African finds remain among the most significant in the history of human paleontology. At Calico, let's say his previous luck may have gone to his head.

Like the Washington eagle museum specimens, the Minnesota iceman disappeared. The frozen corpse described in gruesome detail by Sanderson was replaced, the story somewhat conveniently has it, by a more durable latex replica. As in an episode of *The X-Files*, the case, blockbuster discovery and all, was closed without resolution. Though the legend of Bigfoot, like that of his Himalayan counterpart, has proven remarkably durable, somewhere along the way it became obvious to me that the purveyors of such mysteries tended to overplay their hands, finding traces of Sasquatch in Minnesota and Upstate New York and just about everywhere else they looked as well as in the creature's traditional Pacific fastnesses. I suppose many a Bigfoot rumor has been hung on little more than a two-legged crunching of twigs or an ear-level growl in the night. Besides, the natural world is manifestly less untrammeled than when I was a child. The Northwest was subjected to aggressive clearcutting in the seventies and eighties. Hundreds of people climb Mount Everest each year. Everybody and his brother has dropped a minisub into Loch Ness, and still no monster.

Or maybe I just grew up.


2

The story is by now familiar, and has been told in detail elsewhere, so it should suffice to offer just the briefest sketch. On April 28, 2005, spokespersons representing the United States government and the Cornell Laboratory of Ornithology announced that *Campephilus principalis*, the long-lost ivory-billed woodpecker, was alive in the White River/Cache River bottomlands of Arkansas, said to be contiguous with the "Big Woods" Old Ben stalked in William Faulkner's "The Bear." The morning I heard the news, broken first on National Public Radio, I was on my way to a meeting with an ecologist with whom I was editing a book. I ran a copy of the official press release, complete with the seals of the United States Fish and Wildlife Service and the Interior Department, and handed it to him, asking him if he'd heard. He read the announcement, folded the paper, unfolded it, looked it over again more closely, folded it once more, and, patting it into his shirt pocket, asked "Can I keep this?" I like to think it's been in his pocket ever since. The "rediscovery," as it's now known, was hailed by just about everyone except land developers as close to a miracle. Even in the middle of the United States, there was still room for something unexpected in the woods.

Or was there? Since those heady days, neither Cornell nor anyone else has been able to confirm the woodpecker's presence. Cornell teams spent five winters combing the swamp forests with admittedly unimpressive results. In the wake of the Big Woods rediscovery, an Auburn University ornithologist and his graduate students zeroed in on a second site well southeast of Arkansas in the Florida panhandle, but Auburn's efforts followed Cornell's pattern: a burst of enthusiasm, then a slow erosion of confidence. Spurred by the more famous and better-funded expeditions, a colorful cast of independent searchers has turned up scattered sightings from Texas to southern Illinois. Each time a bird has been "found," however, followup efforts have yielded diminishing returns, the trail gradually growing cold. The ivory-bill, it seems, has withdrawn its support from the search.

The analysis of physical evidence gathered by searchers has been hampered by the paucity of knowledge about the species and by the ambiguity of the evidence itself. Arcane bark-peeling comparisons and cavity measurements have been inconclusive, due mostly to the number and variety of arboreal animals and the random effects of decay and weathering. *Kent* calls similar to archived ivory-bill vocalizations have been heard by searchers and recorded by remote listening stations; blue jays and nuthatches, however, make similar calls. Alternative explanations for "double-knocks," a diagnostic *Campephilus* drilling pattern, range from colliding duck wings to gunshots to tapes played by other searchers. Photographic evidence consists of a few blurry and fleeting videos subject to multiple interpretations and an automatic Reconyx camera image of a group of flying birds that Auburn ornithologists tagged as ivory-bills. When *Birding* magazine included this image as their monthly "Photo Quiz" feature, readers advanced a variety of interpretations; ivory-bills were among the guesses, as were eighteen other taxa, including a variety of ducks and wading birds, pileated woodpeckers, gannets, starlings, and exotic Cuban parakeets. Quiz participants differed over the number of species represented and even over which way the birds in the photo were flying.

All this is in keeping with the history of ivory-bill encounters over the decades since the woodpecker's 1940s disappearance from Louisiana's infamous Singer Tract, or rather the disappearance of the Singer Tract from it, the result of intensive logging on behalf of indifferent sewing machine magnates. Since then, the ivory-bill has engaged in a now-you-see-it-now-you-don't act that puts the Brighton Beast to shame. Every so often a bird is spotted in Mississippi, or South Carolina, or Florida, or Texas, then nothing. A photo is snapped, but the photographer prefers to remain anonymous. A bottomland farmer attests to ivory-bills in a hurricane-flooded woodlot just a few years back. In retrospect it isn't all that surprising that even the elite Cornell Laboratory of Ornithology met its match in this phantom bird of southeastern swamps.

Few people are more invested in the Arkansas rediscovery than Bobby Harrison. It was Harrison, along with Tim Gallagher and Gene Sparling—invariably described as the "local kayaker"—who brought their Big Woods sighting to the attention of the CLO, Gallagher's employer. Characterized in Gallagher's *The Grail Bird* as a paunchy, loveable everyman, the ubiquitous Harrison maintained a high profile in the years following his initial sighting through lectures, slide shows, and interviews, and through innovative attempts to attract the birds with skillfully carved decoys he makes himself. Perhaps in part because his day job as a mild-mannered college professor parallels my own, I was delighted to attend one of Harrison's talks, at central Florida's Historic Bok Sanctuary. Harrison was spellbinding, constructing his case for the ivory-bill while vicariously guiding the audience into a kayak to relive his first glimpse—he claims several—of the legendary woodpecker. Harrison has a lot riding on that initial encounter; as with Calico Early Man Site enthusiasts, it has been suggested that he and Gallagher may have become entangled in their own tale with no way to extract themselves. But, judging by the eager, informed questions and comments following the talk at Bok Sanctuary, Harrison's listeners expect a trustworthy recollection of events as they happened, and Harrison is enough of a raconteur to understand the importance of his "contract" with his audience. He shows no signs of backing away from his original account.

Harrison's confidence, however, is not shared by all. As befits the generally polarized atmosphere of the times, it wasn't long after the Arkansas rediscovery was announced that ivory-bill aficionados divided into opposing camps of "skeptics" and "believers." Perhaps miffed at being left out of Cornell's loop, Jerome Jackson, the reigning dean of ivory-bill hunters, coined the phrase "faith-based ornithology" to account for the university team's conclusions. Though his comparison of Cornell scientists to religious zealots galled believers, his doubts are focused mostly on the Big Woods rediscovery. He's had his own close encounters of the ivory-bill kind—a couple of fleeting glimpses and, in Mississippi, a tantalizing 1987 response to a taped ivory-bill call; he has grown more pessimistic over the years, but his dubious opinion of Cornell's evidence didn't prevent him from striking up an unlikely across-the-lines friendship with Harrison, who tapped him as science advisor to his Ivory-billed Woodpecker Foundation. Says Harrison, quoted in a 2007 *Huntsville Times* article, "I had heard that he was 'the enemy,' and he's not."

Jackson may not be one of them, but Harrison's enemies are easy enough to find. In blogs and Internet fora—by 2013, the BirdForum thread devoted to the subject had generated a whopping 14,096 posts, most from the years immediately following the rediscovery—skeptics regularly pepper believers with comparisons between ivory-bill seekers and the teams of camouflaged "researchers" roaming forests and swamps with camcorders and nets, certain that this time they will strap Bigfoot in all his smelly glory into the bed of a pickup and cart him back to town. In response to a BirdForum post noting that a new woodpecker sighting was being considered by the TBRC—the Texas Bird Records Committee—one skeptical wag responded with "TBRC? Oh right, Texas Bigfoot Research Center." In case you're keeping track, that was Post 11,860, accompanied by a link to the Bigfoot Center's rather sensationalistic website.

The message behind such ridicule is clear. Believers are at best silly romantics with overactive imaginations, latter-day Ichabod Cranes ready to jump at the first pumpkin, the first sign that there are more things in Heaven and Earth than in your philosophy. Which, as near as I can tell, the skeptics say there aren't. In fact, one leading skeptic was so confident that his position would prevail that, while keeping one eye on the ivory-bill, he opened his blog to a bigger target, the nefarious machinations of the Intergovernmental Panel on Climate Change. The current alarming meteorological trends, he assures us, are nothing new under the sunspot-flecked sun.

If skeptics brand believers as gullible dreamers, believers are quick to dismiss skeptics as armchair experts too lazy to venture into the swamps themselves. They point to other "Lazarus species"—the black-footed ferret, the Vietnamese rhino, the Yangtze River dolphin—each of which has at least temporarily survived its declared demise. Indeed, the ivory-bill itself had been feared extinct before James Tanner's 1940s Louisiana find. Believers make a fable of the story of the coelacanth, that strange fish that, just as the ivory-bill was reappearing in the Singer Tract, swam out of millions of years of extinction into a South African fisherman's net. The plain implication is that closed-minded skeptics would have missed it completely if a coelacanth had floated into their seafood market. The distant British addresses of some BirdForum skeptics—whether the word should be spelled with a *k* or *c* was for a time itself a subject of debate—has perhaps helped perpetuate this stereotype of the skeptics as detached know-it-alls, but in truth the skeptical ranks include such master field birders as Kenn Kaufman and David Sibley. Like Jackson, Sibley, the field guide heir to Roger Tory Peterson, has been a reluctant warrior. He writes that he "felt like I had been kicked in the stomach" when he came to doubt the Arkansas rediscovery; his critiques are substantive, measured, and thoughtful, far from the scathing sarcasm found on skeptical websites such as WorldTwitch, which lambastes the rediscovery as "Peckergate: The Ivory-billed Woodpecker Hoax."

Though not above resorting to stereotypes, believers are generally more temperate in tone than their counterparts. One notable exception is a self-proclaimed "well-trained scientist" with "a knack for solving challenging scientific problems." While employed at a government laboratory within paddling distance of an ivory-bill "hot zone," he claims to have repeatedly seen and videotaped the birds. BirdForum wags find him an inviting target, mostly because they know he'll take the bait. When his efforts are disparaged, he'll dish out invective with the best of the skeptics, if without their sense of humor. His special target, though, is the "birding community." Not known for his lack of ego, he has alienated many in the competitive but genteel circles of upper-echelon birders with his unseemly self-promotion—in the interest of science, of course—and with a history of questionable sightings. British skeptics have gleefully but mercilessly labeled him a "stringer," a tag of dishonor applied to a birdwatcher who puts together a string of unlikely reports. Elite birders and professional ornithologists mostly ignore him, at least in public, a neglect he finds particularly infuriating—understandably so, assuming that his day-to-day online journal accurately accounts for the time and resources he regularly expended on the search from 2005 to 2013, with occasional excursions since then. I personally can't pick out any kind of bird in most of his video footage, even with the full complement of colored boxes and arrows he provides as aids to interpretation, but he enjoys considerable credence, even a kind of hero status, among independent believers.

~

Part of what drives both university and wildcatter searchers is the ivory-bill's status as perhaps the rarest of the rare North American birds, a blank on even the most accomplished living birders' life lists. Eyebrows were raised when Auburn's Geoff Hill suggested there might be as many as six to eight pairs—hardly a thriving population—at his Florida site. Though I would certainly not go so far as the Bush administration official who encouraged military bykill since "bird-watchers get more enjoyment spotting a rare bird than they do spotting a common one," the knowledge that beholding a "difficult" bird—a *rara avis*, if you will—may constitute a once-in-a-lifetime experience accounts for a significant element both of birding's aesthetic appeal and its sporting character.

Sibley, Jackson, and others have concluded that the bird in the brief, out-of-focus "Luneau video," a key piece of the Arkansas evidence, is actually a more common pileated woodpecker. Believers point out that diagnostic plumage differences should make it easy for a practiced eye to distinguish between these two large, crested birds. Skeptics counter that lighting conditions, individual variation, and the possibility of "aberrant" birds, along with wishful thinking, complicate the situation. Even believers readily admit that a number—perhaps a majority—of alleged ivory-bill encounters have likely involved pileateds. While it's obviously easier to find and identify a common species than a scarce one, rarity can cut both ways. Kenn Kaufman notes that exploding numbers of invading Eurasian collared-doves were missed by Florida birders for years because they were new and unexpected, while a similar bird inhabiting the same range, the ringed turtle-dove, was considered an "uncountable" and therefore unworthy domestic type. Who knows how many times over the years a conservative observer has seen a not-quite-right looking flash of black and white disappearing into the trees, shrugged, and written off an ivory-bill as a pileated?

For bird listers and endangered species advocates, the boundaries of recognized possibility are shaped indoors, far from any remaining ivory-bills, by professional societies, environmental organizations, and what Aldo Leopold characterizes as government "alphabetical conservation," bureaucracies which, even if careful and well-intentioned, cannot help but be influenced by a variety of agendas. It's not surprising that the Arkansas Bird Records Committee moved to accept the Big Woods sightings, putting the state on the birding map and fostering ecotourism in an economically depressed rural region. The Nature Conservancy enthusiastically embraced the CLO's rediscovery, which instantly raised the profile of bottomland forests the group was already engaged in protecting. Other, more distanced committees and organizations have adopted a circumspect "watch and wait" position. The American Birding Association, for example, still classifies the ivory-bill as "Code 6," defined as "probably or actually extinct." Such a pattern suggests that the process of interpretation, especially when based on limited and equivocal evidence, is inevitably influenced by the beliefs and desires, noble and otherwise, of the interpreters.

Bird records committees and umbrella organizations like the ABA are subjective by their very nature, deliberative bodies of interested observers charged—in addition to evaluating individual sightings—with funneling periodic revisions of the august American Ornithologists' Union, the final authority on matters of avian classification, into the life lists of birders across the country. Together, the AOU and ABA reorganize taxonomies, regularly "creating" and "disappearing" species administratively. This abstract, esoteric process of defining and recognizing—or ceasing to recognize—species affects even amateur birders in the field. Some years ago, while attending a writers' conference in Tempe, Arizona, I neglected to get a close look at the local flickers, then considered, despite differences in plumage and habitat, a "morph" conspecific with the northern flickers I regularly saw in my neighborhood, and therefore not a listable new species. My mistake, as the birding powers-that-be have since enshrined—reinstated actually—the gilded flicker of southwestern deserts as a "full species." I did, in fact, see flickers around Tempe, but, concentrating on "new" birds, I let the authorities shape my perception and consequently lost my chance to actually *experience* this beautiful and interesting desert woodpecker.

In the case of the ivory-bill, human decision makers hold considerable sway over the ultimate question of whether the species is extinct or extant; a records committee can simply vote to not accept a report, in effect declaring that an encounter didn't really happen. Government agencies, meanwhile, make their own determinations regarding species status, a process that has become notoriously politicized in recent years. Even when integrity is assured, a subjective element permeates such deliberations, as consultants and committees wrangle to produce something like consensus. In 1986, the ivory-bill was "saved" from bureaucratic oblivion not as a result of new sightings or physical evidence, but by Jerome Jackson's forceful assertion that a proposed United States Fish and Wildlife Service extinction declaration was premature.

With the video evidence tangled perhaps irredeemably in an arcane hermeneutics of wing camber, pixels, and artifacts, the ivory-bill case rests primarily on sight records, a cause for jittery soul-searching among birders. I suppose even the most meticulous life list must include at least a few identifications made confidently and carefully, but not under circumstances allowing for absolute verification. Pondering the validity of sight records brings into play uncomfortable questions about whether the whole endeavor is "citizen science" or merely educated guesswork, and about how completely birders' experience, judgment, and honor-system ethics can be trusted against the compulsion to see, identify, and list rare species. Especially when the species happens to be a "grail bird."

~

The lack of accord among ornithologists and records committees has left the entrenched camps with no shortage of published articles and conference papers to turn to for support, and placed a premium on the opinions of high profile "agnostics" like Sibley and Jackson, who have been courted by believers and skeptics alike. Both men's statements, stripped of context, have been used to endorse mutually exclusive positions. As with many contemporary issues, the truth seems dependent on one's predilections and worldview. One believer headlines his blog with Carl Sagan's conviction that "somewhere, something incredible is waiting to be known." A skeptic counterpart answers with his own Saganism: "Extraordinary claims require extraordinary proof." It seems ironically fitting that both attributions require qualification. The first was written about Sagan by a *Newsweek* reporter. The second is simply Sagan's phrasing of a long-standing, though not universally accepted, scientific principle.

If there's one thing that skeptics and believers agree on, it's the sanctity of empiricism. Despite their gritty optimism, believers certainly don't want to be taken for romantics entranced by ivory-bill mythology. It's science they admire, real science, the kind practiced by the good doctors of Auburn and Cornell (in general, both sides affix the honorific *doctor* only to those scientists backing their positions). James Tanner, who for several years studied ivory-bills in the Singer Tract, is held up by skeptics as a kind of Aristotle, his findings constituting something like ultimate authority even though he observed only one dwindling population in one isolated place. A report's being perceived as at odds with Tanner is enough to lead a skeptic to reject it out of hand. Believers also appeal to Tanner, defending their confidence in the woodpeckers' uncanny elusiveness by pointing out that Tanner himself needed a local guide to find them.

Though not so categorically as skeptics, believers, too, are uncomfortable with mysteries, at least those that strain a bit too hard at the bounds of possibility. They hold to the hope that, with time, logical explanations will dispel the ivory-bill's almost Fortean aura. They note that habitat in parts of the Southeast has been improving for years as farmers retire and loggers move on. Besides, while it has long been accepted as a given that ivory-bills require extensive tracts of old-growth swamp forest, the actual research behind this supposition is thin. The pileated woodpecker was once characterized as a declining deep-forest bird, but has proved more adaptable than expected. Why couldn't the same be true for the ivory-bill? Continued systematic searching in the maturing bottomland woods, believers maintain, will reveal something essentially normal, without the *para*—just a woodpecker, not a "legend come to life." Really, they tell us, there's nothing very strange about such a large, flashy representative of a noisy, conspicuous family sustaining an underground existence for decades in a populous industrialized country. Ivory-bill habitat is hot, uncomfortable, infested with snakes and mosquitoes, they remind us, and few birders go deep into the swamps. The ivory-bill is simply an animal that has found a way to survive by avoiding humans.

The same claim, of course, is made by the Sasquatch searchers, who temper the more outlandish aspects of their quest with photos of pipe-smoking scientist types measuring tracks and examining hairs under microscopes, though the effect of these images is often more campy than authoritative. Bigfoot hunters refer to their quarry as "the animal" as often as possible, as if attempting to reduce a seven-foot man-ape to an expected if undiscovered component of the North American biota. Some years ago when we lived in northern Maine, an obscure late-night public radio show accompanying my family home from a trip to the coast broadcast what was purported to be a confrontation between a cabin full of hunters and a band of Bigfoot (Bigfeet?). Even the recording's interpreters had been flustered to discover, in garbled but discernable words, one of the creatures spitting out, "You're not welcome!" As I recall, their conclusion was that "the animal" must be a clever mimic indeed. There are some places, it appears, that even cryptozoologists fear to tread. Their quarry may challenge the distinction between humans and other animals, but today's watered-down adventurers, apparently enthralled by the chimera of scientific acceptance, prefer to keep niceties intact. Not their intrepid forebears. Think what you might about him, Sanderson, like Louis Leakey at Calico, was not afraid to flout conventional wisdom, to say nothing of common sense. *Abominable Snowmen: Legend Come to Life* is subtitled "The Story of Sub-Humans on Five Continents from the Early Ice Age until Today." Sub-humans. No namby-pamby "the animal" for Ivan T. Sanderson, explorer.

～

I'm not among those who equate Cornell and Auburn with the TBRC (not the bird records committee). Aside from an understandable if ill-advised attempt by Cornell laboratory director John Fitzpatrick to "bribe" Jackson by offering him coauthorship of a CLO article, I see no evidence that the university ornithologists acted in an irresponsible or unprofessional manner. Moreover, I have no reason to suspect that the majority of independent searchers are anything but particularly obsessed birdwatchers on the trail of an extraordinarily challenging "lifer." As believers are wont to point out, there are considerable differences between the case of the ivory-bill and the natural history aspect of the paranormal. Ivory-bills, after all, are not unknown, just unseen, or not often seen. Scientists have studied them, on occasion, at close range. Many, perhaps too many, museum specimens remain. Both Audubon and his rival Alexander Wilson painted ivory-bills, the latter, an oft-repeated anecdote recounts, harboring one in a hotel room. And the bird's existence has been "officially sanctioned" by organizations like The Nature Conservancy and government agencies like the United States Fish and Wildlife Service. Ivory-bill searchers consider their quest high-minded and urgent, envisioning another Singer Tract falling to the chainsaw, this time because of failure to confirm the bird's presence rather than Singer's "we are just money-grubbers" indifference to its fate. What chance does such a rarity have without a known population to protect? Even being found doesn't guarantee that a Lazarus species will survive. The Vietnamese subspecies of the Javan rhino, for example, descended to, perhaps over, the brink after its 1989 rediscovery resulted in the establishment of a national park around the remaining animals. With such long odds, to recover the ivory-bill would make an inspiring conservation story with few equals.

The debate between believers and skeptics has been going on—often without much new information—at least since 2005, though fervor on both sides has flagged in recent years. I suppose skeptics, knowing they can always get a rise out of their foes, can't really be blamed for occasionally hauling out the Bigfoot card. After all, nothing gets to a believer like the specter of Sasquatch. The believers' reaction to being lumped with Bigfoot hunters is based on the desire to be taken seriously, to defend the turf of presumed legitimacy they've occupied since the rediscovery was endorsed by United States Secretary of the Interior Gale Norton. Faith-based ornithology sounds close enough to cryptozoology to make believers cringe. They point to a long shabby history of reputations being ruined following ivory-bill claims. LSU ornithologist George Lowery was ridiculed for buying into ivory-bill photos taken in the 1970s, and for John Dennis, the story goes, it was even worse. I've seen the Lowery pictures, which were eventually revealed as the work of a Louisiana boxing commissioner named Fielding Lewis; they look like snapshots of an ivory-bill on a tree to me. Dennis, who had previously observed ivory-bills in Cuba, claimed to have glimpsed and heard them in the Big Thicket of Texas in the 1960s; when his birds couldn't be relocated, his findings slipped into disrepute, and he fell from an acknowledged expert on the species to a kind of embarrassment to the ornithological community. According to Gallagher, wildlife-management student David Kullivan, whose 1999 sighting brought the ivory-bill back into the public eye and arguably led to the Arkansas rediscovery, won't even talk about his encounter any more.

Given the career-damaging abuse heaped on Lowery, Dennis, and Kullivan, the believers' self-conscious allegiance to empiricism is understandable. But how can they explain the pull of the grail bird? Believers may talk of the imperative to learn, but surely there are other scientific conundrums, and other pressing conservation causes, that could be pursued with less risk to reputations and more dependable, maybe even more potentially far-reaching, results. For believers, however, what's at stake in the quest is nothing short of redemption. Huge swaths of "original America" have been squandered in just a few centuries. The passenger pigeon and Carolina parakeet may be gone for good, but the ivory-bill's resurrection would perhaps restore some measure of innocence. In an age of environmental problems so overwhelming there seems little chance that the future will honor the current crop of Americans as anything remotely resembling a greatest generation, the saved ivory-bill could provide new hope, or, at the very least, living proof that we weren't all bad.

Skeptics, representing themselves as appalled at the waste of scarce conservation dollars on such a will-o'-the-wisp, are ostensibly even more devoted to empiricism than believers. But they too have been captured by the ivory-bill mystique, sometimes offering sheepish apologies for their continued interest. And, even while ardently asserting the ivory-bill's extinction, more than a few confess in unguarded moments that they would like to believe in its survival if they could. It's safe to say that even the most skeptical skeptic is a little jealous of the Gallaghers and Harrisons, and most would trade a year of birding, or even a year's salary, for the opportunity to mark their lists with a John Hancock–size *x* in the box next to ivory-billed woodpecker.

~

I like birds. My own life list, maintained for over thirty years, has grown to a respectable number of species. Though my list is rarely if ever examined by anyone other than myself, I'm careful about my claims, noting possible and probable sightings but excluding them from my "official" tally. Some years ago I filed my first rare bird report—black-throated blue warbler on the Billings Rimrocks, a "good bird" for the area if not in the ivory-bill league—with the Montana equivalent of the Texas Bird Records Committee. I've even tagged along at times with high-powered listers who communicate by two-way radio and cell phone so no rarity goes uncounted. But I have little interest in becoming a world-class birder of the trophy-hunter variety, even if I could afford the necessary trips to remote locales like Attu Island in the Aleutians, where hard-to-get Asian vagrants are ticked by the birding elite.

It doesn't take a Roger Tory Peterson, however, to find the grail bird compelling. I first learned about the ivory-bill from a grade school *Weekly*

*Messenger* article proclaiming that John Dennis, at the time still a noted expert, had rediscovered the lost woodpecker in the Big Thicket of Texas. I suppose the story shared the romantic appeal of Sanderson's cryptozoology, but its higher, adult, level of credibility has given it more staying power with me. Though I've never been obsessed like Bobby Harrison, I've always been alert to the bird's appearances and, alas, disappearances; it seems the world is a little younger, a little more intact, when the ivory-bill is "on." If I lived in the vicinity of an ivory-bill hot zone, I might find myself tromping, as quietly as possible, through the swamps with the local "team," even though at heart I share Theodore Roethke's suspicion of overly organized, single-minded listers.

And why not follow Roethke's example? My background is in literature—poetry even—so I have little to gain from claiming the mantle of science or entangling myself in the legalistic stipulations of sport birding. When it comes to the thing in the woods, what kind of poet would I be if I didn't side with mystery? Any veteran of a college workshop knows that writers value a kind of show-don't-tell empiricism—one of my professors advocated carrying anything I thought might be an original insight around in a pocket to test whether it was "true in the world"—but the conclusions and connections drawn through poetry are provisional, useful, as Emerson has it, for "conveyance," not "homestead." Poets are more interested in evoking immediate impressions—finding objective correlatives, if you will—than in having the last word; in my experience, poets aren't much inclined to believe in final answers. The ivory-bill is a virtual embodiment of Keats's principle of negative capability: it dwells in uncertainty. A few advocates have suggested that the bird would be better off preserving its current shadowy status, which may, anyway, have kept it alive so far. Meanwhile, we humans could, perhaps indefinitely, hold out hope for its survival while maintaining the exquisite apprehension engendered by its presence at the edge of existence—both there and not there, both real and imagined, like an image in a poem.

I don't wish to suggest that there's no difference between an ivory-bill in the flesh and one used as a metaphor, or that the latter is in any way a viable substitute for the former. In fact, I recoil whenever I hear that some animal, place, or other natural feature is "not only important for its own sake," but is also, and, by implication moreso, valuable for some human, usually economic, purpose. Of course, the concept of importance itself reflects a human ordering of value. I see no essential reason, however, why humans can't conclude that nature is more significant in its own right than for what we make of it; indeed, many people have, and still do, believe so. That being said, it seems reasonable to suppose that the ivory-bill's durable presence at a ragged boundary of our collective reality might have something important to tell us about ourselves.

The ivory-bill's uncertain status has opened a lane of perception that is appealing, troubling, and usually unavailable to eyes limited by Western notions of knowledge and possibility. In Simon Ortiz's poem "Comprehension," "two Indian men" encounter a creature that is both a coyote "crossing the highway. / Right before us" and the great trickster Coyote. The animal's spiritual aspect "is illusion, true, but real." The poem defines *comprehension* as the ability to combine "this illusion / and the reality we must know" through a kind of myth-conscious perceptual acuity. Our European-based post-Enlightenment culture, on the other hand, insists that something must be either real or imaginary, but not both. Contemporary anthropologists acknowledge the importance of belief systems in shaping cultural identity, but in common parlance we still reduce the word *myth* to mean something like a false belief that has been or should be replaced by scientific fact or law, or, at best, a nostalgic aura generated by humanity's past reverence for iconic creatures like bears and wolves. Skeptics label the ivory-bill a myth, which, in Ortiz's sense, seems obvious enough. But to both skeptics and believers, reporting a myth crossing a highway, or flying across a bayou, would be tantamount to "seeing things," as the saying goes. By connecting ivory-bill believers to Bigfoot hunters, skeptics are pushing their rivals over a conceptual precipice separating respectable reality from the lost valley of superstition, the land of the "old wives' tale" where Ichabod Crane, versed in Cotton Mather's *Wonders of the Invisible World*, turns pumpkins into ghosts.

Whether adhering to the standards of science or those of bird listing, a claimant must provide proper credentials and documentation to acknowledged gatekeepers—peer reviewers on the one hand and bird records committees on the other—whose inherent subjectivity is controlled, or masked, by a framework of established precedent and criteria. So often rollicking when needling believers, skeptics get serious, dour even, when discussing *Science* magazine's apparent "fast-tracking" of Cornell's original ivory-bill report. Such opportunistic fraud, they assert, constitutes an attack on the bastion of empirical positivism at a time when the scientific method is under assault from religious fanaticism, commercial influence, and political manipulation. Protecting the integrity of science is timely and even noble, but can the search for the ivory-bill really be compared to organized attempts to market new drugs based on falsified test results? At the very least, the comparison seems to lack perspective, to suggest some hidden anxiety. It may be wise to remember that, in the midst of such pious allegiance to the banner of science, support for climate change denial is coming—not universally, to be fair—from within the ranks of ivory-bill skeptics, not believers.

Perhaps the skeptics are chasing a phantom as elusive as the ivory-bill. Undermined by everything from bureaucratic "editing" of unpleasant findings to the profoundly unsettling insights of theoretical physics, the idea of scientific objectivity has emerged into the new millennium with habitat problems of its own. Ortiz's coyote partakes of a multilevel existence while the ivory-bill resists commitment to either side of a duality, but the result in each case is to throw into question the whole notion that something must be either nature, that is scientific, or culture, that is mythic. On its own terms science deals only with quantifiable data, while culture must "bring facts to life" through impure but exhilarating subjectivity. The border between the two, however, has become a treacherous postmodern no-man's-land, where science is cultural and myth natural. The telescope and the particle accelerator, those precise instruments of objective observation, turn out to be double agents, revealing a world shot through with apparent subjectivity. No wonder science seems a bit addled by its own revelations. The universe, we are now told, may be something like an idea, a story even, maybe an "illusion, true, but real."

If the ivory-bill were a subatomic particle or a creature of dark matter, it could, like Rene Daumal's Mount Analogue, be inevitably perceived if one could only discern when and where, and especially how, to look. Of course, the ivory-bill is not a denizen of the quantum world, or, for that matter, of the French novel; it shares in our own conventional but generally reliable limitations of time and space. Skeptics sometimes accuse believers of, in effect, creating the ivory-bills they claim to see in dappled woods and blurry videos, an accusation that stings at BirdForum even if it wouldn't hold much weight in the annals of quantum mechanics. Believers counter by asserting that skeptics are blinded by their own preconceived notion of the ivory-bill's extinction. Perhaps Jerome Jackson said more than he intended when he accused Cornell of faith-based ornithology—this coming from a man who, armed with little more than hope, has spent most of his adult life chasing something he fears may not really be there.

With Jackson's equivocal, perhaps partly fabricated, endorsement, hardcore skeptics patrol a backwater of the conceptual borderlands in a rearguard attempt to preserve a fragment of stable objectivity. If the ivory-bill wants to be part of the real world, it will have to pass reestablished checkpoints, surrendering its other, mythic identity in exchange for renewed, valid *Campephilus principalis* identity papers and a spot with the living woodpeckers in the next edition of the major birding field guides. Tricksters must not be allowed to have it both ways. The coelacanth was bad enough, but at least it had the decency to remain found.

In the event that indisputable proof, often characterized impatiently by believers as a "*National Geographic* glossy," is unveiled, the ivory-bill will presumably take its place among the "regular" animals, a new coelacanth reminding us that we live surrounded by mysteries we have only begun to fathom. A valuable lesson to be sure, more definite and universal, if less profound, than what the ivory-bill is telling us now.

## 3

It's late December and the ivory-bill search season is just getting underway. Maybe even at this moment one of the Reconyx cameras already working the swamps is snapping off a definitive photograph. Hopefully, though, confirmation of the bird's presence will come not from an anonymous machine but from some human devotee. It would be gratifying to see the "peace team" of Harrison and Jackson credited with the big find. I'd just as soon pull for the independent searchers, who, though they would understandably reject the comparison, carry the exploratory legacy of Ivan Sanderson into the twenty-first century. Wouldn't it be grand if the ultimate piece of ivory-bill evidence came from someone like Mary Scott, who once patrolled the woods with a "bird whisperer"? That would be enough, paraphrasing Wallace Stevens, to make rationalists reach for their sombreros.

In all likelihood, representatives of the Texas Bigfoot Research Center will also be afield, perhaps sharing the Big Thicket wetlands with ivory-bill hunters following in the footsteps of John Dennis. The Bigfoot team has at least one advantage over their counterparts: since they are chasing a mystery that, let's face it, will never be solved, they will be able to return year after year, their quest forever unfulfilled. What will the ivory-bill searchers do if the woodpecker's presence is confirmed once and for all? For some, discovering the limits of its range—whether it still flies in Texas, Tennessee, South Carolina—will be enough. Others, inspired by the ivory-bill's example, will no doubt turn their attention to the Bachman's warbler, a tiny songbird they could seek in familiar ivory-bill habitat. In quest of the Eskimo curlew, a wide-ranging shorebird, American searchers might even join forces with former "sceptics" from the British Isles. A far worse fate for all would be a final admission that the ivory-bill is gone. Proving a negative, however, is notoriously difficult, a principle under cover of which the discouraged university-backed teams have mostly withdrawn. The irrepressible Bobby Harrisons and Tim Gallaghers, having glimpsed the grail bird, are likely to carry on indefinitely, even at their own expense. Of course, the wild card in all this is the woodpecker itself, that great trickster. Where, when, and to whom will it reveal its flashing white wings, its distinctive nest cavity? What story will it choose to inspire next?

⌒

As for me, I can't claim a revelatory moment as sublime as Harrison's, and I may not be the storytelling equal of my college friend, but I know from my own experience that there's something out there in the woods, or at least there has been in my lifetime. I suppose I'll never know what we encountered that evening at Shades, or even how many legs it had. I can say with confidence that it wasn't an ivory-bill. I have no reason to suspect that it was Bigfoot. The Brighton Beast? Not a chance.

Whatever my thing in the woods was, it remains in my memory as a humble embodiment of the profound mystery that, emanating from the creation, is the source of both science and art, a mystery that beckoned Audubon and Wilson into the wilderness, and that must have led a backwoods sculptor to carve a likeness of the devil on an Indiana ridge. Assuming that he was more than a cynical enabler of hoaxes, that same mystery drew Ivan Sanderson into a shadowy world of wild subhumans. I may not be able to follow him there—I'm apparently "not welcome," anyway. But somewhere in Arkansas or Florida or Mississippi or Texas, someone is parting a screen of kudzu and fallen timber to reveal a flooded forest of tall cypress and tupelo, gloomy but split by sunshafts. And there, in the biggest, oldest tree, a flash of black and white disappears into a large oval hole.

Maybe. But, at the very least, during an otherwise unremarkable outing at a popular midwestern state park—a leftover remnant of original forest surrounded by alternating squares of corn and soybeans—I heard something growl.

II

## Travelers

Thorough the fog it came;
—Samuel Taylor Coleridge

On a typically cool, overcast summer afternoon on California's North Coast, I steer our rented Sentra across a misty spit of dunes toward the south jetty, one of a matched pair ushering the open Pacific into roughly hourglass-shaped Humboldt Bay, the state's second-largest ocean inlet. Dodging potholes requires careful attention; under a constant barrage of windswept sand and salt spray, the narrow road has deteriorated in the twenty-seven years since I've been here. Finally, the sandy peninsula gives out, the dunes grudgingly ceding a small parking lot, the bay's channel before us.

During the mid-1980s, Cara and I spent a year in Eureka, on the inland side at the hourglass's narrow waist. We were recently married, having met in a Louisiana Master of Fine Arts program from which, disillusioned, neither of us had graduated. Our plan, such as it was, called for me to finish an incomplete or two that stood between me and a pre-Louisiana master's degree; Cara, after establishing residency, would take up wildlife management at Humboldt State University, just up the bay in Arcata. Meanwhile, we'd piece together a living as best we could. It would be an adventure.

That's not exactly how it worked out. I did finish my incompletes, and even did a little teaching—my class was "Personal Editing"—for the university's extension program. Making a living on the North Coast, however, proved a challenge. I shuttled between part-time jobs, resurrecting an adolescent career selling shoes at Montgomery Ward's by night after manning the store for a hot tub and greenhouse dealership. These pricey items appealed to Humboldt County's backwoods marijuana farmers, who'd show up in downtown Eureka at harvest time with wads of illegal but welcome cash. On Sundays, I put in a few hours at a tobacco shop, mostly handing out free sample cigarettes to the small city's transient population. Cara, meanwhile, did office work for Mid-County Truck until, like so many North Coast businesses, the concern folded. After that, she kept the often-alarming books for an unprofitable Eureka lumberyard.

The North Coast economy was traditionally centered on extractive industries, particularly redwood logging. As explained to me by an employment counselor at the Eureka Job Service office, for decades timber companies had been liquidating labor-intensive groves of ancient giants so they could streamline operations in automation-friendly second growth. When the "save the redwoods" movement succeeded in preserving most of the remaining pockets of mature trees, about 4 percent of the original forest, the corporations blamed the environmentalists for killing the very jobs they themselves had been striving to commit to obsolescence. Though the Humboldt area is known as a liberal bastion—locals talk about living "behind the redwood curtain"—there's still an undercurrent of resentment against tree huggers. The anger may be misplaced, but it is understandable; the scarcity of good jobs in this neglected corner of California has become chronic, if not permanent.

An unexpected pregnancy and the birth of our son broke our tenuous Northern California hold. After a year in Humboldt County, we knew virtually no one. We were pretty independent, I suppose, and the fog-wrapped North Coast tends to cocoon residents in a gentle if vaguely survivalist isolation. A family, we knew, meant a whole new level of responsibility and care. In short, it was time to grow up. I applied and was admitted to Purdue's PhD program in American literature. Pending the start of the next fall semester, we moved to Cara's hometown, Salt Lake City, where our son, named Thomas for relatives on both sides, could be welcomed into the world by grandparents and cousins. A quarter century later, that same son returned to his fleeting first home, comparing himself to a salmon in his application to study environmental resource engineering at Humboldt. Here we are, then, just a few days after his wedding, with a dim midday sun holding off the fog, setting out into the Pacific on the south jetty.

When we lived in Eureka, I enjoyed walking the jetty; like my familiar Ontario Beach Park pier, it offered a way to penetrate the deep waters, at least a little, without a boat. Unlike Lake Ontario, the Pacific is standoffish, churning distant and aloof behind long skirts of foam, but even the world's biggest ocean was right there under your feet when you got out past the surf line. Of course, a walk into such a powerful, essentially foreign element can be treacherous. A bright red Danger sign cautions that the south jetty is "unsafe for walking," which in fact is not far from the truth. At a stormy high tide, this walk would indeed be unpleasant and maybe worse, the warning sign insisting that "deadly waves," are possible "at any time."

Along with the sense of being in the ocean's midst, we used to come here for close encounters with marine life. I saw a gray whale once, actually inshore from where I stood about halfway out, and I remember on another occasion a huge bull sea lion, probably a Steller's, tilting his head toward me for a moment like a human swimmer while forging a powerful, effortless course out of the bay. The life list I've maintained since I was in my twenties includes several new birds attributed to this jetty—snowy plover, common murre, wandering tattler, ruddy turnstone. Today there will be one more.

At the outset of our maritime saunter, we stop to watch a flight of shorebirds—western sandpipers with a few semipalmated plovers—collapse onto the beach only to swirl up and settle again like a blanket in almost the same spot. Beyond the surf, under the grating calls of elegant terns, starfish cling to the jetty rocks. Sea palms, absent from the bay, clump the ocean side. Seals surface in the channel, perhaps drawn by the hubbub of Heerman's gulls harassing the fishing pelicans. A harbor porpoise arcs, and again, farther out.

Small flotillas of scoters and duos of murres—usually an adult and a juvenile—ride the crests closer to the jetty's end. Here, the rocks are supplemented by a rough framework of dolosse (from *dolos*, a South African term for a kind of game counter) pitched about like massive concrete jacks. In addition to shredding the waves, the jumble of blunt spikes offers handy perches for western and glaucous-winged gulls, brown pelicans, and Brandt's cormorants, with surfbirds, maybe a black turnstone or two, decked along a lower prong.

I lag behind Cara and Tom on the way back, immersed, as it were, in the sea's hollow rhythm, punctuated by the foghorn's lifeless yet evocative pulse, a sound I seem to have always known. When I heard the Ontario Beach horn on cloudy nights through my childhood bedroom window, it meant that the big lake was just beyond our tame suburban neighborhood. Out there, intrepid sailors were making their way through all that darkness and wave.

What's this, though?—my reverie interrupted by excited pointing and binocular waving coming from ahead. There, over the channel, a bizarre brown-and-white cross-shaped apparition hangs with head high for a long moment, now plunges forward, wings swept back, knifing bill-first into the water. It's a brown booby, forsaking its tropic seas for this cool sun-deprived bay. None of us have ever seen one before, though we know its North Atlantic cousin, the gannet, well enough to surmise pretty quickly what sort of creature we're looking at.

After a few minutes, the booby has had its fill of channel fishing, and turns west, straight out to sea. We won't see it again. And, as far as we know, neither will anyone else. There will be no corroborating reports on the Redwood Region Audubon telephone birding hotline or the California Birds Internet list. A brown booby was observed near San Francisco in June, but that was over a month ago and hundreds of miles to the south. As dramatic as it seems to us, our bird's sudden appearance at Humboldt Bay will go as unremarked as our own brief tenure decades earlier.

Each summer, a current of pelicans and terns flows from warm, nutrient-poor breeding grounds to the rich wind-stirred waters of Northern California and the Pacific Northwest. The same bounty draws an occasional booby, but these ocean vagabonds are not given to venturing close to shore. The brown is the most likely to turn up on the North Coast, but that only means the others are rarer still. A brown booby was recorded at the jetties in 2006, another in Mendocino County just south of Humboldt in 2003. One or two additional North Coast records note boobies of undetermined species, and a smattering of sightings has occurred farther north in Oregon, Washington, and British Columbia. That's about it. Anecdotal evidence—not much more than speculation at this point—hints at an incipient northward shift of these tropical plunge-divers, perhaps in response to warming-driven changes affecting breeding islands. Whether climate refugees or simply off-course wanderers, North Coast boobies, like lone pioneers, are a long way from others of their kind. Birds seen so far from their usual haunts are labeled *accidental*. To be at the exact spot where one of these wanderers shows up, to be on hand for such an accident, is one of the amateur naturalist's singular and memorable pleasures.

~

If the booby's appearance was brief and obscure, the same can't be said for another ocean denizen gracing the North Coast at the same time. On June 23, a gray whale and her calf entered the Klamath River. Migrating grays frequent the region's inshore waters; an overlook at the Klamath's mouth is a noted whale-watching perch. These marine journeyers might linger in the productive zone where river nutrients blend into the sea, but they usually stay in salt water. This particular cow and calf, however, caused something of a sensation, swimming upriver about three miles and settling right below the Highway 101 "Golden Bear" bridge. After weaning a month later, the calf abandoned its mother, who remained in the river. Concerned that she might run out of food or deep water as the summer progressed, local, state, and Yurok tribal authorities (the lower Klamath banks are reservation land) attempted to nudge her back to sea with everything from firehoses to taped orca songs. But hazing caused little more than momentary jitters, and her prospective benefactors stepped back, stumped, while she remained stubbornly in plain view of passers-by on California's Redwood Highway, the major coastal route between the Pacific Northwest and San Francisco.

No one knows why she chose to stay in the river. Perhaps she suffered from the inner-ear disorder thought by some to lead to whale beachings. Maybe she was spooked by predators or simply confused. One theory held that the tsunami following the previous spring's Japanese earthquake had swept an avalanche of crustaceans and other sea life into the river, leaving behind an easily accessible banquet of quality whale chow. Grays are flexible in their diet and habits, including, research shows, their travels. The species is known for its long seasonal migrations between Mexico's Baja lagoons and the Bering Sea. But several hundred whales, not necessarily the same ones each year, stick around at various places along the way, especially where food is plentiful. The Klamath animal, assigned number 604 in what the weekly *North Coast Journal* calls "the official catalog of gray whales," had not been previously documented in California waters, though she was well known farther north, from Washington to Alaska; she had spent considerable time around Vancouver Island, where Cara and I saw a gray whale, possibly even the same one, two summers before.

By the beginning of August, when we drove down the coast en route to Tom's wedding, the Klamath River whale—a Redding blogger pegged her with the rather uninspired name Mama—had become a celebrity. A digital highway sign at Crescent City (and another, we later found, in Arcata) alerted drivers to "people on the bridge" without specifying what they might be doing there. Despite the highway department's evasiveness, the pulloffs on each side of the Klamath, pressed into service as parking lots, were almost full when we joined the line of eager leviathan seekers snaking along the bridge's narrow sidewalk. And there she was, not just a fleeting hump rising from ocean depths, but a complete, if cloudy, outline cruising right below the surface. When she came up to spout, we could see her face, narrower than I would have guessed, showing no particular inclination to explain her presence to humans. But no agitation or hostility either. If she objected to whining cameras and leaning shadows, she didn't show it.

With their perceptive intelligence and uncanny long-distance communications, cetaceans have long fascinated a legion of admirers, and Mama chose, after all, New Agey Northern California for her entrada into the American interior. So it's not surprising that she was soon sought out by pilgrims, a few serenading her with flutes and ukuleles. Unlike belugas or humpbacks, grays aren't considered particularly gifted musically, and whether she liked the attention or found it a nuisance is anyone's guess, although she didn't attempt to avoid the performers and tourists who flocked to her. Eventually, one overly enthusiastic boatload of well-wishers got a bit too close and bumped her, thankfully without apparent harm to either party.

Yurok reactions to Mama's presence were complex and ambivalent. Bolstering Redwood Coast tourism, she provided a short-term economic boost to this chronically strapped area, along with something like Andy Warhol's fifteen minutes of fame. "It was like a rock concert," according to innkeeper Reweti Wiki, a Maori from New Zealand who had married into a Yurok family. Tribal people attempted to understand her appearance in the light of indigenous tradition. Recalling "The Inland Whale," a story told by her ancestor Fannie Flounder to anthropologist Theodora Kroeber, Wiki's mother-in-law and business partner Janet Wortman thought, "When the whale is in the river, it means the world is out of balance ... things aren't the way they should be." Yurok chairman Thomas O'Rourke concurred, but in true political style praised the community's efforts, however ineffectual, to come to her aid. "It is acts like this that are going to happen if we are going to stabilize the environment," he pronounced. Elder Walt Lara Sr., offered a contrary perspective, asserting that "to us, a whale in the river is a good thing. It is a spiritual move that says, 'You people are doing things right.'"

The stir turned out to be short lived, and, for the whale herself, the inland adventure ended badly. On a mid-August evening, just a few weeks after we saw her, Whale 604 beached herself on a gravel bank and succumbed. She had lived in the river for fifty-three days. She had shown no signs of illness or injury before respiratory distress set in that afternoon. Given the ordinary pressures associated with calf-rearing and migration, she did not appear undernourished or overly stressed; scientists trying to determine her physical condition kept concluding that it was just about normal. It would take months of forensic sleuthing to identify a freshwater fungus infection as the cause of death.

The ebullient atmosphere abruptly dispelled, Mama was given a dignified memorial ceremony by tribe members. Her death saddened her many callers, from flute-bearing New Age acolytes to scientists like Humboldt State zoologist Dawn Goley, who valued the rare opportunity for herself and her students to get to know an individual whale. No doubt even anxious highway safety officials felt a melancholy emptiness when their warning signs were no longer required.

The day we stopped at the bridge, the obligatory self-appointed expert was explaining to whoever would listen that Mama and her calf were not the first of their kind to swim up the Klamath. During the 1980s, he said, another cow and calf passed beneath the highway. Other accounts of that 1981 visitation don't mention a calf, perhaps an irresistible embellishment for the sake of narrative symmetry, carrying for us the delicious implication that Mama was retracing a route she had plied in her youth, returning like our son to a place where parental wanderlust had once brought her before.

Honeymooning up the coast, Tom and his bride were among the Klamath River whale's final visitors.

~

That summer was a time of restoring lost connections. On several occasions, circumstances reunited me with people and places I hadn't seen for many years, Humboldt Bay's south jetty among the latter. These months also brought a spate of encounters with wild travelers. Not long before our California trip, Cara and I took in a pastel violet sunset from another spit, this one at the mouth of Braddock's Bay on Lake Ontario. On a still, almost windless July evening, rocky Manitou Beach offered a welcome asylum from the bay's persistent deerflies and mosquitoes. Suddenly, however, the placid mood was split asunder as a dark inexplicable shape coursed purposefully across the mouth of the bay. Far out from shore, it looked darker than the darkest gull, but was not flying at all like a goose or cormorant. It struck me as an anomaly, not anything I could easily place into a landscape I know as well as any in the world.

"Did you see it?" This from a breathless, binoculared pair who had materialized behind us. After asking if we were birding or just watching the sunset—not a distinction we had thought to make—they told us that a friend had called to report a long-tailed jaeger winging inexorably toward our viewpoint. A jaeger makes a dramatic, even uncanny, impression. The minute they told us what they were looking for, I was sure it was the apparition we had just beheld moments before. Though it wasn't close enough to count—I had never seen a long-tail—I'm just as certain today. The couple, whose names we never got, said that while a few of these birds are reported from the lake each fall, July sightings are unheard of. Or so it seemed. Their friend's posted pictures show, beyond a doubt, a long-tailed jaeger cruising the lake off Braddock's Bay.

Once home to harbor seals, Lake Ontario is the closest Great Lake to the Atlantic. Gannets and other seabirds are seen occasionally, navigating, along with ocean-going freighters and tankers, up the vast Saint Lawrence estuary. I had previously encountered parasitic jaegers while whale watching offshore from Rivière-du-loup, Quebec, on the Bas-Saint-Laurent, where migratory finback and minke whales summer with an endangered population of belugas. It seems reasonable, then, to expect an occasional jaeger to track the great river all the way to the freshwater sea at its source. Decades of observational records, however, show that jaegers reach the Great Lakes by traveling overland from James Bay. Moreover, long-tails, the most pelagic of the three jaeger species, seem peculiarly drawn to Lake Ontario, the smallest of the five lakes.

Jaegers, like boobies, are solitary long-distance vagabonds, their travels understood by ornithologists and birders only as general patterns and tendencies. The sudden manifestation of one of these far-flung wanderers can seem portentous, almost metaphysical, like the albatross in *The Rime of the Ancient Mariner*. Who can say what leads a jaeger across hundreds of miles of boreal forest while most return to sea after the tundra nesting season? Is Lake Ontario on an ancestral route passed down in some Lamarckian fashion from an original explorer? Scientific study might reveal and categorize advantages the rare inland migrants gain, but what can be made of the impulse that leads an individual bird to trade the open water for an ocean of trees?

～

Birds are built for mobility, and even those least inclined to wanderlust sometimes turn up in unexpected places. At first glance, Florida scrub-jays have little in common with roving jaegers and peripatetic boobies. Stay-at-home landlubbers loyal to small plots of relict scrubland, most jays are content with a few acres around the natal nest. An occasional adventurous sort, however, forsakes its homeland and heads for parts unknown. Like the Klamath whale, such brave souls lead risky lives, but, researchers surmise, "every once in a while, a jay heads over the horizon and hits the jackpot: an empty territory bursting with acorns and beautiful patches of white sand in which to bury them." Small parcels of jay habitat dot interior Florida like a scattering of islands —many scrub patches *were* islands at one time. Scrub tends to give way to hammock or pine savannah, and the birds need wildfire—grown less dependable with the spread of orange groves, golf courses, and tract homes—to keep territories open.

In effect, the rare explorer jays may function as a "Hail Mary" safety-valve for the species. That's what ornithologists conclude, based on a big picture analysis that can't begin to explain what moves an individual jay to set out, acting against the weight of inclination and evolutionary heritage.

Perhaps whatever drives the explorer jays may also move whales to swim up rivers, boobies and jaegers to penetrate strange regions of sky and shore. Roaming individuals may have no clearer sense of destination than, say, the early Polynesians, who followed migrant birds en route, as it turned out, to Hawaii. For some creatures, human and otherwise, the urge to seek out new places somehow simply overwhelms the desire to trust to proven ways.

～

I feel a deep affinity for the Yellowstone region. Though I will never be a native, this windswept land of prairies and mountains has become my home. But it's not at all like the orchards and viney woods of the Lake Ontario plain or the coastal environs I seem naturally drawn to. Revisiting someplace like Humboldt County can be disorienting, and Rochester always is. After that summer's travels a few days camping on Big Pryor Mountain, lights of small Wyoming towns to the south and Billings to the north, brought me back, in short, to my present world. A town edged against water, with gulls on pilings, knocking boats, and haunting foghorns, may be my *kind* of place, but this Montana-Wyoming borderland has become my *place*. At least for now.

When I left Upstate New York in the early eighties, my plans were open-ended, and for several years I considered myself a traveler, moving from home to home with only the vaguest of plans. Four states, including California, in four years. Tom's arrival made us more future-conscious, but even then our wanderings weren't at an end. Five years of graduate school in Indiana, followed by a series of jobs in Wyoming, Maine, Florida, now Montana. It hasn't been the kind of life that someone like Wendell Berry would seek or approve of. But the way it has unfolded might have something in common with the travels of a wandering booby or Great Lakes jaeger. As must be the case for a windborne seabird, mine has been a life to ride rather than to inhabit.

I'm not sure that the ride is over yet. Scattered across the continent, our families pull us in various directions, and each place we've lived exerts a kind of obscure gravitational attraction. But our move to Billings was our most conscious relocation. It was, first off, a return to a place that had set hooks and called us back. Circling back is different from setting out to points unknown. Before 1984, when we moved to Eureka, Cara's Humboldt County experience was limited to a couple of brief stops during childhood family vacations; for me the entire West Coast was terra incognita. When we visit now, that initial displacement is overlain with the aura of return, a harmony wrapped around a dissonance. Eureka has sprawled a bit at its edges, but fanciful Old Town facades still lure passing tourists. Arcata's bronze William McKinley stands as stern as ever against the framing palms. And there, where we left them, are the wise redwoods, the soulful, inquisitive faces of harbor seals.

Unlike Montana, where the effects of today's climate disruption are as obvious as a beetle-killed forest, the North Coast seems pretty much the same as it did three decades ago. Studies show redwood-nourishing sea fog gradually diminishing, and, more ominously, the ocean growing more acidic. Not exactly Shangri-La, then, but there is a sense of at least relative stability. Even the "plazmoids" hanging out in Arcata's central square must surely be avatars of predecessors whose sixties garb and spacey mellowness were already anachronistic in 1984. Some of the older ones may, in fact, be the same people. One gets the impression that their society is loose, fluid, the square a gathering place for vagabonds who might be gone tomorrow, or who might stay, one day at a time, for thirty years. Like the North Coast as a whole, Arcata's plaza retains a remarkably singular and durable identity as a haven from both spiraling out-of-control change and the dreary sameness that stifles contemporary life.

One of the things I like best about the North Coast is how it grips its eccentricity as tenaciously as a starfish clings to a rock. The region emanates an unforced weirdness able, it seems, to incorporate cell phones, computers, and the university's hydrogen-powered cars while keeping big box expansion in check. The new-to-us mall in Eureka has a hangdog look, as if it desperately wishes it had tried a less intransigent neighborhood. If not overly vibrant, gilded-age downtowns endure, odd boutiques offering Humboldt State Lumberjack sweatshirts alongside Bhutanese prayer flags. Generations past Woodstock, hippie vans still park in front of quirky Victorians on side streets. Humboldt County speaks to a capacity, perhaps inherent in place itself, to survive the steamroller of contemporary development, and even, possibly, the looming chaos of the future.

I used to trace my leaving home to a rejection of the generic suburb—not much like Wendell Berry's family farm—where I grew up. But place, I now see, can only be suppressed by such so-called development, not eliminated altogether. I didn't know this then, but I can recognize a Rochester neighborhood, maybe even my childhood tract, by the quality of light alone. At least I think I could. Looking back, I have to admit that my decision to take off was as much instinctive as intentional, and not, in and of itself, irrevocable. Plenty of Rochesterians, including a friend who went to Louisiana with me, have returned to the city from colleges, workplaces, or military hitches, presumably taking up their old associations as if they'd never left.

We might also have stayed in Florida, where in seven years we had found friends, accumulated belongings, and become conversant with the landscapes and wild inhabitants that defined the spirit of that place: the mysterious Red Red Silver, for example, named for her leg band colors, an outsider among our local scrub jays. Or the displaced Pacific coast Heerman's gull, known, inevitably, as Herman, who bothered pelicans up and down the Gulf from the Panhandle to Manasota Key, sharing the trade winds with tropical frigatebirds and wide-ranging winter gannets. But then something—the call of the Yellowstone, if you will—came up, and there we were, well past youth, gearing up for one more cross-country move. "Way leads on to way," as Robert Frost has it, making a life-defining pattern revealed only in retrospect, an idiosyncratic map that has brought us, unlike Frost's famous man at the crossroads, back to a place where two roads diverged long ago.

A booby miraculously appearing out of the sea reminds us that we too have emerged out of personal, cultural, and evolutionary histories, our paths meshing with those of other journeyers like momentary alignments of planets—*wandering stars* in Greek—bound for destinies and destinations not yet set and only dimly foreseen. As the climate warps, even those of us who are most rooted in one spot will in a sense become travelers, the known world shifting around us. A friend in Maine, a state noted for the pugnacious loyalty of its residents, once lamented to me that his native woods "will be somewhere up in Quebec fifty years from now." How will we react to such a world-scale unmooring? Will we seek new habitat like explorer jays or hunker down and wait for restoring fires?

⁓

The Adirondack Mountains were, I think it's safe to say, my father's favorite place, and my family's summer trips almost always landed in or at least managed to pass through the giant state park that encompasses them.

Like Yellowstone a landmark of American environmental history, New York's ancient rising mountains may share something else with the first national park, current geology placing the Adirondacks atop a deeply buried volcanic hotspot. The ragged young uplifts on our Billings horizon are a far cry from the rounded contours of those eastern highlands. But every so often, say at Shoshone Lake in Yellowstone Park or maybe along Rock Creek in the Beartooth Mountains, I'm struck with an unmistakable if elusive sense of "Adirondackness." It may be that something about a tumbling river or a wooded slope resonates with an eidetic memory. Perhaps the deeper regions of one's consciousness seek out such ephemeral links in the process of composing the narrative that underlies our sense of who we are. Or maybe places really do partake of something like atmospheric connections, mountain calling to mountain, forest to forest, lake to ocean. Could it be that certain individuals, animal and human, might overhear their conversations? Following at best uncertain signals, a scrub jay explorer somehow knows or feels the presence of distant scrub, an outbound Polynesian the call of uninhabited islands thousands of miles away. Of course, it goes without saying that some travelers, maybe most, never find what they seek, or fail to recognize it, or find it only to lose it again, or find it too late. Or never even figure out what it was they sought. The world is big enough for even a whale to get lost in.

I have no quarrel with the Wendell Berrys of the world, and I'm well aware of the high cost inherent in the rootless depredations of what Raymond Dasmann calls "biosphere peoples"—cultures that consider the entire planet their rightful territory. We grow through close association with a place—from being *in place*—and places, now more than ever, need their familiar defenders. When Berry showed up on the Frankfort capitol steps to protest mountaintop-removal coal mining, he was backed by generations-worth of loyalty to his Kentucky farmland. More power to him. There are things about a place that a nonnative, let alone a traveler, may never be privy to. But Berry is being hyperbolic and ethnocentric when he asserts, in *The Unsettling of America*, that European adventurers "invented the modern condition of being away from home." Imagine how our distant ancestors felt, striking out from Africa, eventually, for better or worse, to people the planet. Like it or not, Berry's European gadabouts were in line with a major feature of our species's history.

Humboldt County, California, takes its name from a nineteenth century Prussian nobleman who never saw the North Coast. Embarking on a South American "plunge into a vast solitude" that would paradoxically make him a legend around the world, Baron Alexander von Humboldt sought "to study the great harmonies of nature," in which, along with all "organic beings," he was enmeshed. Aaron Sachs, in *The Humboldt Current*—my copy, a Christmas present from Tom, was purchased at an Arcata bookstore—credits Humboldt as a formative influence on American environmentalism. For Humboldt, to cast oneself adrift with a scientist's careful eye and a mystic's intuitive mind was to experience nature and all its connections anew. Out there in the numinous could be found the exact opposite of the arrogance Berry critiques. Quoting Humboldt, Sachs concludes that "the most important lesson of 'communion with nature' was an awareness of 'the narrow limits of our own existence.'"

Human wanderings may not at this point represent the evolutionary safety valve that leads scrub jays to untapped acorns, whales to food-filled estuaries, and jaegers and boobies to distant shores, but it might feel the same for the individuals involved. No creature is conscious, after all, of its deep-seated biological imperatives. And even when a traveler's goals are as simple as untapped acorns and virgin sand, the place where, in an apt phrase, one "finds oneself" is, whether one is human, whale, or bird, likely an unpredictable result of circumstance and blind choices. But not quite blind. The Klamath River whale stuck to her bridge as if she knew where she had to be. We might as well say that when a long-tailed jaeger forsakes the ocean or a brown booby swings into the Humboldt Bay channel, it's heeding a guiding inner voice. Such awareness may not be conscious, but, for the individuals involved, it must be compelling.

Perhaps a wandering life is a necessary, or at least useful, counterpart to the settler's way. It may not, after all, be such a large step from speaking from the center of a community to believing that one *is* that center, or from advocating for one "special" place to discounting the value of others. Besides, cultural and land-use traditions don't always translate to place-conscious stewardship, and multigenerational abuses may be as common as indigenous wisdom, at least in displacement-haunted North America. And changes in land-based lifeways can be insidious. Liquidation logging firms are practiced in passing off ruthless exploitation as the way things have always been. Too often, they're at least partly right.

Already there when he or she arrives, remaining after he or she fades from local memory, places insinuate themselves into a traveler's consciousness. The world is more used up now than in Humboldt's day, all our "vast solitudes" marked by the footsteps of the baron and his compatriots and scarred by the unholy forces of exploitation that followed in their wake. Even space exploration is old hat, nothing remotely in reach but so much empty, soon, no doubt, to be sold to the highest bidder. Yet, for all that, wonder persists: Leviathan appears beneath a highway bridge, a young man wakes up one day in the unfamiliar landscape of his birth. From time to time, in the face of the great mystery our lives take us through, the ego still gives way, if only for a fleeting instant, to something larger, as a continent might shape itself around a river-going whale or a seabird emerging from fog.

# In Wonderland

I

In 1991, I left graduate school to take a position teaching in the English department at Northwest College in Powell, Wyoming, a small agricultural town in the Bighorn Basin east of Yellowstone National Park. Beginning my career at thirty-six, I was a slow starter, but with a child in first grade and a "real job" at a community college in a state where any college was rare enough to be noteworthy, I was finally, it seemed, on the verge of becoming an adult.

Two years earlier, I had begun searching for a faculty position, hand-copying addresses and instructions from job announcements I tracked in library copies of the *Chronicle of Higher Education*. I considered the opportunities and duties the ads described, but I found it more important, certainly more enjoyable, to consult the atlas for a tentative appraisal of what each place would mean for my family and me. Was it reasonably close to either of our hometowns in Utah or New York? Near the mountains or the sea? Was it at least not in northwestern Indiana? As is often the case, the job search was discouraging. My first interview was on the Virginia coast, my second near Saint Paul, Minnesota. Though both passed the first atlas check, neither was in a place where we had any real reason or desire to live. No matter, because I didn't get either job. Later, during the summer, I drew little more than a perfunctory response following an interview at Snow College in Utah. In short, I came out of my first year on the market emptyhanded, except, of course, for the "interviewing experience" that more successful job seekers always touted as a kind of consolation prize.

Most of the second year was much the same. Northwest College's position had run into some sort of administrative hangup, and by the time I got

the call inviting me to campus I had pretty much written it off as just an-
other of the two hundred unsuccessful applications I had tossed in the mail.
It was late in the season for academic jobs, and I was just about resigned
to another year at Purdue, chipping away at the dissertation and wading
through *Chronicle* and *MLA Job List* ads.

Though we had learned by then that an interview generally meant at best
a 33 percent chance of success, with the call from Powell we again got out
the atlas and flipped to Wyoming with considerable interest. There were
mountains. There was the mottled shading of national forest. There was
*Yellowstone*, a solid green square where geysers and grizzly bears played.
Cara had been there once or twice as a child. My own Wyoming experience
was limited to the long windswept drive between Denver and Salt Lake
City on Interstate 80. Now, while Tom read about the park and its hydro-
thermal features in books he borrowed from the West Lafayette public
library, I prepared for the first interview I thought really mattered.

I had applied at Northwest College the year before with no luck, so I had
reason for caution. On the other hand, at least I knew that they didn't take
my repeated attempts as evidence that I was having trouble landing a job.
Maybe there really was something to that interviewing experience, after all.
I felt that I could read this committee's intentions, that things were leaning
my way, and the welcome I received from my Powell interrogators further
bolstered my confidence. One of the first places on campus they showed
me was a kind of one-room natural history museum where elk, antelope,
and black bear stared out of surprisingly effective dioramas. The faculty
seemed a bit self-conscious about having "the animals" in the middle of the
administration building, but there was no question that the mountains and
deserts lapsing into the hazy diorama distance were central to the life of the
community. Since I was ABD—all but dissertation—with little experience,
I knew I was out of my league in the buyer's market of the universities.
Northwest College was just the kind of place I was looking for, and I found
that the committee, including the successful candidate from the previous
year's search who fortuitously knew one of my dissertation readers, was,
in fact, pretty friendly. I soon realized that barring some unforeseen mis-
chance the job would be mine.

Following the interview's final planned social/professional activity, I
took an early evening walk. Powell was small and square, a compact knot

embracing just enough stores, schools, offices, and homes for not quite five thousand people. With the houses ending abruptly at barley and sugar beet fields, it wasn't all that different in layout from a typical Indiana farming hamlet. Where the fields began the residential streets gave up their pavement, picked up irrigation ditches, traded names for county road numbers, and lost themselves in the cropland grid. It was still early in the agricultural spring, and the fields were dressed only in the dried flags of last year's stubble. To tell the truth, the place wasn't much to look at. Except, that is, for the horizon. North, behind the long flat desert escarpment called Polecat Bench, rose the blue hump of the Pryor Mountains, snow-whisked, striped with the dark seams of runoff canyons. To the east, the basin was bounded by the white snowcloud of the Bighorns, serenely suspended atop vertical cliffs some six thousand feet above the valley floor. Just southwest of town were the red and gray bentonite badlands of the McCullough Peaks. To the west behind the foreground shrug of Heart Mountain the hunched ranges gradually turned purple and black as the sun slipped behind them. Over there were the Absarokas, the Beartooths, and ultimately the high plateaus of Yellowstone. Counting the Bench and the McCulloughs, which my Indiana-adjusted eyes were inclined to do, there were mountains just about anywhere I looked. And all that sky! Fire-tipped plumes and lavender lenticular saucers launched over the mountains, gradually dissipating into wisps and swirls in the clear dry air of the Bighorn Basin.

I was taking stock of a decision that, for my part, had already been made. Since Cara longed to return to her native West and Tom was just going into first grade, it was for all intents and purposes a done deal. As I walked back toward Powell, my path marked by distant lightning over the Absarokas, a coyote doggie-gliding its way across the dirt road in front of me served, despite undoubtedly having more pressing things to do, as a portent.

～

We arrived in Powell in August, enrolling Tom at Westside Elementary School, settling temporarily into a rented house (we would become first-time homeowners the next year). Our yard was frequented by a stray white cat with frostbitten ears who soon became our cat. In the weeks before Northwest College opened, we explored the anachronistic downtown where Kragler's five-and-dime offered Aunt Jemima figurines and John Wayne clocks, none of which had been dusted, let alone sold, for years. We searched for tepee rings, rock circles marking Indian lodge sites, scattered across the sparsely grassed, badland-edged, windy expanse of Polecat Bench.

Labor Day weekend we camped in the Absarokas along the North Fork of the Shoshone River. Passing cars we could hear from our tent held lucky travelers bound for Yellowstone Park's east gate. There wasn't nearly as much traffic as we had feared, most schools having abandoned the traditional end-of-summer holiday in favor of mid-August starting dates. And so, a change of plans—we had intended to casually hike up one of the North Fork drainages—brought us over Sylvan Pass to Yellowstone Lake. From Lake Junction, we tracked the shore past West Thumb and crossed the continental divide—twice—to Old Faithful, eventually following the south half of the Loop Road to the Upper Falls at the head of the Grand Canyon, and then back through the Hayden Valley dusk, returning to Powell far later than we had intended.

That was the first of many such visits, mostly day trips, with occasional overnighters at the Old Faithful Inn or Mammoth Hot Springs. Sometimes we aimed for a hiking trail, sometimes just for a walk around the geyser basins. Tom, a born engineer, studied the underground links between thermal features. Once, at Old Faithful, he called out that Beehive, across the Firehole River on Geyser Hill, was about to "go" moments before a ranger huffed along the boardwalk alerting tourists to the infrequent eruption. Both knew the compressed two-hundred-foot-high column was soon to play because its "plumbing" linked it to another, smaller spout. During the four years we lived in Powell, we hiked to Shoshone Lake, Lost Lake, Riddle Lake, Lone Star Geyser, Garnet Hill, Fairy Falls. We climbed Mount Washburn and Avalanche Peak. We would arrive shortly after the plows at the end of April when otters played in riverside snowbanks, return in June for cutthroat trout battling their way up LeHardy Rapids, and again in September to hear the elk bugle. Somewhere along the way, we developed extravagant "mountain man" personas to amuse Tom, and ourselves, on the two-hour ride from Powell; in the absurd dialect our characters employed, my name was Lork, which may have had some etymological relationship to Luke, or perhaps "look," as in "lork at that thar." And we adopted the local custom of referring to Yellowstone simply as "the park."

Wyomingites, we discovered, had a generous conception of the neighborhood; ours included places as far away as Thermopolis, a hot spring swimming hole one hundred miles from Powell that we visited once or twice each winter. We sometimes hiked in the Montana Beartooths near Red Lodge, or camped as far away from home as Red Rock Lakes, tucked against the Idaho-Montana border. We braved the 10 percent grades of the "Oh My God highway" to reach the Bighorn Medicine Wheel and hiked above timberline in the Bighorn National Forest's Cloud Peak Wilderness. One August, we combined a day at Crow Fair, one of the largest intertribal Native American gatherings, with a stop at the Little Bighorn battlefield, where Custer, along with Crow allies, had met his famous fate in the persons of Sitting Bull and Crazy Horse. Perhaps our most frequent outing destination was the nearby Bighorn Canyon National Recreation Area, not far past the massive sugar beet refinery at Lovell. The canyon view was almost southwestern in scope, and the sere grass flats and brushy side canyons supported wild horses—not the ordinary escaped ranch animals but, Lovell promoters boasted, genuine descendants of the original Spanish mustangs. There were abandoned ranches and at least one intact ghost town, a sampling of frontier architecture once inhabited by colorful figures like pioneer journalist Carolyn Lockhart and Grosvener W. "Doc" Barry, a man of many exploits and dubious capitalist enterprises.

Looking back now, the whole experience seems hopelessly scattered, with daytrips and occasional weekends forced to substitute for the kind of familiarity that marks the indigenous experience. I couldn't claim to know even the park itself very well. There were whole regions—the Gallatin Mountains, the Pitchstone Plateau, the Thorofare—still way beyond my limited backcountry experience. But none of that mattered at the time. Yellowstone was sacred ground; its aura extended all the way through Powell, east up the canyons of the Bighorns, south to the hot springs at Thermopolis, even north to Billings, a refinery city along the banks of the Yellowstone River over one hundred miles from both Powell and the park border. The desert cliffs of Bighorn Canyon, the history-haunted grasslands of the Little Bighorn, the hidden marshes of Red Rock Lakes surrounded the park like luminous satellites. For me, Yellowstone suffused a territory less defined but far larger even than the ambitious "Greater Yellowstone" designated by ecosystem managers and environmental groups. Our final time in the park, after we knew we were leaving Powell, was a kind of ceremony—the last geyser eruption, the last walk by the lake, the last buffalo.

~

Eleven years later, I'm flying above the lightless landscape of northern Wyoming. From what I've read about the latest energy boom, I half expect the whole place to be just one garishly glowing methane well. But at least what I can see from the plane is all black. The Wyoming landscape had always felt harsh and otherworldly from the air, but after seven years in crowded Florida I find the darkness below reassuring. I'm on my way to another job interview, which I hope will be the last one I'll ever face. It's in Billings, and I'm guardedly optimistic about my chances.

In the summer of 1995, we left Powell, voluntarily but inevitably, caught up in a complex net of circumstances I still don't understand completely. Chalk it up to inexperience with the quicksand of academic politics. We ended up in Fort Kent, Maine, so far north that we lived between the Canadian border and the Welcome to Maine highway signs. Yellowstone seemed like a lost home. I knew I'd go back if the chance presented itself, but I also knew that such an opportunity was unlikely in the college-poor Rockies. Maine's Saint John Valley, self-contained and as close to self-sufficient as such a cold, remote land could be, proved a hard place for people "from away" to live. For Valley natives, everywhere else was "just the rest of the planet," as novelist Cathie Pelletier told me. Like few contemporary American places, the Valley belonged to the people who had settled there generations ago, who shared and cherished the legend and heritage of Acadia and New France. Outsiders were not disliked or distrusted; we were simply irrelevant. University people came and went, and no one was really surprised when, after a few years, I started applying for other positions. We were looking for the same things we had sought eight years earlier at Purdue: access to our families, to mountains or the sea. I had interviews with schools in Montana and Idaho, but nothing came of either one. Instead, we found ourselves in Lakeland, Florida, just as Tom was entering high school.

We developed a comfortable routine in Lakeland. I worked at Florida Southern College, noteworthy for its beautiful and historic lakeside campus complete with the world's largest collection of Frank Lloyd Wright buildings. The most rewarding experience of my professional career occurred when I taught Florida Southern classes in Greece, Turkey—with a stop at the Mammoth-like Pamukkale Hot Springs—and, the next year, Italy. Cara supervised work—doing much of it herself—on the old house we had bought, wrote novels, and eventually she too secured employment at Florida Southern. Tom flourished in high school, graduated with honors, and, in keeping with his long-standing interest in systems and electronics, applied to and was accepted by Caltech.

With Tom spending most of his time in Pasadena, we again began to think about the future. Did we really want to spend the rest of our lives in Central Florida? We had good friends in Lakeland, a house we'd put considerable work and money into, a garden with oranges for us and forage for various kinds of butterflies. We took long walks in the nearby scrublands and open pinewoods, encountering gopher tortoises and swallow-tailed kites. Each summer, we monitored scrub jay populations at a local preserve, getting to know individual birds by their leg bands. I had grown up with the water horizon of the Great Lakes and liked having the ocean close at hand, closer, despite the intervening urban congestion, than it had been in northern Maine. Though we hadn't fully realized it, we had begun to settle, to put down roots.

One thing we did know was that we wouldn't move again unless we were convinced we'd stay in our new home indefinitely, with luck permanently. But we didn't really worry about it much. At Purdue, I had responded to hundreds of ads, virtually saturating my small corner of the market. Now, I was applying for two or three jobs each year. At that rate there was a pretty good chance I would never have to consider an actual offer. I knew that most college teaching positions were entry level, and while the academic ranks didn't mean all that much to me, especially since Florida Southern had no tenure system, I could understand why a potential employer slogging through stacks of applications would pass mine by. *Hmm. What's wrong with this guy that he wants to start over again?* In short, we didn't expect much for my trouble, but we weren't quite resigned to staying where we were either.

Now, as the plane flies north toward Montana, I review what I know about Billings, the self-proclaimed "Magic City." If you live in Wyoming, the magic consists mainly of merchandise. From Powell, going to Billings was going to town; those excursions tended to be practical in nature—shopping, driving the two hours home after dark with supplies ranging from winter coats to tropical fish. Billings was the hub of the region, plausibly claiming an urban zone of influence stretching between the metropolitan spheres of Minneapolis and Spokane, and extending from Denver and Salt Lake City to Calgary. What I remember about Billings itself doesn't amount to much. I can picture a park by the Yellowstone River with cottonwoods and waterfowl, and, I think, an odd canopy over one of the downtown intersections—maybe I just saw that in a photograph. When the city lights at last emerge in the distance, I'm ready for the sudden landing on the Rimrocks, the downtown buildings still a few hundred feet below.

～

The May air is cool and, by Florida standards, dry, even on an overcast morning. My motel window looks out on the Rimrocks, where magpies and ravens range along ochre sandstone cliffs. Fruit trees are blooming, and the cottonwoods and willows along the irrigation canal wear the delicate effusion of early green that I haven't seen in seven years in Florida. At first, though, I find Billings disorienting, perhaps partly because it's always strange to return to a place after long absence, but also because the city is, well, urban. Despite my past experience as a reluctant shopper at Rimrock Mall, over the years my version of Billings has become inextricably embedded in my memory of the wide open Bighorn Basin. So the standard city downtown and oozing shopping centers are disconcerting. With office towers, refineries, and helicopters, it's obvious that Billings isn't another Powell.

During an afternoon break between interview-related events, I wander downtown, taking in Rodin's bronze *Adam* and some striking forest fire photography at the Yellowstone Art Museum and pausing under the open metal framework that hovers, half awning, half monumental sculpture, over the corner of Broadway and Second Avenue. I pass Barjon's Books, a New Age shop where Cara once purchased a Zen flute CD, a suitably cosmopolitan token to bring back to Powell from the city. I discover the baseball stadium where the Billings Mustangs play. I begin to like the city, even the fact that it is a city, which does give it certain advantages over a place the size of Powell. As much as I love the open spaces and the wilderness, I am, I suppose, urban, or at least suburban, myself.

En route to the airport, a potential faculty colleague and I take a walk along the Rimrocks at Zimmerman Park, where a popular hiking and biking path wends through ponderosa pines on the clifftop. From the Rims the city is reassuringly finite, neighborhoods lapsing into ranches and irrigated farmland beyond a shimmering new Mormon temple. Even in these sprawl-ripe expanses, the obvious evidence of modern human settlement soon thins out. The southern horizon holds the unassuming north nub of the Bighorns; the Pryors, gentle undulations from here; and the great floating snowline of the Beartooths, northeast of Yellowstone Park. When I fly back over Wyoming in the daytime, I see more landmarks—the deep slash of Bighorn Canyon, the abrupt mountain wall east of the Bighorn Basin, the snowy tundra of Cloud Peak.

As it turns out, leaving Lakeland proves more difficult than we'd imagined. Saying goodbye to home and friends and moving even a modest household's worth of belongings, as well as an arthritic elderly dog and two kittens, across a continent is not an easy thing for a middle-aged couple of limited means to contemplate, much less attempt. But in the end, the lure of the Yellowstone wins out, and I accept the position. Two months later, on a tropically humid Florida morning, we close our house sale. As we leave the realtor's office, two swallow-tailed kites unexpectedly land in a live oak by the parking lot, calling back and forth and gesturing with their wings in the language of avian ritual. "Kites are about surprise," says naturalist Susan Cerulean. They make occasional appearances in Lakeland, but they are birds of the open sky, and I've never seen one alight before. Though these two are preoccupied with each other, it's hard not to see their presence as a symbolic gesture of farewell.

By nightfall, we're in Dothan, Alabama, headed north and west.

2

To get to Mammoth Hot Springs from Billings, you can switchback up Beartooth Pass, or, as we do today, cross Paradise Valley to the Gardiner entrance. In Yankee Jim Canyon, we encounter our first "charismatic megafauna," a band of bighorn rams. Nearby, we find displaced Yellowstone buffalo in a quarantine facility at Corwin Springs, hostage to cattle industry fears concerning the spread of brucellosis, a notorious ungulate disease. Or perhaps more accurately, ranchers' reluctance to share grazing rights with bison. Finally, we fulfill the goal of our pilgrimage, passing under the Roosevelt Arch, complete with the obligatory posing tourists. Just inside the park, we're flagged over by a cheery graduate student from Idaho State, who explains that Cara has been chosen to fill out a visitor survey. He hands her the questionnaire and sends us on our way across the Wyoming line, past the sign still marking the midway point between Equator and Pole. A lone elk far from the high summer ranges puts in an appearance along the Gardner River.

It's July, and Mammoth is crowded. It takes twice around the lot to find a parking space. The lunch line at the snack bar extends out the front door. And it's hot, hotter then we remember, hotter, maybe, than it should be. Even so, there's no place I can think of that I'd rather be.

In Florida, I tried with reasonable success to avoid the Orlando hype festering an hour away from our home. Whenever school or family events brought me to the theme parks, I was impressed by the lack of genuine happiness among the revelers, beset by long lines, crying kids, hot pavement, additional costs escaped from the package deal, and maybe mostly just by self-induced pressure: *We're finally here, it cost us a fortune, and, hey, it's Disneyworld; we'd better be happy, damn it, what's wrong with us?* It always seemed that most of the faces in those crowds were grimly forcing their way through to some future day when, safely returned to their distant homes, they would believe they had had the time of their lives.

I always found the theme park "worlds" dreary and unpleasant. And I knew from my students that under each grinlocked character's head there was an underpaid sweaty teen shamelessly exploited by a powerful and autocratic corporation, the same high-handed entity that had strongarmed the state's bullet-train plans by insisting that the firm would support this voter-approved, badly needed public transportation initiative as long as the trains stopped only at Disney, that is, at none of the competing parks. Though I still thought *Fantasia* was pretty good, any illusion I had ever had about the benevolence of the Disney Corporation was long gone by the time we left Lakeland.

Yellowstone, of course, has its own history of commercial exploitation by figures ranging from Buffalo Bill to Jay Cooke of the Northern Pacific Railroad. Tacky tourist traps cluster around each gateway town, and the "attractions" and concessionaires continue to exert a not-always-healthy level of influence on park policy. But the crowd at Mammoth Hot Springs seems happy, maybe the most genuinely relaxed bunch of people I've seen in eleven years. Some bypass the lunch line completely, instead opting, as we do, to purchase snacks at the somewhat less packed general store and head for picnic tables or the springs themselves. Though the terraces have, characteristically, changed in the dozen or so years since we've seen them, drying in some places, expanding in others, water still filters through glistening orange and yellow pools in classic Mammoth Hot Springs fashion, the effect enhanced by that infernally glorious Yellowstone smell.

Accompanied by our twelve-year old lab/blue heeler mix—a Wyomingite herself—we spend more time in the car than we'd like. After taking turns walking the terraces (no dogs allowed in thermal areas), we drive east toward Lamar Valley. The sage hills are peaceful, the successfully reintroduced wolves, and the caravans of devoted wolf watchers who follow them from pulloff to pulloff, apparently enjoying afternoon siestas. We stop to spend some time with a herd of bison, mostly cows and calves talking to each other in low rumbles. A few pronghorn antelope frisk along the edges of the herd. Ground squirrels whistle and rustle in the brush. From the river bars, the calls of Canada geese and sandhill cranes drift on the wind, mingling with the roadside chat of a few summer travelers comparing chili at various resorts. They seem especially fond of the restaurant at Signal Mountain in the Tetons, which I like myself, though it's been a long time since I've eaten there.

∼

The Basin Creek Lakes Trail in the Beartooth Mountains northeast of the park represents another return, this time to the place where we took Tom to learn the pleasures of backpacking. Basin Lakes has a waterfall, some history in the form of a dilapidated cabin or two, and the lakes themselves, the lower of which is greened by conifers and lily pads. When we overnighted here in the early nineties, probably in June, we camped just above the lower lake, close to the receding snow line, and picked our morning way across eroded drifts to the still half-frozen upper lake. Two months later in the season and a little over a decade later in the insidious process of global warming, there's still a patch or two of snow in the bowl above the upper lake. Eschewing the splintered turrets of many Beartooth Mountain lake backdrops, the cirque is flat across the top, just like a sidewalk, as Cara observes. A sidewalk with a thousand-foot dropoff, that is. But her point is well taken. The simple rim gives the impression that a hiker on the Silver Run Plateau above could just walk to the edge and look over at the lakes below.

The prominent characteristics of the trail come back to me—the lakes themselves, the falls—and some less obvious things, like the trailside kinnikinnick. But there are other things I don't remember. Just above the falls, the forest seems to be struggling a bit, some of the needles browned, perhaps by beetles or drought. And, oh yes, the trail is steep. Of course it always has been, but Basin Creek requires a different kind of walking than the sandy plowing of our hikes in the Florida scrub, and the trail seems a lot more demanding than we recall it being.

The sky above the lakes is clear enough by mountain afternoon standards, but over to the west, a brown-bellied white sheet marks the Derby Mountain fire, a drought-fed conflagration covering over two hundred thousand acres, that will still be burning weeks later, consuming summer homes and inspiring heroic mobilization by a small city's worth of firefighters and support staff. Fire is endemic to the Rockies, essential, even, for the long-term health of grasslands and coniferous woods. But wildfire size and intensity have spiked alarmingly, a development keynoted by the infernos that swept Yellowstone in 1988. I've never seen the park without the burned slopes, and, like most park visitors, I've generally accepted the scarred landscape with equanimity as befitting the grand and violent forces that shape and define the place. But a study published in *Science* in 2006 concludes that increased temperature is the dominant factor in the prevalence of both drought and fire during the last few decades. Nature's adjustment to human-generated changes can be catastrophic, as people living under Derby Mountain, and elsewhere in the West, are finding out.

The gateway to the Beartooths is the town of Red Lodge. Bogart's, our traditional after-hiking spot, is so unchanged that I probably would have known instantly where I was even if I had been taken there blindfolded. The food, a mix of Mexican and traditional American dishes, is still good, especially after a mountain ramble.

~

At the beginning of August, I travel east to see my mother in Rochester. When Tom, who has been spending his first summer in Pasadena, decides to visit his grandmother, I take advantage of the opportunity to see them both before he starts his senior year and I begin my new job. Occupied with the move to Montana, I have not been to my hometown since my father's funeral over a year ago, when I was only able to stay for a weekend. My mother has recently moved across town to a senior citizens' apartment complex, where she's found new friends—we're introduced, without names, as "my son and grandson." Son and grandson do most of the requisite Rochester things—stroll out the Ontario Beach Park pier, visit with my old friends around an evening picnic table, enjoy a Sunday dinner with my sister's family. Neither Tom nor I have seen my father's grave before. We pay our respects, then roam the grounds of Holy Sepulcher Cemetery with Anne, who has taken to stitching the generations together through genealogy charts, old photos, headstone maps. Surrounded by so much family history, I can't help but think about my relationship with this city, my first home. Will it still be my home, will I come here at all, when the last of my parents' generation is gone? And will the Upstate New York voice I was born with ever say *canyon* and *coulee* with the ease with which it says *pier* or *gorge*. Maybe, as novelist Harry Crews believes about his own experience, everything important in one's life dates from childhood. At a conference earlier this summer, a Rochester native asked me if I ever wrote about the city where I was born. Without hesitating, I answered "all the time." I suppose I've been writing about my birthplace from elsewhere for decades. Nothing's really changed, then, except that I now have an adopted home. Far from the marshes, woods, and fields of New York, the gray skies and cobble shores of Lake Ontario, I intend to stay.

There was a time, just after high school, when I thought I might spend the rest of my days happily enough in Rochester. I still return to New York State regularly, and I read everything I find about the Great Lakes. No doubt, I'll always be a bit of a foreigner in the Rockies—an easterner to boot. It seems more than a bit presumptuous for me to say anything about such iconic places as Yellowstone, the Tetons, the Little Bighorn. Unlike Hayden and Moran, by the time I got to Yellowstone, everyone already knew about it. I had known about this fabulous place myself since, at maybe eight years old, I discovered a public library copy of National Geographic's *America's Wonderlands: The National Parks*, with its page-spread glossies artfully framed to eliminate all but the most benign human presences, these consisting mainly of smiling circa-1960 car-camping families seeing the great West for the first time. There were all of the obligatory views—Old Faithful, the Mammoth terraces, the Lower Falls—and a considerable wildlife sampler as well. Fashioning an absurdly ambitious itinerary that would probably have given us at best a couple of hours in each park, I launched a bid to convince my parents that we too should see America's Wonderlands. But my plans never panned out, broken on the reality of my family's limited finances and the close horizons defined by our eastern perspective. My parents enjoyed summer weeks in the Adirondacks and New England, as did I, but felt no great need to go farther, especially westward, where distances were so hopelessly vast. When at twenty-seven I rode the Greyhound to Louisiana, my personal western horizon was already expanding by the time I reached the Pennsylvania-Ohio border.

The night before I fly back to Billings, my mother and I watch a Travel Channel documentary about Yellowstone. Wonderland again. I know the sights, the issues, even recognize one or two of the interviewed experts. I haven't had time to adjust completely to living in Montana, but, crammed as we are into my mother's tiny apartment, it also seems a bit strange to be in Rochester. I can easily imagine circumstances in which I would return to Upstate New York to live, but I have no real pressing desire to do so. It's almost as if Rochester, confident in the primacy of childhood and resigned as a northeastern city to losing parts of itself, has made room for the series of other homes that have become "my places."

On our way to the airport to catch our separate planes, Tom says he will soon be a human being again. I think I know what he means. We've been camped in chairs and sleeping bags in my mother's living room, after all. When it comes right down to it, I guess he'll probably feel more-or-less the same way when he returns to California after visiting us this Christmas. He hasn't been to Billings since those occasional shopping trips when he was in grade school. Even with the traditional household objects and his four childhood years in Powell, it's not likely that our new place will seem like home to him. His childhood disrupted by continental-scale relocations, Tom grew up without the reliable connection that Crews calls an "anchor in the world." But perhaps under any circumstances, the end result of a trip to the past—one's own past—is something like a release into a temporarily revitalized present. And despite the best efforts of memory, the present is where we inevitably find the places we return to.

The gray expanse of Lake Ontario follows alongside the plane until, over what I know must be Hamilton, Ontario, it turns back to the east. By that point, Lake Erie has already cut under Ontario's south shore, the two lakes linked by the silver tether of the Niagara River. A while later, the plane's shadow crosses Lake Michigan like the ghost of a voyageur, headed west.

~

The day before classes start, Cara and I drive to Powell on a warm early September afternoon, the Bighorn Basin sky filled with smoke from the still-blazing Derby Mountain fire. The Bighorns, Beartooths, and Absarokas are reduced to vague scrim shapes. Heart Mountain slouches, distinct in form but stripped of dimension and color.

Northwest College's once-vibrant flower gardens have grown a bit shabby, but, except for the dorm that burned down a few years ago, it's all pretty much the same. I find my old department just where I left it. We visit friends on campus, make tentative plans to meet in Billings, still the "Magic City" where needed supplies can be obtained. I stop by the "new" science building, under construction when we left, to look for a biologist friend, but my unannounced visit finds him not in his office.

Some downtown businesses—Powell Drug, Hansel and Gretel's Restaurant—have somehow survived this far into the age of chains and chain wannabes. Kragler's five-and-dime has finally been put out of its misery, its dusty artifacts no doubt packed away in boxes cluttering the former proprietor's attic. The War Surplus Store has updated its name and inventory. The most significant new development is the Powell "Merc," for Mercantile, an independent cooperative community business venture that has endeared Powell to reformers across the country and that even earned the town a featured spot on *Good Morning America*.

Of course, we pass "our" house, which, equally of course, has been ruined by an eclectic array of alterations that seem to us completely at odds with the original 1914 structure: there's a long, absurdly varnished front stairway replacing the graceful framing columns, a boxy addition overwhelming the back yard. The old neighborhood has been invaded by faceless contemporary housing. More interesting in a macabre way is the "Coffins of the West" outlet that has ghoulishly appeared around the corner from the house. We don't go in, opting instead for Polecat Bench, where our stay is shortened by biting gnats we don't remember being there before.

A Northwest College friend predicts that the twenty miles between Powell and Cody is filling up so rapidly that in ten years it will all be one big housing tract. So far the sprawl peters out a mile or two west of town, though the stretch between Powell and its outlier Ralston has been ominously five-laned. Some government entity has been busy posting wildlife-watching binocular signs and historical markers—not only for genuinely noteworthy points of interest like the Heart Mountain Relocation Camp, but also at obscure places like Willwood Dam and Ralston Reservoir—perhaps in an effort to slow down some of that Yellowstone tourist traffic now zooming by on the widened road. For whatever reason, it seems the whole valley has become one big amorphous designated historic site.

For me, ordinary little Powell will always be a place with great personal resonance—my first job, my first house, my son's elementary school. And Powell was the base from which I first experienced so many things—geysers and badlands, mountain lions and grizzly bears. The Powell Valley was the looking glass or rabbit hole that led to Wonderland. In a different way it still is. Not surprisingly, the community has gone on without us, but versions of Cara, Tom, and me will always be trapped in their own bit parts in its receding history, just across the century divide.

~

As a late September afternoon slips into evening, we sit on driftwood logs above the gravel shores of Mary Bay on Yellowstone Lake. It has been raining all week in Billings, and fresh snow dusts the Red Mountains and Absarokas. It's evident that a hot blaze has surged east of the lake sometime in the past few years, long after the 1988 fires, but only the fumaroles of Steamboat Point are smoking now.

Cloudbanks left by the week's storms strain color from the sunlight, leaving lake, mountains, and sky shades of a metallic silvery gray. A ridge of burned trees holds onto some yellow, but the live pines across the water etch black mirages of island and promontory. Even the goldeneyes scattered on the bay have given up their crisply pied markings to the season and the general silver gilding.

From somewhere far behind us Cara picks up the bugling of an elk, at this distance melodious, almost thrushlike. After a while, a closer answer sounds over our left shoulders. The nearer bull, stationed atop the lakeshore ridge, unleashes jazzy runs, high trumpet squeals breaking downward into deeper treble registers, all underlain by bass huffing. A long howl turns our heads. Wolf? Again the canine voice preempts the elk music with another searching howl, this time collapsing into the insane giggles that separate coyote from its larger, reintroduced cousin.

Earlier in the day, we had driven through robust young forest growth, naturally reseeded, an interpretive sign informed us, after the great 1988 fires. At Norris Geyser Basin, we stopped to immerse ourselves on this cool fall day in the steam and smell of the park's hottest hydrothermal site. Norris roiled with the sounds of various features: the spitting of tiny boiling springs, the hiss of steamvents, the popping of hot mud, the oceanic heaving of Steamboat Geyser, the streaming of its runoff channel. Overhead, the occasional *quork*—Bernd Heinrich's onomatopoeic term—and heavy flap of ravens, along with the small chips of chickadees and juncos, added organic notes to the geophysical, mineral music of geysers and springs. Cara and I took turns, one of us hiking the boardwalks while the other read or ambled around the parking lot so Rita could get her fill of the scents of buffalo and elk. Whether these essences recalled her to the puppyhood before her doggie-lifetime absence I couldn't tell, but she certainly seemed to be enjoying herself. A passerby commented that she was "doing well for a senior citizen."

Leaving Mary Bay, we cross Sylvan Pass before the nightly closure turns the road into a work zone. The east entrance reconstruction is still not finished after eleven years, the summit a semipermanent building depot and a reminder of how dependent our travels are on that singularly destructive means of transportation, the private car. Today we will drive about four hundred miles to, through, and from the park. The more frequent, shorter trips for Beartooth hiking trails, prairie birding, and visits to Cody or Powell also add up. We adopt mitigation measures, minimizing in-town driving, avoiding buying gas from the most vicious oil companies—good things to do for certain, but bearing a taint of rationalization. Of course, we would support and use a Denali-style shuttle if one existed, but such a fundamental reform would have to break through the region's stubborn and not altogether charmless traditionalism. Besides, we'd still have to get from Billings to wherever the shuttle routes started. The inveterate wilderness hiker and advocate Bob Marshall claimed that some people need access to wild places to retain sanity and spirit. I can't be much use to anyone, I suppose, without either, but the fact remains that the car that brings us to Yellowstone—with its never-ending demands for oil and its universal invitation to a world of irresponsible mobility—represents an insidious danger, far more formidable than grizzly bears, fires, or the terrorists who have cast such a pall over American actions and ideals.

Construction conditions on the pass are hard, with snow falling from September to May. Even during the summer building season, work shifts are limited to the night hours to allay the fears of tourism cloutmasters in Cody, some fifty miles down the North Fork canyon. In truth, despite the challenges, progress has been made. The roadway is basically smooth and graded, if as yet unpaved. The stone walls built to keep the road, and the Winnebagos that lurch along it toward the RV camp at Fishing Bridge, from sliding into the creek below evoke the WPA remnants of twentieth-century American history I've seen in parks throughout the country.

I have to admit that the Wyoming Department of Transportation has done a pretty good job modernizing the North Fork road, our original and most frequent route between Yellowstone and Powell. Eleven years ago, this road was slated for a controversial upgrade. Highway engineers and Cody tourism interests wanted a safe, fast, modern parkway to Yellowstone while wildlife and status quo defenders, myself included, feared that a new high-speed road would fundamentally alter the canyon. The finished product, according to Cara, who is driving, is easy and safe, while the fifty-mile-per-hour speed limit maintains a fair semblance of the mountain drive atmosphere the road had before the project (by contrast, the approach to Mammoth through wildlife-rich Paradise Valley carries a speed limit of seventy).

But if the highway hasn't altered the canyon profoundly, the North Fork has changed nonetheless. After feasting on dying timber left from the 1988 Yellowstone fires, Douglas-fir beetles careened into the canyon, leaving mountainsides a mosaic of dead and living conifers, with the skeletal ghost trees predominating. An estimated fifty thousand North Fork trees were killed by beetles between 2000 and 2002. A 2003 Forest Service assessment estimates a Douglas-fir mortality rate of 40 to 70 percent in some areas. The beetles are native, an expected agent of ecological renewal. But they are encouraged by drought and fire, and shorter, milder winters have led to major outbreaks of a variety of destructive forest insects.

By the time we've lost the mountain clouds and made the lower reaches of the canyon, most of the remaining daylight is locked in the gold of riverside cottonwoods. We spill through the three tunnels—the bear and cubs we used to call them—into the Bighorn Basin. At Cody we seek out Zapata's, which has relocated to a downtown storefront right across the street from the comparatively elegant, long-established La Comida, a business risk exhibiting chutzpah to match the restaurant's name and the photos of rebels from Robert E. Lee to Ché Guevara that adorn its walls. The enchiladas and rellenos are covered with enough hot green chili sauce to make us glad we have some water left for the ride home. On our way back to Billings, we stop several times for deer and pull over twice, first to lose ourselves in the basin stars and a second time to watch an eerie green sheet pulsing just above the horizon ahead of us, our first northern lights since we left Maine.

~

The Wonderland tinfoil wrapping geysers, canyons, wildlife, for a hundred and fifty years, shaping and shading my own experience since *America's Wonderlands: The National Parks*, makes, on the face of it, a cheap and silly way to think about a real place presumably indifferent to our adulation. But is it really so unfortunate to think of such a place as "full of wonders"? For myself, I can't say whether the nature of the Yellowstone country declares its own sacredness—its impressive array of singular features is after all pretty unusual—or whether its global status as a landmark of environmental conservation is the source of its power. In *Searching for Yellowstone*, Paul Schullery, whose books and articles about the park have made him something like its official literary voice, reflects on a "popular arguing point among historic preservationists," that "we humans decided to set Yellowstone apart because it was valuable to our culture." But he concludes that park "exploration is always a mixture of wonder and wondering, of awe at the place and excitement at what it has come to mean to us." All of our experience is phenomenological in the sense that the past, both cultural and individual, shapes and defines our perception as well as our ideas.

Yellowstone mists and steams in dynamic beauty at the center of a field of experience and landscape so inextricably intertwined that, even if I thought it was important to do so, I could not separate the elements of what it means to me. The National Geographic books, the Thomas Moran paintings, an evening walk around Geyser Hill, a mountain lion slinging itself like a rope across the Chief Joseph scenic highway late one night in Sunlight Basin, a covey of sharp-tailed grouse poking through tall grass on the hill where Reno waited for Custer, the oddball dialect we developed to play mountain man on the North Fork road from Cody to Sylvan Pass— my own idiosyncratic constellation of place, event, and experience forms a pulsing aurora I could not dispel even if I wanted to.

3

Most years, the road leading through Crow Reservation farmland toward the northern end of Bighorn Canyon National Recreation Area would have been rattling for a month with trucks bound for the sugar refinery in Billings, but today it's nearly empty. Flocks of Canada geese drift across beet fields, the harvest dangerously delayed by inopportune rains. There's plenty of bitter irony in agriculture, especially in this marginally arable land; in the midst of a ten-year drought, farmers are unable to bring in their crops because of mud. Election Day was two weeks ago; colorful but obsolete signs pushing United States Senate candidates Conrad Burns or the winner, Jon Tester, cling to fences and tatter in the wind.

Most of Bighorn Canyon's sites of interest—the wild horse range, the historic ranches, the thousand-foot overlook into Devil Canyon, are to the south, accessible only through Wyoming. At the north end visitor's center, closed for the season, imperative signs warn us that the Department of Homeland Security will apprehend anyone approaching the Yellowtail and Afterbay dams. Overkill to be sure in such an obscure place: Fort Smith, Montana, its few streets muddy, dusty, and icy by turns, seems an unlikely target for foreign terrorists. Such diligence is probably just standard procedure in the post-9/11 world, although the Bighorn River between the dam and its confluence with the Yellowstone is the epitome of a western blue-ribbon trout fishery, attracting well-heeled sports, among them a certain Wyomingite vice president of the United States.

Today it's unseasonably warm. A few small gnats waver in the air as we descend the Beaver Pond Trail past Lime Kiln Creek's extensive beaver workings. The short path ends at an overlook view of the distant "Afterbay," its mergansers apparently untroubled by the water control structure that defines their refuge. Later, we try the official scenic drive through the Bighorn foothills to Yellowtail Dam, which, of course, we've already been warned not to approach. The dam is a 1960s Bureau of Reclamation project, its environs managed by the National Park Service "with input from the Crow tribe," part of a history of cooperation which, if it served tribal members poorly on the Greasy Grass in 1876, has arguably worked mostly in their favor. The reservoir has been somewhat controversial in Crow Country. While not an opponent of the project as such, Robert Yellowtail, a tribal chairman for whom the dam is named, considered the federal government's approach to Crow water rights exploitative. Other objections were more fundamental. As with many such developments, lands were condemned and graves were inundated. Like other Indian nations, the Crow are beset by a variety of economic and social problems, and the tribe has been involved in long-standing legal disputes on issues ranging from water policy to coal mining. Still, the extensive Crow Reservation—the largest in Montana—incorporates a prime portion of the people's traditional homeland, and the tribe is at least able to influence policy not only in the National Recreation Area, but also at the Little Bighorn Battlefield, which, ironically enough, is surrounded by Crow land.

Scenic drive motorists are instructed not to wander away from the road without tribal permission. A pulloff interpretive display, designed by Northwest College art students and faculty while we lived in Powell, explains the people's heritage, reprising the oft-repeated assertion by a Crow leader variously called Eelapuash or Arapooish that "the Crow Country is exactly in the right place. Everything good is to be found there. There is no country like the Crow Country." The open range and brushy meadows, with early snows already dressing the forested slopes of the gently rounded mountains, attest to the justice of his evaluation.

At the bottom of a harrowing descent, the road dead-ends at a lackluster reservoir picnic area. We grab some snacks and follow the paved lakeside path around the parking lot. The daylight fading when we get back to the car, we climb back up the grade and are soon heading north along the Bighorn. After a twilight walk through bare cottonwoods at one of the many fishing access sites—only locals or die-hards working the river this late in the day and season—we turn west, following the Yellowstone toward Billings, racing to beat a storm front looming in from the Pacific. The temperature is already falling, and there will be snow on the ground when the sun rises tomorrow morning.

~

The river, so they say, was named *roche jaune*—yellow stone—not for its cream and butterscotch canyon in the park but rather for the Rimrocks, a hulking layer of Eagle Sandstone stacked on crumbling slopes intermittently on either side—mostly the north— of the Yellowstone around Billings. The cliffs are fissured by runoff and ice, and the centuries have strewn a frozen landslide of boulders across the prestigious neighborhoods at their base; some room-size rocks have been incorporated into the designs of opulent homes and decks.

Just across the river from the city, Coburn Road follows an old stage line down Bitter Creek to a hollow in the South Rims secluding three "Indian caves." The identity of the people who created the eponymous pictographs of Pictograph Cave State Park is something of a mystery. They weren't the Crows, who arrived from points east some two thousand years after the earliest pictographs were rendered.

Like the others, the biggest cave—Pictograph Cave itself—is actually more like an alcove or rock shelter than a true cavern. The rock-art panel has been damaged, in part by WPA-funded excavators who showed more enthusiasm than skill, at one point sandblasting the artwork in an attempt to clean it. Still, a few ancient lines and forms can be made out, enhanced when viewed through binoculars and compared to the park's interpretative display. In better shape are images of horses and rifles, added—sometimes superimposed on the originals—by later people, perhaps Crow or Cheyenne artists or historians.

Burdened by all those ghosts, the dry landscape seems meditative and quiet, but there is plenty of life here. Swifts flick across the Rims, disappear into creases of stone. A redtail lands in a ponderosa pine. High above, a golden eagle floats, a solid black speck against the glare of sun and cloud. A passing pair of ravens breaks the quiet. Down in the ravine where springs ran as recently as twenty years ago, cottonwoods and box elders still find enough moisture to make a home for chats and brown thrashers.

Cottontails graze near cover, occasionally dashing through open stretches between patches of brush. The ubiquitous rock wrens pick dragonflies off the grilles of cars in the parking lot.

On our way home, we stop at Four Dances Natural Area, a windswept grass and prickly pear plateau where the Rims break abruptly down to the river. William Clark, the intrepid Corps of Discovery captain, passed this way in 1806, temporarily separated from Meriwether Lewis. Maybe he banked in close to this cliff, sculling against the flow, examining the riparian flats for deer or camping sites. Some hold that he carved his name in the Billings Rimrocks as well as downstream at Pompey's Pillar National Monument. Here also, the obligatory legend has it, a party of Crows, discovering that their village had been stricken by smallpox while they were away, leaped to their deaths in the river below (In recent times, however, Billings boosters shifted this story to Four Dances from a less imposing Sacrifice Cliff that was itself sacrificed for construction of the city's MetraPark arena). The Yellowstone, for its part, is settling into the willow and cottonwood life of a prairie stream, carrying the last undammed river's worth of water from its mountained youth to the mid-continental lowlands.

Seen from Four Dances, the riverfront is far from pristine. In fact, it is the city that is framed by the view, the foreground dominated by the tanks, the filtration ponds, the hollow hum of a substantial water treatment plant. Its hotels and offices nudged by refinery works, downtown peers from behind parked boxcars and oil tankers. Interstate 90 hauls lone business travelers toward Seattle and vacationing families toward Mammoth Hot Springs. On the North Rim across town, the airport tower blinks in an occasional plane. The Billings area may not be scenically spectacular by Wonderland standards, but its ponderosa-topped ridges and riparian bluffs are marked by thousands of years of human passage—pictographs, explorers' graffiti, stagecoach trails, battlefields, railroads, highways, fire scars. The Yellowstone Valley remains a traveler's country, as it's been for millennia.

Spurred by the surface waves of career and by deeper, more mysterious currents, my own journeying has swept me back into the Yellowstone's long history of migration, carried upstream by an accidental gravity or magnetism, an unconscious alchemy of circumstance through which America's Wonderland called me home.

## The Woods Are Burning

The Basin Creek Lakes Trail climbs steeply and steadily from the West Fork of Rock Creek. We weren't breaking new ground: we'd loved Basin Creek for many years. We'd hiked to Upper Basin Lake two years before, and Cara had more recently been as far as Lower Basin Lake with her sister. There's an unassuming quality about Basin Creek. The lakes aren't included in the designated Absaroka-Beartooth Wilderness, perhaps because the trail follows the ghost of a road past cabin ruins. The lower lake's not much more than a pond crowded by conifers, their crisp reflections interrupted by flotillas of lily pads. The cirque glacier-carved into the Silver Run Plateau above the upper lake is impressive but not overwhelming, a perfect spot to spend a relaxing mountain summer afternoon.

Our time at Upper Basin Lake was not completely peaceful. Occasional clouds of mosquitoes or passing showers kept us alert, especially the latter, as such afternoon rains are often punctuated by lightning. After a couple of hours, we wandered a narrow fisherman's path around to the other side of the lake. Lincoln's sparrows flitted across what looked like mountain muskeg. The lowering sky, the boggy lakeshore, and the ubiquitous moose sign gave the place a kind of Maine feel, and, as is often the case in the Maine woods, it was a change in the weather that sent us down the mountain. Thunder echoed around the cirque. It was time to go.

Two weeks later, the West Fork was on fire.

~

It started at an abandoned camp, the cause initially listed by the interagency InciWeb wildland fire information site as "under investigation." When smoke billowed over the canyon, friends and relatives of hikers along the popular West Fork trails began to worry, and homeowners in the smattering of new subdivisions above Red Lodge aimed garden hoses at their roofs and hung on updates about what had already become an "incident." One of my co-workers, a business professor at Montana State University Billings, was hiking with his children at Quinnebaugh Meadows, on the wrong side of the fire; they had to climb out over Sundance Pass and down to Lake Fork, emerging twenty-five miles by road from where their car waited at the West Fork trailhead.

The Cascade Fire had just ignited, but Forest Service spokespersons were already talking about it burning until the first snow. Characterized by an official interviewed on the Billings evening news as "decadent timber," century-old lodgepole pine and Douglas-fir in rugged terrain combined with a major blowdown the previous fall to create conditions ripe for "the big one," a "megafire." The West Fork forest was doomed.

*Doomed?* We use words like that. Fire "destroys," "consumes," "incinerates" the places in its path. Or does it? We also know that in the West wildfire is endemic, even essential, the region's fire-adapted ecosystems having evolved in a world of dry lightning, heat, and drought. And perhaps those trees really are decadent—beetle-riddled elders doing the conifer equivalent of doddering around the landscape. A forest is a living entity and must be able not only to grow, but to die when its time comes. In a year or two, under the black spars of burned trunks, elk will chew their cuds in rich fresh grass, surrounded by a riot of lupine and fireweed, while the bell notes of mountain bluebirds and the drumming of black-backed woodpeckers echo *all's well* through the canyon.

Maybe. There certainly is a sense of inevitability about the Cascade Fire, and about the Gunbarrel Fire working through gray slopes of beetle-killed trees across the Beartooths in the Absaroka Mountains west of Cody, Wyoming, at the same time. But, though forest fires have always blazed across the West, this era of megafires—acre on acre, square mile on square mile, state after state, summer after summer, feels like a new thing.

Not that the ongoing spate of large conflagrations is without precedent. In much of the West, wildland fire tracks with recurring dry cycles. George Wuerthner, whose many books on the western environment include *The Wildfire Reader*, notes in a *NewWest* column that drought-fed fires consumed over 39 million acres in the 1930s, and cites a single 1910 blaze that scorched "3.5 million acres of Idaho and Montana in a single month." Wildfire occurs throughout the United States from Alaska to the Everglades. New York's Adirondacks endured logging- and railroad-triggered firestorms in the early twentieth century. Similar circumstances touched off America's most devastating forest fire, which killed over a thousand people around Peshtigo, Wisconsin, on October 8, 1871, the same day as the famous Great Chicago Fire. Megafires can be traced through the geologic ages. Imagining a time-travel journey of 300 million years back to the Carboniferous period, paleontologist Peter Ward describes a sky "yellow-brown, irrespective of weather," polluted by "smoke from giant fires perpetually raging and new ones set alight with each lightning strike hitting the extensive forests of the temperate and tropical regions." Even in the relative calm between megafire outbreaks, smaller blazes play a significant role in diversifying wooded environments: mountain meadows and aspen groves spring up in the wake of the flames, relieving extensive single-species stands. The varied beauty we find in montane forests is in part a legacy bequeathed by the history of wildland fire.

~

Why do the woods, especially if not exclusively in the West, burn? The situation is complex, involving several major factors, the most obvious of which is the interplay between climate and western ecosystems. Warm-weather precipitation in much of the region is notoriously unreliable, and seasonal thunderstorms often bring more lightning than rain. Various western plants have evolved to cope with, even profit from, periodic burning, and, drying in the summer sun, can even be said to encourage the flames. Grassland fires sparked by lightning or set deliberately by Native Americans helped maintain the Great Plains buffalo prairies. The thick bark of mature redwoods and ponderosa pines allows them to survive all but the most intense infernos; typical grass fires sweep right past big ponderosas, leaving open parklike woodlands with well-spaced trees positioned to take advantage of limited nutrients and water. Northern Rockies species like lodgepole and whitebark pine are also fire adapted. Something like 80 percent of Yellowstone Park is covered by lodgepole forest. Many individuals of this short-lived species are equipped with specialized serotinous cones that burst open when heated. They are, in effect, Phoenix-trees. Examining the relationship between fire history and forest ecology, biologists William H. Romme and Don G. Despain concluded in 1989 that megafires like those that swept across about a third of Greater Yellowstone the previous year are an inevitable part of the life cycle of such a forest.

Much has been said—most of it derogatory—about government fire-fighting philosophy and practices. After the Yellowstone fires, controversy flared around the infamous "let-burn" policy, though the majority of Yellowstone's conflagrations were not covered by that directive. In 1988, Greater Yellowstone experienced 248 wildfires, only twenty-five of which fell under let-burn guidelines. Three of the seven largest blazes were fought immediately if ineffectually. Firefighters, even hotshots, will tell you there's no way to stop a megafire once it gets going. Such an inferno follows its chosen path as if by will. The best firefighters can do is try to herd the flames away from buildings and communities. In his poem "Animals," Robinson Jeffers envisions creatures of the sun with "bodies of living flame." Managers talk about fire itself as a living thing, and anyone who has ever gazed into the writhing center of a campfire has a sense of what they mean. A wildfire "makes a run," it "behaves" one way or another, it "tries" things. Sometimes it hides out for a while, buried in the duff and litter of the forest floor. A wildfire's actions, like a bear's, are unpredictable. It might turn away from human habitations, or seek out something to consume on the outskirts of a town—something like the Red Lodge Mountain ski resort, for example, nervously blasting its snow-making cannons against the leading edge of the Cascade Fire.

But let's not let government agencies off the hook just yet. Following intensive clearing by miners and settlers, a century of fire suppression—Smokey Bear and his shovel—has reduced many mid-elevation Rocky Mountain forests to virtual plantations with little species or age diversity. An expansive panorama of identical conifers draped beneath snow-capped peaks makes a calendar image of wilderness. Such forests are cool and green; they "feel right." The first western burn I came upon was in Colorado's Rocky Mountain National Park. The fire had probably occurred about a decade earlier, and the charred area was substantial, though not in the megafire range. It was June, with lush grass and plenty of wildflowers. Mountain bluebirds and woodpeckers flashed among blackened hulks. I was a bit surprised to find the burn zone a hub of activity in the quiet surrounding forest. Still, it was a relief to pass back into the shade of living trees.

Wildland fire expert Stephen Pyne has attributed such aesthetic reactions to a misplaced urban animosity toward fire, a cultural prejudice leading to the reflexive snuffing of potentially cleansing minor burns and the concomitant overload of combustible fuel in mature forests like those in the path of the Cascade Fire. Even Romme and Despain acknowledge that, if not for aggressive suppression, midcentury Yellowstone blazes might have left natural firelines inhibiting the amalgamation of 1988 infernos with names—the Clover-Mist, the Snake River Complex—evoking the corporate mergers that, like the fires, roared across the American scene during the Reagan era.

A long-time foe of knee-jerk fire suppression, Pyne, writing in the Spring 2008 issue of The American Scholar, regards with equal skepticism the current conventional wisdom casting wildfire as simply a natural force to be fostered or left alone. Such trust in nature to work things out despite the heavy hand of human influence Pyne characterizes as "faith-based ecology." "In fire-prone settings," he concludes, "big parks become permanent habitats for fire; left to themselves they will burn, often more ferociously than at any time in their history." Pyne advocates directing fire toward desirable ends, but worries that agency fire management as practiced is likely to generate more heat than light. Employing a particularly acerbic analogy, he compares contemporary government managers' enthusiasm for burned acreage to the reckless determination with which their commodity-focused predecessors "got out the cut."

Though some early reports blamed lightning for the Cascade Fire, the day's clear skies and the blaze's origin near a community of summer cabins led both local residents and the Forest Service to suspect, rightly, a human source. Either deliberately or accidentally, people start fires. Arson, occasionally by unemployed firefighters drumming up business, has been implicated in a share of recent major wildfires. Careless mistakes are less dramatic but, one hopes, more common. Famous for his practical as well as philosophical skills, Thoreau nevertheless accidentally burned three hundred acres near Concord, Massachusetts, and Sam Clemens—aka Mark Twain—confessed in *Roughing It* that his campfire sparked a substantial wildfire near Lake Tahoe. Even if we see fire as an enemy to be defeated, there's a certain hypnotic attraction to such an elemental force when freed from our control. At one of my first boy scout "camporees" I was what might be called a material witness at the dawn of a small grass fire. Most of the older boys were off somewhere, and I was left with another tenderfoot to watch the campfire while John, a more experienced scout, chopped wood. Despite his savvy, John axed a gash into his leg, and while he accomplished most of the stanching and wrapping for himself, my friend and I were distracted enough to let the fire escape into the surrounding field. But that's not quite the way it was. In that moment before the others returned—now replayed in slow motion by memory—both of us saw the creeping flames on one side and John's bleeding leg on the other, unable or unwilling to do anything about either. It was almost as if the world had its heart set on catastrophe and it would have been wrong to interfere.

The human influence on wildland fire need not be a matter of management policy, carelessness, or overt or passive pyromania. In private holdings abutting national parks and forests, changes resulting from human land use have also fed the flames. People intentionally or inadvertently replace relatively hard-to-burn native plant communities with eminently flammable grasses. Invasive cheatgrass—downy brome—gets a jump on native competitors by setting seed early, leaving tinder-dry yellow shreds to bake in the sun until ignited by lightning, fireworks, or sparks from passing cars. Residential development in the wildland-urban interface has upped the stakes, making it more difficult to let fire play its natural role. Nobody wants to see an expensive dream house or multigenerational summer getaway converted to ashes, and buildings burn even more readily than trees. Pyne, channeling combustion itself, points out that "houses . . . as viewed by fire, are indistinguishable from piles of logging slash."

A 2006 study by University of Arizona dendrochronologist Tom Swetnam and three Scripps Institute researchers cites drought and increased heat as causes of the recent spike in wildland fire activity. Climate cycles are notoriously hard to interpret, but a consensus is emerging that the West is subject to alternating dry and relatively wet periods that might last decades or centuries each. Despite the proliferation of more glamorous theories, evidence persists that it may have been extended drought that drove the Anasazi from their southwestern farms. In *One Long Winter Count*, Colin Calloway details the formative role of rainfall cycles in the cultures of Native American peoples inhabiting the West before the region was "discovered" by Lewis and Clark. According to Calloway, Indians responded to fluctuations in climate and water supply by shifting back and forth between agrarian and hunter-gatherer lifeways. The Euroamerican settlement of the West corresponded, it seems, to a wetter-than-average swing now in the process of reversing.

Anthropogenic climate change adds an unprecedented wild card to the mix of forces influencing wildfire patterns. During 2007, the city of Billings recorded forty-two days with highs of ninety or above, two more, in fact, than the number of days in which the temperature stayed below freezing. Of course, extrapolating from limited data is fraught with uncertainty. Even as our power to warp our planet's systems increases to sorcerer's apprentice levels, a humiliating lack of understanding makes it impossible to say for sure just what is attributable to us and what is not. We know that drought and fire have risen with the temperature over the past few decades, but, as Pyne concludes, "Nobody can say for sure how much of this agonizing bout of aridity is attributable to man-caused climate change and how much to the inevitable reappearance of dry spells in a region that has endured prolonged droughts for millennia."

In Montana, there aren't many outright climate change deniers left, at least outside the media and the political establishment, and not much doubt that summers have lately been longer, hotter, and dryer throughout the region, giving mountain wildfires plenty of time to grow and ideal conditions for taking off on the wind. Swetnam calculates that "the fire season in the last 15 years or so has increased more than two months over the whole western U.S." Organisms in arid regions may be adapted to dry conditions, but the effects of drought in the West tend to be magnified since "water budgets" are strained even under optimum circumstances. The sooner the winter snowpack melts, the lower the summer level of creeks and rivers, and the quicker the forest dries out. The drought that fed the 1988 Yellowstone fires took place in a context of heat waves and low water across North America. With the moisture content of park forests reduced to that of cured lumber, the first major blazes were underway by the middle of June and the last were not extinguished until snow fell in mid-September.

*Los Angeles Times* reporters Bettina Boxall and Julie Cart, interviewed on NPR's *Here and Now* public affairs program, observe that western wildfires have not increased in number—there were more, in fact, in the 1960s—but the intensity and behavior of wildfires have changed in disturbing ways.

Their findings resonate with recent hurricane studies; it appears that basic elements and forces currently in play will continue shaping a region's climate, but storms are likely to be more severe, droughts more protracted, cyclical shifts more sudden and extreme, like weather on steroids. In the face of human meddling on the planetary scale, it's hard not to see stand-replacing infernos as elements of the apocalypse of the natural world that Bill McKibben calls "decreation."

Ultimately, even the most expected phenomena—drought, fire—may become frighteningly foreign as effects compound. Global warming threatens to accelerate the rate of change beyond the adaptive speed of plants and animals, an evolutionary potential that encompasses the ingrained limits of human understanding. The conventional wisdom holding that the weather may shift "every five minutes" but significant climatic variations stretch out over geologic or at least historical eras is simply no longer tenable.

∼

Applied to nature, what do words like *regular*, *stable*, *normal*, mean? If spared by the development sprawl we grumble about but think we understand, things—natural things—are supposed to remain more-or-less as they are. If that's too much to ask, we expect ecosystems to advance through predictable stages of change toward equally predictable goals. The notion of orderly forest progression to a stable climax state is challenged by the history of the Rockies, where forests come and go distressingly abruptly in what seems like haphazard fashion. In Irvin Shope's *The Four Georgians*, displayed at the Helena, Montana, Regional Airport, the city's namesake mountain hunches open and grassy above horseback prospectors. The painting, familiar to me from university business trips to the capital, is based on historical accounts and early photographs. If the artist had used the Mount Helena I climbed one morning as a model, the modest slopes would be covered by a thick cloak of conifers. Relying on the mountain as a landmark, the founders might not be able to relocate their claim today. The evergreens, however, have come under bark beetle attack, which could ultimately restore something like the view depicted in the painting.

The Beartooth Mountains around Red Lodge are moose country. Tourism-promoting magazines show these giant deer roaming residential streets. I once encountered a moose trotting down Red Lodge's main drag, leading a small parade of curiosity-seekers. Faced with ubiquitous commercial images ranging from the stately antlered silhouette gracing the doorway of the elegant Pollard Hotel to the considerably less formal sneaker-clad bullwinkle representing the annual Fun Run for Charities, it's easy to forget how rarely moose were reported by early travelers. In fact, their abundance around Red Lodge may prove to be historically ephemeral. Yellowstone Park Northern Range surveys estimate a 75 percent population loss since 1988. What's behind this precipitous decline of such a well-loved member of the charismatic megafauna? There's a quick reflex answer—the reintroduced wolves have, obviously, eaten them all. But research suggests a different explanation. Moose in the Rockies winter in dense woods, precisely the kind that a century without wildfire brought to places like the West Fork of Rock Creek. As flames have raged across northern Yellowstone, moose have been dispossessed, retreating south of Yellowstone Lake, where, despite the 1988 fires, the landscape remains mostly wooded, and where post-fire recovery seems likely to result in a moosey paradise of lush forest punctuated by wet meadows. But the migration hasn't stopped there. In fact, moose have been moving rather rapidly southward down the Green River, perhaps following a route blazed by early twentieth-century forebears who established a small population in the Uinta Mountains. During the 1990s, I was surprised to find a moose along the Green at southwestern Wyoming's Seedskadie National Wildlife Refuge, named for the more expected sage grouse, and even more startled by a cow and calf crossing a highway not far from Logan, Utah.

Despite the innate regional suspicion directed toward government land-management agencies, for generations national park visitors and area residents alike have accepted as a given that the world we see around us is basically as nature intended—the way it should be—especially in a carefully protected place like Greater Yellowstone. But the "natural state" envisioned in the influential 1963 A. Starker Leopold report as "a vignette of primitive America" when first seen by Europeans is perhaps unrealistic given the dynamism of a place like Yellowstone. And of course, the initial set point is somewhat arbitrary, as has the theory's application been in practice. For one thing, national parks, like the rest of "primitive America," were inhabited places in which untold generations of humans had played various roles in shaping the landscape and biota. Natural processes—avalanches, earthquakes, storms, fires—have also altered park environments, and will inevitably continue to do so. As Yellowstone writer Paul Schullery has it, "we obligate ourselves to preserve the wild setting as it was when first discovered," but "the wild setting may not want to stay as it was."

The 2008 season marks the twentieth anniversary of Yellowstone's ordeal by flames, labeled by CBS News "the first mega-fire." Romme and Despain might disagree with that assessment, but they wouldn't deny the impact of those conflagrations on our perceptions. Park publications and ranger programs bravely address fire ecology alongside such favorite topics as geysers and grizzly bears, and a commemorative "Yellowstone Fires of 1988" insert accompanies the Summer 2008 edition of *Yellowstone Today*, a newspaper distributed at entrance stations. Despite the fanfare, it's apparent that, after two decades, the Park Service hasn't fully recovered from the bitter, often patently unfair criticism hurled its way in the wake of the flames. "Fire scares most people—and that's a big reason why wild fires make such news and why much misinformation is spread," the newspaper insert somewhat defensively pronounces. Park administrators seem gratified, or maybe just relieved, that the "Children's Fire Trail" constructed after 1988 has had to be broadened in interpretive scope to "The Forces of the Northern Range" "because the trees grew back so quickly and strongly." The message, an implicit rebuttal of Starker Leopold's base assumption, is clear enough. The 1988 fires have shown that, whatever harmonies exist over biomes and eons, viewed on a human scale natural systems are fundamentally unstable. We can influence or trigger change, but we can't prevent it.

⌒

The Grebe Lake trailhead is on the Norris-Canyon road, close to the center of Yellowstone Park. As Cara and I pull into the parking lot, we're startled by the simultaneous arrival of a fleet of yellow hotshot transports. Energetic young firefighters leap out of the vehicles, but we soon notice that they're laughing, apparently just on an outing or perhaps taking a quick break en route from one assignment to the next. A few engage in truckside calisthenics, keeping in shape, ready for action. For now, though, all is calm.

The trail, an old fire road, crosses small meadows and forest burned in 1988. Some areas feature dense regrowth, the deceased parents leaning in Freudian fashion over a sea of head-high offspring. In other places, more sunbaked or steeper or thinner-soiled, the process seems painfully slow, with young trees scattered, framed by the crisscross trunks of fallen fire victims still whole after twenty years. No hordes of woodpeckers today, but families of mountain bluebirds drift from burned snag to burned snag, chasing plentiful grasshoppers and gulping an occasional mosquito. Chipmunks and chipping sparrows glean around and across the grid of logs. Gray jays patrol the shadows of living pines and Douglas-firs. An odd touch is provided by an osprey nest high in a scorched-naked treetop we pass long before the lake comes into our view.

Grebe Lake sits against a backdrop of Washburn Range hillsides, old growth threading the lighter green of new trees and the gray remains of 1988 in a textbook burn mosaic. Around the lake, monkshood, gentians, and "Rocky Mountain yellow flowers" crowd the occasional silky elk thistle in bright grassy meadows. Gadwalls, goldeneyes, Canada geese, cormorants, even a pair of loons join the namesake grebes—eared grebes, to be exact— on the placid water, and ospreys eye the surface, perhaps for grayling that, reputedly easy to catch, have brought a smattering of fisherfolk, including children, to the lake. Spotted sandpipers work the shoreline, along with song and Lincoln's sparrows. Bear tracks attest to other, bigger denizens.

We eat lunch in a shady place by the shore, eager to see where the loons will surface next, whether the sandpipers will lead their fledglings past our spot, if one of the osprey pair will snag another grayling. An idyllic after-noon unfolds in what Wendell Berry calls "the peace of wild things," but, as usual, the summer sky eventually gathers threatening clouds. Before we get back to the trailhead, we're walking through light rain and pea-size hail, one terrifying thunderclap echoing off the heights of Observation Peak behind us.

Our way back to Billings will skirt the LeHardy Fire in the park and the Gunbarrel Fire in Shoshone National Forest. Despite the LeHardy's un-natural genesis—it was sparked by a downed power line—both are "good fires," we are assured by a ranger at the cavernous new Canyon Visitor Center, clearing standing deadwood left from earlier blazes and insect out-breaks. After consulting with the park authorities, we drive south, delayed for a time in a traffic jam we fear might signal an unanticipated shift by the ostensibly well-mannered LeHardy Fire. But as we inch forward the obstacle is revealed to be a sizeable herd of rutting bison cavorting in the road, heedless of the nerve-jangling rattle blasted through truck-mounted speakers by a frustrated ranger. Between Hayden Valley and Yellowstone

Lake, the fresh black of the LeHardy Fire spears through the still-green surrounding forest, the flames having moved northeast, apparently harmlessly, into an earlier burn. Without the interlacing branches necessary for the dreaded crown fire, a blaze in previously charred timber essentially goes one tree at a time, "torching" its way slowly, clearing the ground and conditioning the soil, providing light and nutrients for the burgeoning seedlings.

The Gunbarrel Fire has grown to over thirty thousand acres, largish even by current standards. Signs warn travelers between the park's east entrance and Cody of "wildfire activity ahead." At one point we're close enough to see a column of smoke over the canyon, and the sun is dimmed for several miles along the North Fork road. A fire headquarters at the Big Game campground looks like a miniature Crow Fair comprised of a field of colorful firefighter tents surrounded by larger military-style messes and a sprawling assortment of tankers and equipment, both for firefighting and for the maintenance of the camp itself. But the headquarters is quiet, the personnel on a watch-and-wait standby.

It's been a good day for my personal concept of wildland fire. In the midst of a Greater Yellowstone protected by diligent but confident public servants convinced that this latest round of burning is necessary, useful, and, given the local conditions, normal, I've wandered through a spirit-restoring national park robustly regenerating a healthy, resilient forest of the future.

∼

Or so it seems. A few days after our hike to Grebe Lake, skepticism again rears up. I came to the Yellowstone country as a new resident just a few years after the 1988 fires. My first experience of Greater Yellowstone was, therefore, of a landscape replete with the aftermath of wildfire, whole mountainsides devoid of living trees, a situation which, according to the Park and Forest Services, was pretty much the way it was supposed to be. Such an assessment was neither ill-informed nor unrealistic, but given the intervening summers of megafire, there is perhaps more reason today to doubt the assurances of well-meaning experts.

Wildfire may be natural, but it's probably safe to say that human influence of one kind or another has exacerbated the current outbreak. And as climate change brings longer, hotter summers with worsening droughts, western megafires may be revealed to be as much an artifact of industrial human civilization as the firestorms that swept eastern and midwestern forests a century ago. In an article about the Adirondacks, McKibben once wondered if people could love the mountains enough to stay away from them. I can't bring myself to think that our best response to places important to us is to avoid them. Not yet. I like my job, my colleagues. I accept and for the most part enjoy being a part of my community in Billings. But I didn't come back to this part of the world for Billings. I'm here because of Greater Yellowstone, because in the early 1990s something told me that this is where I belong. I didn't listen closely enough then, but I'm listening now. During my time away, I kept track of the Yellowstone country—conditions in the Northern Range, the interactions of wolves and prey—but distance and preoccupation with things and places nearer at hand clouded my view. Without renewed experience, the region's mountains and forests were inevitably suspended in memory as they existed when I last immersed myself in their immediate living moment. How can I return only to my mind's-eye Yellowstone of 1995, or of 2008, without dimming my awareness of the vibrant, troubled, mutable—in short, real—place silhouetted on the Billings horizon?

Veterans of titanic uplift and erosion, the Beartooths will endure the legacy of climate change, and, though its individual manifestations may fall victim to a desperate search for energy sources, the Yellowstone hot spot will continue its inexorable churning far below the earth's crust. McKibben's belief that global warming signals "the end of nature" notwithstanding, the processes of geology and evolution remain in force. But how we come to grips with our role in decreation may be as important to us as how to deal with all that carbon dioxide we're releasing into the atmosphere. Indifferent to Starker Leopold's noble preservationist sentiments, nature can be ruthless in its solutions, replacing moose with mule deer or pronghorn, shade-loving trout with less-fastidious catfish, ponderosa pine with cheatgrass. Such ecological adjustments don't appear to play favorites. Montana calls itself the "Last Best Place," but nature may not make such distinctions.

～

The 2007–2008 winter left a generous supply of water in the Northern Rockies. Creek flows remained robust, the snowmelt late and gradual.

Rather than the previous year's pervasive heat and hydrologic drought, the course of 2008's Montana and Wyoming wildfires has been dictated mostly by local conditions. With new snow almost certain to crest the mountains and dust the high meadows of Yellowstone in a few weeks, we still have days with a hint of smoke in the air, but the etched outline of the Beartooths has returned to the Billings sunset horizon.

InciWeb's "last update" has the LeHardy Fire still peaceably "smoldering in heavy fuels" in an old burn. At over sixty thousand acres, the Gunbarrel Fire has grown genuinely large, its sheer size leading to increased urgency as firefighters attempt to steer the flames away from lodges and homes. From the Gardiner Lake trailhead on the ten-thousand-foot plateau near Beartooth Pass—mostly tundra, at least for the time being, and unlikely to ignite—the Gunbarrel looks like a volcanic eruption, motion frozen by distance, smoke pluming thousands of feet above the Absarokas in a curving pennant undoubtedly causing air quality alerts in Cody. Still, officials continue to regard the Gunbarrel as a good fire with relatively predictable behavior and largely beneficial results.

The Cascade Fire near Red Lodge has also calmed, reaching a final size of a moderate 10,173 acres, with crews "continuing to demob," according to the final InciWeb report. The West Fork Road won't reopen for general use until, at best, sometime in September, but inholders have been allowed to find what's left of their summer refuges, the fortunate structures intact amid slopes of burned timber and the ruins of neighboring cabins. The fire spared the Red Lodge Mountain ski resort, and fears that it would "sweep all the way into town" appear to have been unfounded. It seems not to have been "the big one" after all; it may in fact prove useful in slowing the spread of future blazes.

～

Late in August, in the Bull Mountains north of Billings, a wind- and heat-driven blowup swelled the perimeter of the thought-to-be-contained Dunn Mountain Fire, roaring through dry grass and ponderosa pine, to one hundred thousand acres. But over the Labor Day weekend, heavy rain and the first high-elevation snow reduced all area blazes to smoldering. At what looks like its finish, the 2008 fire season, even including Dunn Mountain, pales against 2007, when, according to *High Country News*, 740,000 Montana acres burned.

Most West Fork hiking trails remain closed because of hot spots and the danger of falling trees. But there are other places to hike. There might still be time for a walk or two before deep snow seals off the Beartooth Plateau, and there's no place quite like Yellowstone Park in the fall. We may not see Basin Creek until next summer, when fireweed should already gentle the young burn with a lush magenta carpet. We'll prepare ourselves to note the profusion of wildflowers, the influx of woodpeckers and bluebirds. And— since most wildfires are erratic, patchy—we'll hope. Newspaper maps of the fire zone, more illustrations than actual representations of the situation on the ground, show the preponderance of the burn across the canyon from the lakes. Perhaps the old cabin ruins along Basin Creek will somehow have been spared. Maybe the boggy shore of Upper Basin will have discouraged the flames. Maybe not. But the overall atmosphere of the canyon will be different in any case. One of my university colleagues recently returned to Billings from traveling and, unaware of the fire, drove up the West Fork to the roadblock at Basin Campground. What he saw beyond was a "big black mountain."

Twenty years after the Cascade Fire, if the climate holds in something resembling its present state—admittedly a major if—a new crop of lodgepoles and firs will crowd the rejuvenated forest floor. Beetles will have settled back into their pre-plague role opening spaces by eliminating weaker trees. Aspen groves will flourish in post-fire meadows. By then, I'll be seventy-three, with a little luck still capable of climbing through saplings to the Basin Creek Lakes.

Romme and Despain estimate that the first stage of regeneration in Yellowstone will take about fifty years. That will make me—what, 103? Not long after the Yellowstone infernos, a lifelong resident told me that he knew all about wildland fire's inevitability and ecological role, but the burned landscape just would never be the same for him. I could understand what he meant, but I'm learning it firsthand now. One of my significant places has become a different place entirely. The moose-haunted forest is gone. Not for good, we hope—the moose and I—but for the rest of my lifetime.

~

In the wake of the Cascade Fire, moose may withdraw from another localized portion of their regional range. If it happens that their appearances on village streets eventually become less frequent, wolves are likely to share the blame with the federal government. But perhaps for the time being we'll still find moose tracks near Red Lodge.

When Tom was a boy—I remember him as about nine—we were confronted by a moose in a trailside meadow at East Rosebud Lake, a drainage or two from the West Fork. This was no cheery Fun Run bullwinkle, but a frustrated adolescent enduring, perhaps, an unsuccessful first rut. It was dusk, and bear country, no place to be out walking after dark; wedged between moose and lake, we had no alternative route back to the trailhead. Bunched into a tight phalanx with responsible adults in the lead, we ventured into the moose's meadow. As we passed out of his sight behind a willow, the bull came on, antlers lowered, plunging through the lakeside brush. Rita the dog, always more intelligent than heroic, reached the other side of the clearing first, followed in short order by Cara and me, unaware that Tom, behind us, had been cut off by the moose's charge. Fortunately, the bull, having made his point, had resumed his desultory browsing. With parents relegated to sideline gestures of encouragement, Tom was able to inch across without further difficulty. For Cara and me, it was of course a parental nightmare, but the fleeting moment when we became undeniably the focus of one moose's world was also destined to become part of our family legend, an adrenaline-pumping encounter with nature in the raw indelibly imprinted on all of our memories. That's where it will have to stay. In 1996, East Rosebud Lake was in the path of a midsize blaze much like the Cascade Fire, an "incident" that destroyed some summer homes and, I'm afraid, that particular moose's winter refugium.

A couple of months before the Cascade Fire ignited, Cara and I—along with Tom, who was visiting from California—parked by an idle plow at the West Fork Road's still-in-place seasonal barricade and started up the glistening asphalt path between the pitted drifts. Snow cornices hung balanced waves above the creek. A dipper bowed on a midstream boulder. A month earlier, when the roadway was still groomed for Nordic skiers and snowshoers, Cara and I had watched golden eagles flying in and out from an overhung ledge high above Wild Bill Lake, a couple of miles past the gate. We thought they might be nesting.

But we didn't get that far this time. About a mile above the barrier, the road ahead was claimed by the first moose we'd seen since returning to the

Rockies. It was getting late; what daylight there was on an overcast evening was climbing the canyon walls, leaving us in deep shadow. The eagles could wait for another time; a moose was plenty for one walk. For a while we watched her sampling what was left of last year's willow growth along the creek, then we turned back toward the car in a cool spring rain.

## Red Summer

It's been a splendid July day in Yellowstone. Cara and I have hiked through a blaze of wildflowers: elephant heads, monument plant, rein orchid, larkspur, monkshood, and more; watched a coyote pouncing its way across a meadow; and looped down Dunraven Pass as a thunderstorm spun a rainbow over Tower Falls. Now, on our way home, we scan through late-afternoon light for bears, maybe a moose or great gray owl. As always, the park has delivered a generous share of the wilderness "glad tidings" that the naturalist John Muir called on his readers to get firsthand, an invitation that has brought acolytes to places like Yellowstone for well over a century.

The road between Tower Falls and Mammoth Hot Springs crosses the western reaches of the park's Northern Range, country famous for its elk and bison, and for the wolves that follow them. Parts of the range were seared by the great 1988 fires, but on the Blacktail Deer Plateau northeast of Tower Falls, wet depressions, sagebrush hills, and open groves of Douglas-fir and lodgepole pine are laced together by strands of aspen into one of Yellowstone's most diverse and striking landscapes. At least that's how it was. Today, driving toward Mammoth, we're surrounded by an alarming panorama of reddened needles extending out from both sides of the road. We can't say what's attacking the Blacktail Plateau trees, but north of the park boundary we find the Absaroka mountain slopes draped with a more uniform red zone, the distressingly familiar mark of the ongoing mountain pine beetle epidemic that has been sweeping through western conifers for the last two decades. Environmental writer George Wuerthner cautions that such outbreaks don't really kill *all* the trees, and generally look worse than they are. That may be, but the effect is shocking nonetheless, the bugs advancing through Greater Yellowstone's sacred space like an invading army.

Which, in fact, they aren't. The native insects ripping through western forests have coexisted with their conifer hosts for millennia, usually going about their business unobtrusively at "endemic" or "background" levels, turning weak and diseased trees into useful snags and nest sites. Occasionally, however, *Dendroctonus*—Latin for "tree-killer"—beetle populations surge, scattering the insects across the mountains in plague numbers. Bark beetle outbreaks occurred during the 1930s, 1950s, and 1970s, but those were small potatoes compared to the pandemic now engulfing montane forests from Arizona to British Columbia. In Colorado, there's talk of lodgepole pines, a favorite insect target, becoming functionally extinct, and across Idaho, Montana, and Wyoming, slopes of dead trees are coming to dominate formerly wooded landscapes. Real estate hucksters are scrambling to market "new view lots," and ski resorts are taking chainsaws to what used to be their ambience, a liability- and public relations-driven preemptive strike against any potential convergence of tourist and toppling deadwood. The outbreak is being called the biggest event of its kind in North American history. Trained by experience to suspect human agency—of late especially climate change—in rapid wholesale environmental disruptions, it's hard not to see these bugs as a kind of fifth column, allied to unholy forces from without, that is to say, us.

Not denying the human signal in the red slopes, Wuerthner views beetles as the forest's way of pruning woodlands that, in a warming, drying West, have become "overstocked" with mature conifers. He reminds us that, despite their comfortingly timeless name, evergreen forests are dynamic systems. Our present-day woods are a snapshot moment in a complex co-evolutionary history linking climate, trees, and insects. Systematic weather and forest-health records covering a century or two offer little perspective when placed in the long-term context of what might be called a forest's own reckoning of time.

In *Of Rock and Rivers*, Colorado State University scientist Ellen Wohl parallels an epidemic of hemlock looper bugs in the Northeast some forty-eight hundred years ago with the current mountain pine beetle surge. Those woods were thinly peopled, but the insects didn't need human help to catalyze wholesale changes in forest ecology. Loopers decimated eastern hemlocks, leaving scattered remnants from which the species eventually rebounded, eventually being somewhere in the neighborhood of fifteen hundred years. Now relegated to cool, humid pockets in hardwood-rich woodlands, hemlocks are once again under insect attack, this time by the introduced woolly adelgid. Who's to say what another millennium will bring?

Rooted in the meager soil of unstable slopes and routinely subjected to weather extremes, Rocky Mountain evergreen forests, especially those dominated by lodgepole pine, are prone to apocalyptic renewal cycles. The natural lifespan for a Rocky Mountain lodgepole ranges from one hundred to four hundred years. Ultimately, the mature trees fall victim to canyon windstorms, drought-induced wildfires, or insect infestations, often in single stand-replacing events. The woods reddening and dying throughout the West are largely even-aged old-growth stands dominated by one or two species, the kind timber industry PR used to label "overmature" to justify clearcutting. Such forests come and go across the fossil record, and even in recorded history. Some old timers shrug off the latest insect outbreak as more of the same, though most people who spend time outdoors in the West admit that they haven't seen anything quite like this epidemic in scope and duration. I found, and still find, the slopes of red trees the single most jarring and discouraging difference between the Yellowstone country I left in 1995 and the place I returned to in 2006. Sometimes it seems best not to revisit a particularly magnificent stand of pines, for fear that they might be dead. As we descended Avalanche Peak near the park's east entrance late one day in the early 1990s, we hiked through a gorgeous pine stand, though my son Tom found the gnarly trees a bit haunted-looking, more so, perhaps, because grizzlies frequent such high-elevation forests at times. Despite the amazing view from the top, I don't think I want to hike that trail again. Those slopes have, according to the latest addition of Yellowstone's most comprehensive trail guide, "experienced almost 100% mountain pine beetle kill in recent years." Haunted, indeed.

Sprouting nutritious calorie-rich cones, an autumn staple for creatures ranging from Clark's nutcrackers to grizzly bears, the whitebark pine is a particular concern in the high mountains framing Yellowstone Park, legendary ranges such as the Tetons, the Gallatins, the Beartooths, and the Absarokas. The haunted forest on Avalanche Peak was old-growth whitebark pine.

~

The Beartooth High Lakes Trail winds through a bouldery world of sub-alpine ponds suspended thousands of feet above the surrounding valleys and just below the Beartooth Pass tundra. It's the kind of place John Muir would have liked. It's also ideal whitebark pine habitat, which explains the grizzly-warning signs at the Beartooth Lake trailhead. But looking across the lake at the slopes of Beartooth Butte, an eccentric tawny sedimentary mesa afloat on a granite base, we can already tell that all is not right with the pines.

The trail begins with a steady climb through colorful wildflower mead-ows—mostly yellows and blues by mid-August—but it's another color that grabs our attention. Unlike densely packed lodgepoles, mature whitebark pines develop spreading crowns, giving these "stone pines" a striking ap-pearance perfectly suited to the dramatic talus-strewn mountainsides where they grow. When a centuries-old whitebark is killed by beetles, it makes a rusty sunburst—spectacular but disheartening. We find such ragged explo-sions blazing throughout the Beartooth lakes, with silvery previous victims interspersed like giant dandelions gone to seed among firs greenblack in the glare of high-elevation sun.

Whitebarks form distinctive groves or mingle with other timberline spe-cies in Yellowstone's mountains and in similar places from northern Canada south to Muir's Sierra Nevada. Though mountain pine beetles have histori-cally infected whitebarks during unusually warm, droughty periods—the 1930s, for example—these long-lived slow-growing pines have not evolved the vigorous defenses characteristic of more common hosts; in a Greater Yellowstone study by Jesse A. Logan, William W. McFarlane, and Louisa Willcox, "only a couple of the trees (literally two) have been found to be successful in fending off beetle attacks, using chemical and physical re-sponses similar to those in lower-elevation tree species." Instead, white-barks rely primarily on frigid temperatures to keep outbreaks short and self-contained, a strategy only as sound as the winters are cold and long. Willcox concludes that, under present conditions, "whitebark pine is basi-cally a sitting duck to pine beetle." Yellowstone whitebarks are particularly vulnerable in the absence of an extensive fir and spruce barrier separating them from lower-elevation lodgepoles, typically the source of epidemics moving upslope into timberline five-needle pines. The current Greater Yellowstone outbreak, however, seems to have started in whitebarks and moved downhill, perhaps further implicating high-altitude warming. The epidemic may have peaked, but not before reaching over 90 percent of area whitebark forests and causing major losses in over 80 percent of the affected groves. The climate bad news for the whitebark is not limited to beetle depredation; some of the healthiest remaining stands are in Great Basin ranges where their habitat could simply be warmed out of existence.

Despite the daunting complexities of forest ecology, it's pretty clear that, as Teton-based essayist Jack Turner concludes, "to be blunt, the fate of the whitebark pine is our fault." Whitebarks have had a rough century. White pine blister rust, a fungal disease of Eurasian origin accidentally introduced into British Columbia, brought considerable mortality even before the beetles climbed the warming climate to the redoubts where whitebarks grow. According to the Whitebark Pine Ecosystem Foundation, headquartered in Missoula, Montana, a broad swath of the Northern Rockies has lost over half its whitebarks from the one-two punch of exotic and indigenous attackers. Whitebarks find themselves in a classic double bind. Cool, wet summers that relieve beetle outbreaks are conducive to the spread of blister rust. While beetles home in on mature trees, blister rust reduces cone output and can quickly overcome seedlings. Krummholz growth is largely ignored by bark beetles and could serve as a post-outbreak reservoir of healthy trees, but this gnarled, flattened growth form has no special immunity to rust. The Forest Service concludes that, even without the beetles, "white pine blister rust can threaten the sustainability of high elevation white pine stands."

The pines' situation may be dire, but dedicated "whitebark warriors" are stockpiling the cones of rust-resistant trees with future restoration in mind. Whitebarks matter to Yellowstone people, for their beauty, their "ecosystem services" such as slowing and prolonging spring runoff, and their value to bears and other wildlife. Willcox's blog recounts Livingston, Montana, caterer/restaurateur and grizzly aficionado Dan Sullivan's lament, in response to her research group's grim findings, that "the most beautiful bear scats were the blond ones, those filled with pine seeds."

Our Beartooth High Lakes hike ends in a descent through a robust forest of subalpine fir. The Whitebark Pine Foundation lists successional replacement as one of the more insidious threats to the whitebark's long-term viability. Twentieth-century fire suppression may have jeopardized a whitebark competitive edge—seeds cached by Clark's nutcrackers and ready to sprout in the wake of lightning fires. With pinecone stocks and seedling survival further compromised by disease, competing trees are likely to prosper at the expense of the pines. Like the hardwoods that moved into the gap left by looper-blighted eastern hemlocks, subalpine and Douglas-firs, despite their own predatory insects and fire-suppression history, may take advantage of an ecological opportunity spurred by pine beetle kill.

With close to a full complement of native species, the Greater Yellowstone Ecosystem boasts a level of integrity rare in the Lower 48. In the case of the whitebark pine, that completeness is clearly on the line. On July 19, 2010, in response to a Natural Resources Defense Council petition filed almost two years earlier, the US Fish and Wildlife Service announced a belated review to determine if the whitebark merited a place on the Endangered Species List. The agency's website explained that "information provided in the petition, as well as other information in our files, indicates that listing the species may be warranted due to the white pine blister rust pathogen (an introduced fungal disease), mountain pine beetles, and climate change." A year later, the agency designated the whitebark a "candidate species," concluding that the tree needs protection but that listing at the current time is "precluded" by other priorities.

~

For creatures capable of such momentous landscaping, individual mountain pine beetles—glossy black or reddish-brown and less than a quarter inch long—are unassuming and easily missed. In June and July, adults emerge from pupae and begin the work of killing trees, though from their perspective it's the work of staying alive. Often accompanied by a bluish symbiont fungus that suppresses pine defenses, they bore into the living phloem, blocking nutrient channels and thus starving the trees. The red-needled corpses by the road or trail actually succumbed some time ago, perhaps last season. Unless you know what to look for—sap extrusions on the trunks, say—you might miss this year's casualties. But the beetles don't. When a pioneering female follows chemical and acoustic distress signals to a promising victim beset by drought, age, or previous disease, her compatriots descend en masse. When beetle numbers are high enough, even healthy trees in their path are overwhelmed. No one is quite certain how these insects find new, distant hunting grounds. Pioneers have proven surprisingly mobile. Whether riding the wind, stowing away in firewood and rough-cut logs, or weaving along ponderosa ridges, mountain pine beetles have shown up far out on the prairie in places as unexpected as Billings city parks, dozens of miles from the nearest mountain.

Temperature and precipitation can ally with either trees or bugs. Larvae and metamorphosing pupae are vulnerable to extreme cold; a few below-zero days at the fringes of the winter season can curtail an outbreak. Shorter winters, on the other hand, extend the beetle's active season, enabling an annual, rather than two-year, life cycle even at high altitudes. Multiple broods in a single summer have been reported in some places. Sufficient precipitation can provide trees with enough sap to suffocate or "pitch out" the beetles. Hot and dry weather drains the trees and energizes their attackers. Generally, bark beetle populations track with drought cycles, and outbreaks end when moisture is plentiful. If drought persists, an irruption is likely to continue until mature trees are too few and isolated to support it. That appears to be the case in British Columbia's particularly hard-hit montane forests, where an area four times that of Vancouver Island has turned "red and dead." Forests Minister Pat Bell announced in 2009 that "the mountain pine beetle epidemic is largely over . . . . The bad news is that it's because they don't have any food left to eat. The vast majority of our pine stands have been killed at this point." US Forest Service regional forest health expert Gregg DeNitto cites a similar dynamic at Montana's beetle epicenter, noting, also in 2009, that in the Beaverhead-Deerlodge and Helena National Forests the outbreak's energy seems to be flagging in the face of a shortage of mature pines.

Drought is endemic in western environments, and one can see the beetles, as Wuerthner does, as nature's agents adjusting water-starved ecosystems to new conditions. If, whether because of human-generated climate change or the poorly understood "long cycle" governing wet and dry periods in the interior West—probably both—the woods are overstocked, then forests must grow sparser, more open, perhaps withdrawing from some areas completely. This has happened before, more or less. But that more or less is the troublesome thing. Words like *unprecedented, epochal, catastrophic* echo across Rocky Mountain newspapers. It only takes a glance at the twentieth century to expose a hubristic tendency to cast one's own generational situation as unique and earth shaking, and today's sensationalistic news media wholeheartedly endorse hyperbole as a matter of course. As with wildfire coverage, television and newspapers redeploy a few dramatic images at the expense of a more nuanced, complete representation of conditions throughout the region. Wuerthner, his activist instincts attuned to the no-holds-barred salvage-logging dreams of timber interests and Forest Service bureaucrats, warns against "beetle hysteria." As of 2009, the outbreak had reddened 2.7 million acres of Montana pines, well short of the 4 million taken by the same bugs in the 1970s and 80s. Even in beetle-ravaged Colorado, a 2006 study led by W. H. Romme, whose past work included a major analysis of the 1988 Yellowstone fires, states categorically that "there is no evidence to support the idea that current levels of bark beetle or defoliator activity are unnaturally high." Unnaturally high, that is, given what the Forest Service describes as "severe drought during the past decade, accompanied by relatively warm temperatures in both summer and winter."

Still, plenty of testimony suggests that something special is afoot. British Columbia's Bell considers himself the first provincial forests minister in history to face "a very real possibility that we will run out of trees." As formerly unusual temperature and precipitation conditions become commonplace, chronic beetle outbreaks could supplant background population levels as the norm wherever and whenever mature pines are available. Logan, McFarlane, and Willcox acknowledge that fears that a 1930s irruption was driving Yellowstone whitebark pines to extinction proved overblown and premature, but only, they argue, because the return of less beetle-friendly conditions tilted the balance back in favor of the pines. Today, "instead of a short-term weather event, we are experience [sic] a climate trend that started in the 1970s or 1980s and continues unabated."

While the mountain pine beetle is getting most of the press, many tree-eating insects have found recent trends to their liking. According to the Summer 2010 edition of *Yellowstone Today*, the park's visitor newspaper, "Insect infestations attacking trees now include four types of bark beetles and a spruce budworm—a circumstance never seen before. Scientists suspect climate change at work." Park biologist Roy Renkin agrees that past episodes typically involved limited outbreaks of a single species, and "they've never really been that synchronous to the degree they are now." Scientists list insect proliferation among climate change's likely consequences. Along with fires, bugs maintain the forest's natural regeneration rhythms, and shifts in their behavior or prominence mark a scramble to reestablish ecosystem equilibrium as species jockey for new opportunities or adapt to straitened circumstances created by altered conditions.

Like other denizens of the wild, each bug has its own niche and lifeway. Douglas-fir beetles are real catastrophists, their populations exploding in short lived but destructive outbreaks at the edge of wildfires, blowdowns, and other disturbances. The denuded North Fork descent from Sylvan Pass, characterized, with some, but not much, exaggeration by Turner as "an entire [dead] forest on the eastern side of the ecosystem near Cody," was scoured by these insects, along with spruce beetles, after the 1988 Yellowstone conflagrations. Though *Ips* engraver beetles are usually less virulent in their attack, like mountain pine beetles their populations sometimes rise to epidemic levels. Beetles are joined by a variety of arthropod compatriots, such as Douglas-fir tussock moths, pine butterflies, and western spruce budworms.

As it turns out, budworms are the most likely agent behind the reddened trees we encountered in Yellowstone's Northern Range. Park records show a budworm outbreak in the general area of the Lamar and Yellowstone river corridors at that time. Caterpillars of these unobtrusive-looking small brown moths feed on new growth, resulting in burned-out treetops and branch tips. Budworms don't routinely kill their hosts, so it's tempting to take them less seriously than bark beetles, to, for example, feel relief that the Northern Range damage we found was not from a beetle assault. But repeated budworm defoliation can be quite destructive, especially for young trees with fewer needles to spare. In fact, when bark beetles are at background levels, budworms are the most important forest destroyer in both public and commercial timberlands, and the hot, dry conditions favored by beetles are also conducive to budworm outbreaks. Moreover, a budworm surge can leave trees weakened and vulnerable to more lethal bark beetles.

By expanding the number of tree species under attack, simultaneous dep-redation by different insects could compromise a forest's capacity to rebound following a large-scale epidemic, especially in places like Yellowstone, where tree diversity is low; many Yellowstone Park forests are composed almost exclusively of lodgepole pine, and even the more diverse woods of the Northern Range are dominated by a few conifer species. Forests are syner-gistic by nature, and changes in one aspect of forest life will almost certainly have a range of impacts, some predictable, some less so.

A Canadian research team led by W. A. Kurz concludes that in British Columbia, the pine beetle irruption's "impact converted the forest from a small net carbon sink to a large net carbon source both during and imme-diately after the outbreak." Rocky Mountain conifers constitute a timbered peninsula depending southward from similar forests spread across Canada and the entire northern hemisphere. In terms of natural climate regulation, this great evergreen belt is a northern equivalent of the tropical rainforest. The persistence and extent of the ongoing insect epidemic complex has spurred concern that worldwide boreal and montane forests could turn into carbon releasers as dead and dying trees decay or catch fire. The feedback potential is truly mind-boggling. Though it's always dangerous to general-ize from a single, if compound, event, the ongoing tree mortality seems a pretty clear sign that even minor temperature shifts—a degree or two here or there—can have far-reaching effects. We don't know enough to identify a definitive indicator that climatic Armageddon is at hand, but it's not unreasonable to suspect that such a signal might look a lot like a British Columbia's–worth of dead pines.

~

What will Rocky Mountain forests be like in a few decades? In a century? To even venture a guess engages such profound questions as whether the evolutionary imperatives that created human intelligence will mobilize that vaunted force in time to defuse climatic meltdown. In the meantime, a less sweeping application of human ingenuity might be brought to bear on the bugs themselves. As of now, landscape-level responses to bark beetles are impracticable, though individual trees or campground-size parcels can be effectively protected by pesticides and "hormone disrupter packets." A rare upbeat note for whitebarks is that saving some of their more self-contained stands using available means may at least be possible.

Theorizing that auditory cues regulating bark beetle behavior might provide an innovative approach to outbreak control, Northern Arizona University scientists recently bombarded mountain pine beetles with "the nastiest, most offensive sounds." When a mating pair was subjected to amplified and extended beetle "aggression calls," the results stunned even supposedly dispassionate researchers. Resorting to astonished language reminiscent of nineteenth-century entomologist J. Henri Fabre, team member Richard Hofstetter admits that he and his colleagues "watch[ed] in horror as the male beetle would tear the female apart." The Flagstaff discoveries are promising, if gruesome. But given the now-chronic American disdain for expensive scientific research and development, we're likely a long way from erecting a protective wall of sound around the Rocky Mountains. Even given a concerted control effort, basic logistics may well prove unworkable, and complications are almost certain to arise. There may, for example, be a volume or distance limit beyond which beetle vocalizations become unrecognizable to the target audience.

The network of tree-mounted loudspeakers or aerial broadcasts required to mobilize a full-scale sonic assault would place mountain forests under a potentially permanent regime of wholesale human manipulation. In the resulting state of siege, we would hold at best a tentative advantage over adaptively nimble foes: the Arizona team found that their test subjects—unlike the researchers themselves—overcame their initial aversion to Guns N' Roses and radio commentator Rush Limbaugh, and soon resumed their normal activities. Even if acoustic weaponry could be made feasible and effective, the environmental consequences of such total war would be difficult, if even possible, to predict, since bark beetles and their cycles are inextricably tied into the ecology of mountain forests. Like them or not, as much as bears, moose, and the pines themselves, the bugs belong; to eliminate them, even if we could, might beget a nightmare parable against impulsive human meddling. What would Rachel Carson do?

Past insect outbreaks in Yellowstone have been actively fought using methods described in the *Billings Gazette* as "logging, burning and, in the 1950s, spraying infested Douglas-fir with about 62 tons of DDT." Since, as

Renkin puts it, such efforts "tend to be futile," the Park Service has opted at least for now to view the current complex of epidemics as one more titanic force in the park's evolving, dynamic history. There's something to be said for such restraint. The British Columbia Ministry of Forests and Range lists past fire suppression as a major exacerbating contributor to the severity of the province's beetle outbreak, testifying that managerial interference, even if well-intentioned, may be too shortsighted and heavy-handed for finely tuned natural systems.

At least for the time being, Yellowstone managers are staking their hopes on nature reregulating the ecosystem in its own way. Perhaps, aided by growing populations of woodpeckers, predatory beetles, and parasitic wasps, tree-killers and conifers will develop new patterns of coexistence, recalibrating their relationship as they must have done repeatedly since the Pleistocene. Climate change seems to magnify at high altitudes, and just how much stress ecosystems can absorb, and how quickly, and, for that matter, how much the climate will shift, remain to be seen. Nevertheless, the Park Service's decision to basically refrain from mounting a desperate, potentially destructive offensive against bark beetles and their kin may provide one model for the future. At the very least, their response's humility respects the wildness that has brought generations of nature romantics, myself included, to Yellowstone. A. Starker Leopold recommended that "a national park should represent a vignette of primitive America." As Earth warms, Leopold's pristine, static Eden, an ideal image guiding park management since the 1960s, may be primed to fall before a postlapsarian acceptance of nature as constantly, sometimes uncomfortably, evolving process.

Let's say it's a mid-July afternoon fifty years from now. My great-grandchildren stretch out by a grassy stream on Yellowstone's Northern Range. If my superannuated self were somehow there with them, I might recognize the trickling waterway as, say, Blacktail Deer or Hellroaring Creek. I might note how low the stream is, and wonder what happened to the firs and pines that had interlaced with meadows, sage, and the occasional aspen grove in this part of the park. Interpretive dioramas in the venerable Albright Visitor Center could already have informed me that it's been years since elk—or wolves—have been seen on the range in summer, and that moose are reduced to occasional wanderers from more intractably bosky climes. Pronghorn, on the other hand, drift across the brushy grasslands in ever-increasing herds. No boreal chorus frogs call from the dry sloughs, their songs replaced by those of Brewer's sparrows and horned larks, maybe Sprague's pipits. As a herd of bison cows and calves sidle through the sagebrush, passing thrillingly close to my descendants' streamside retreat, my centenarian fingers nervously sifting through dust pull up a footlong shard of barkless wood, a lodgepole remnant.

Would I toss the stick from hand to hand, entranced by its cool balance, wistfully muttering something like "Ah, you should have seen this place then"? At best, my perspective would be historical. At worst, I'd just be one more good-old-days grump. And who's to say that my own—that is to say, the current—version of the Northern Range is "correct"? Historic photographs peg extensive Northern Range conifer stands as a fleeting phenomenon; past centuries saw broad floodplains, with aspens flanking willow and cottonwood beaver meadows. At any rate, what's to be gained by complaining? This grassy vista is what my descendants know, what they have come here for. Maybe I should just let them enjoy their antelope, their larks, their Yellowstone.

Or maybe the trees will have regrown, the forest reasserting itself as it has for centuries, the bugs subsiding to levels optimal for their own survival, which, after all, depends on the survival of the trees. Past outbreaks have ended surprisingly quickly, and it may turn out that the cycle of red to gray to green will continue for some time, perhaps at an accelerated but sustainable pace. Rocky Mountain lodgepole forests, after all, have withstood considerable climatic variation in regions far south of Yellowstone. Areas torched by the 1988 blazes are generally sprouting replacement forests similar or identical in conformation to their predecessors; even in my great-grandchildren's time, the same pattern may prevail in beetle-kill zones. Or, as in the higher whitebark groves, another species, most likely hardy, budworm-resistant descendants of today's Douglas-firs, might supplant lodgepoles, maintaining an evergreen presence on the range—not the same forest, but a forest nonetheless, with enough cover even for a moose or two.

～

Late in June, almost a year after our drive home from Yellowstone past the reddened Absaroka slopes, by now probably mostly gray, a new summer's first mountain hike takes us to the Stillwater River, over the Beartooth Mountains from Yellowstone Park. Along the trail, we encounter several Billings people we haven't seen in town for months, amply demonstrating both the pull of the mountains and the irony of driving nearly one hundred miles to spend a day in the wilderness. It is beyond beauty, this northern fringe of Greater Yellowstone, a land of ragged pinnacles, grand plateaus, creeks plunging through hidden ravines, and the season for mountain hiking is painfully brief. To wander these wildlands is why most of us born elsewhere have chosen the Yellowstone country for our home. "The mountains are calling and I must go," says Muir. Who can resist?

Our destination today is Sioux Charley Lake, a few miles above a dramatic cleft the river pours itself through just beyond the trailhead. Partially compensating for an El Niño winter's meager snowpack, May blizzards and late but generous June rains have swollen the river to a white chaos and left the mountain meadows radiant, paintbrush red and lupine blue punctuating a yellow dazzle of arrowleaf balsamroot. At the lake, really just a broad spot, the Stillwater earns its name, the churning runoff easing enough for a white-tailed deer to swim across as we watch. We don't encounter the moose rumored to be in the vicinity, but the riparian zone is full of life: flycatchers and tanagers calling from cottonwoods, an osprey scouting from a lakeside snag, mergansers napping on a gravel bar, a dipper wrestling a minnow onto a river rock. Though the landscape is verdant overall, a smattering of ominous red patches—the previous year's insect kill—infiltrates the evergreens on higher slopes, especially those not guarded by the black ghosts of lightning fires. If they haven't already, new generations of beetles and budworms will be emerging any day.

Aside from a few surprisingly tall, apparently healthy firs luxuriating in the canyon's ready mist, the Stillwater forests, like most Beartooth woods, are spindly, hardscrabble affairs, stunted conifers gripping bedrock, hunkering much of the year in snow and ice only to be thrust into summers of drought and fire. In the rain shadow of the continental divide, these mountains aren't supposed to look like the ferny glens of the Pacific Northwest. They are, however, our green places. We can hope that the latest epidemic will glance off the Beartooths and move on, or, better yet, that a few cool, rainy summers or a timely arctic blast will tip the bugs into background mode, but we can't look at these woods without thinking of other forests reduced to skeletal patterns against the colossal erosional ruins of the mountains. One thing I've noticed is that the already grayed slopes bother me less than the freshly killed red ones. Maybe that's because I'm used to the aftermath of forest fires. Or maybe it's that the demolition is over and the next forest, the next whatever, is already in the works.

One might argue that a kind of juvenile trust in impervious planetary rhythms has gotten us into our current morass. "God takes care of the universe," a woman working a George W. Bush-for-President table once told me when I asked about her candidate's position on the environment. Such an ideology puts nature's fundamental course serenely beyond our purview and enables a pernicious loaves-and-fishes fantasy that everything from timber and oil to the capacity of Earth to absorb abuse is essentially inexhaustible. That being said, faith in nature is a part of our cultural inheritance that I, for one, hold dear. To John Muir, well aware of the human propensity to damage fragile ecologies, the mountains remained unfailing "fountains of life," high places in which we could sense the universe taking care of us, or at least of itself. We will miss the easy faith streaming like Wordsworthian "clouds of glory" from explorers and naturalists who discovered in Yellowstone and the West a demanding but intact Eden in which to ramble, their confident sense of well-being persisting as a hallmark of later nature writing and nature romanticism in general.

I'd rather be hiking in Greater Yellowstone than doing almost anything else, and I've got to believe that Muir's glad tidings are still out there even in Aldo Leopold's "world of wounds." I can still hear them. But there's no place quite healthy, nowhere we can get away from our own consequences, a complex of intentional and inadvertent effects we'll have to live with, mitigate where possible, forgive ourselves for if we can. It's small comfort to hide behind a divine intent we can neither perceive nor predict. God takes care of the universe? Maybe, but, then again, "the Almighty has His own purposes"—that from an American who knew a thing or two about destruction, responsibility, and renewal.

Places like Greater Yellowstone are not where we go to get away from it all, but rather where we can more clearly see, more deeply feel, our connections, and more viscerally understand the ways in which our lives really do matter. The cost for such enlightenment is high, and it's admittedly shabby compensation to moose and trout, pine and beetle, that will have to pay along with us. The Spanish poet Federico García Lorca credits *duende*, conditioned in part by the felt presence of death in our midst, with providing human culture its fundamental authenticity, a physical gravitas our mediated modernity at best erodes and at worst actively repels. There's a hefty, unescapable shot of something like duende in a slopeful of dying trees.

In urging a full involvement with existence, Thoreau famously warned against discovering when one comes to die that one hasn't lived. Easy for him to say, back when there was still so much flourishing wildness—"the preservation of the world"—just over the horizon, in, well, Yellowstone, for example. But his contemporaries' bemusement shows that even then it was not easy to break the membrane separating what we know from how we live. To do so is to emerge face to face with one's own enmeshment, one's own complicity, in things as grand and beyond comprehension as the birth and demise of forests, life and death on a scale both intimate and planetary. To return, in other words, to the evolving numinous wilderness in which our lives are, and have always been, made. In our time the news emanating from the mountains is ambivalent, even frightening; Muir's call to get those tidings firsthand may lead not only to ecstatic peaks but also to perilous valleys of disillusionment. Never, though, to the dead-end ledge of a false detachment.

# Invaders

## I

At Storm Point, something like Maine surf pulses against something like Maine rocks with a sputtering roar. But when I look up, away from the breakers, there are the fire- and beetle-ravaged slopes of the Absarokas, the snow-traces of Mount Sheridan, the rocket-ship Tetons. This is not Maine, not a coast at all. I am inland, at Yellowstone Lake.

Since Cara and I moved to Montana from Florida and, before that, Maine, our usual route to the park has been to follow the Yellowstone River all the way from Billings to the Gardiner entrance and Mammoth Hot Springs. But during the early 1990s, when Wyoming's Bighorn Basin was our home, the shortest way led through the East Entrance, over Sylvan Pass, and down the west slope of the Absarokas to Yellowstone Lake. My introduction to the strange, wondrous world of Yellowstone was dropping out of the mountains one Labor Day weekend to a glittering expanse of water. A few bison slouched along the shore, disturbed neither by passing cars nor by steam issuing from fissures in the ground. In Mary Bay, my first trumpeter swan towered over a wave-swayed scatter of goldeneyes.

The last time I was at Storm Point, Tom was ten or so years old. Our hike was made memorable by a frighteningly quick thunderstorm, whipping the lake and trees into a dramatic commotion that the great naturalist John Muir, who wrote about riding a Douglas-fir in a Sierra gale, would have found exhilarating. I don't recall feeling much of Muir's ecstasy—what comes to mind is relief that we made it back to the trailhead without falling victim to lightning or toppling pines.

Another century finds us, minus our now-adult son, perched on the austere gray headland of Storm Point, this time, thankfully, without the lightning. A stiff September onshore breeze—trailbooks invariably describe the hike to the exposed point as "windy"—makes our stay on the scoured vantage brief. From there, we follow a semiofficial spur westward across a shore meadow to the next promontory, a stone mini-peninsula separated from Storm Point proper by a scalloped inlet of volcanic sand and tumbled boulders.

Down among the rocks a leeward shelf dips green bangs into a gentle swirl, the private eddy of a mallard hen now paddling her annoyed way into open water. Curtains of tiny silver fish, perhaps native longnose dace, ripple in overhang shadow. Sidelong to the persistent wind, California gulls coast by, a bald eagle, a raven, all headed west toward Fishing Bridge.

~

The official name for the knot of guest services just west of where Fishing Bridge spans the Yellowstone River outlet is Lake, sometimes converted to an adjective before Village or Junction. The moniker is consistent in its simplicity with that of nearby Canyon, and, despite the presence of many other lakes and no small helping of canyons, each is quite sufficient. The Grand Canyon of the Yellowstone offers some of the park's most iconic views. And the Lake is, well, the Lake. Whether you come from Cody, travel south along the river from Canyon, or drop down from Craig Pass and Old Faithful, a sudden sheet of blue water sprawls before you, the other side another place, fifteen, twenty, or more miles away. The mountains over there are a different range entirely, more than one range, in fact. Seen from Lake Butte, a caldera shoulder reached by an East Entrance spur road, the big lake is held in an even grander vastness of Yellowstone backcountry, which, as an overlook interpretive display proudly notes, is the largest roadless area in the Lower 48. The whole prospect is innocent of auto routes except for the Grand Loop, mostly hidden by lodgepole pines, rounding the lake to West Thumb and Old Faithful, with a connector leading to the South Entrance. In a way, the road's presence is itself a statement: modern humans can ensconce our humble workings in right relation to what we know as nature. We can, in other words, still surround ourselves with wilderness, our path appropriately puny beneath the distant towers of Mount Moran and the Grand Teton.

With a maximum depth of 390 feet, Yellowstone Lake is considerably deeper than Lake Erie, though nowhere near as capacious in surface area or volume. Erie, along with its sister Great Lakes, lies where it might be expected in a lowland basin draining a sizeable swath of continent. At 7,733 feet on a high plateau rising from semidesert sage and greasewood flats, Yellowstone Lake is a kind of miracle, a proverbial inland sea complete with whitecaps, pelicans, and "arms" reaching toward hidden coves explored by few park visitors. A mark of the lake's impressiveness can be seen on the National Park Service website: the "Frequently Asked Questions: Fishing Bridge and Lake Village" include—apparently with a straight face—"Is Yellowstone Lake the largest lake in the world?" The answer may be no—not even close, actually—but the lake's size and complex geography provide plenty of habitat not only for a wide variety of indigenous and a few not-so-indigenous wildlife species, but for solitude-seeking humans as well.

Shining water and snowcapped peaks offer a note of accessible beauty amid the weird apocalyptic panorama that is Yellowstone. If you don't look too closely, that is. The lake's northern and western basins occupy a still-hot volcanic caldera. The molten rock below swells and subsides, leaving a "breathing" landscape: lake levels to the south surge noticeably, inundating a backcountry patrol dock, when the thermally active north end domes. At West Thumb, named for its position on the roughly palm-shaped perimeter, boiling pools seethe into cold lakewater. The Thumb itself was blasted out by a colossal explosion the likes of which could happen again with a mere magmatic shrug. Even below the surface, the lakefloor seethes with underwater geysers and fumaroles; placid Bridge Bay, for example, covers a "spire field" of dramatic submerged thermal cones. Considering the titanic geologic forces shaping the terrain, the lake wears its volcanism unobtrusively: a person standing at lakeside faces mostly wind and wave, the hallmark give-and-take of big water everywhere.

～

As it's our good fortune to live relatively close to Yellowstone, at least by Montana standards, we generally forego the midsummer tourist blitz in favor of quick overnighters during spring and fall shoulder seasons. Interpretive programs and visitor services are fewer at those times, but we prefer to explore the park on our own anyway, and the empty boardwalks and unencumbered views more than make up for the lack of official guidance.

That being said, it doesn't take much of an excuse for us to head to Yellowstone, tourist season or not. Our September venture to Storm Point may be more typical, but it shouldn't be too surprising to find us, the following July, contemplating a Bear in Area sign, illustrated with an ominous ursine silhouette, posted at the Pelican Creek trailhead. The rain-rippled cardboard warning doesn't look especially fresh, and the collection of cars in the pulloff lot, along with a family of safely returned hikers gathering themselves with much exuberant shouting, makes a midday bear encounter seem unlikely. Or so we decide.

The Pelican Creek Nature Trail loops along a marshy edge to Yellowstone Lake. At least it should, according to both trailbook and memory. As we zigzag through an unfamiliar maze of downed pines, the lake's soundscape, consisting mostly of the ever-present afternoon wind, is broken by chainsaws. Rounding a bend, we confront the grinding whine's source: a trail crew, burrowing a semipermanent right-of-way through deadfall in lieu of the original marshside boardwalk, which, the crew informs us, has been washed out. *Crew* might be a bit grandiose as a designation for two cheerful middle-aged Park Service employees. Just the night before, they say, a drenching, rafter-rattling thunderstorm poured another inch or two on the already saturated earth, which goes a long way toward explaining why, walking the beach a few minutes earlier, I had stepped ankle-deep into a sucking pit that wasn't there until I put my foot down.

Where the boardwalk used to be, eared grebes and cinnamon teal meander through grass recently reclaimed by the lake. Some of the grebes sit tight as we approach; perhaps they've built nests in the flooded vegetation that had been meadowland before. On a big lake, constant adaptation is the rule, and Yellowstone is especially susceptible to climatic extremes. Even as the lake claims more ground, the burned slopes in the background attest to past droughts.

~

Checking in at the Lake Lodge desk, we're somewhat surprised, in light of the roiling whitecaps we encountered at Pelican Creek, to find our *Lake Queen II* sunset cruise still on. Yellowstone concessionaires have to get what they can from a short season; it would take more than a mere gale to keep the *Queen* in port. With some trepidation we embark on the short drive from Lake to Bridge Bay marina. In sharp contrast to the still-tossing open lake, the piney harbor is deceptively calm, the *Queen* waiting patiently at its slip with hardly a knock.

My maternal grandfather built his own sailboats, but by the time I was born, his adventures—he once suffered a heart attack on a solo sail, rescued only because my teenage uncle fortuitously noticed his erratically drifting craft—had ossified as family legends. Most of my nautical experience beyond rowboats and canoes has, alas, been as a paid passenger on commercial ferries and tourboats. It seems, however, that my early exposure to a water horizon left me eager to prowl about a deck. At least I'm not very susceptible to seasickness. As it turns out, deck prowling on our Yellowstone Lake cruise is proscribed, the passengers confined to a closed cabin, no doubt in deference to the lake's combination of high winds and midsummer fifty-degree water temperatures.

Its gray metallic hull suggesting a military PT boat, the *Lake Queen II* seems sturdy enough, though Captain Jim's safety briefing, including how to fasten your life jacket so that it can be used to lift you from the water when necessary and how to get help should both crew members become incapacitated, is anything but reassuring. It's enough to make one wonder what became of the *Lake Queen I.* A worried child sitting behind me asks her mother, "Do we really have to go in the water?" Fortunately, Captain Jim will be manning the helm, leaving the narration to his colleague, Captain Lindsay, whose lot it will be to shout over the clank and mutter of the boat and the inevitable private conversations among family members and new acquaintances. In high summer, Yellowstone visitors come from all over the world, and our cosmopolitan cabinmates include families from Israel and the Pacific Rim, as well as travelers from elsewhere in the States.

This voyage being an official tour offered under the auspices of Xanterra concessions, a good half of our time on the water is spent coasting beside the Lake developments. Dazzled by the colonial structure's grand sunroom, often spiced by the music of a piano or even a string quartet, Fodor's considers the Lake Yellowstone Hotel's ambience "more Kennebunkport than western." The hotel predates Yellowstone's other still-standing hostelries; a decade or so after the ancestral building's 1891 opening, the simple, elegant edifice we see today was crafted by famed architect Robert Reamer as a "plain Jane" alternative to his rustically ornate Old Faithful Inn. So says Captain Lindsay as the *Queen* wallows against the wind. She tells us that the Lake Village general store features a vintage chandelier suspended from an "unsupported ceiling"—sure enough, we'll feel obliged to drop by and see this vaguely Scandinavian fixture after the cruise. Further along, past the original ranger station, is Lake Lodge, Reamer's 1926 alternative for guests of modest means. Our base is a "Pioneer Cabin" behind the Lodge— no-frills, but graced with the obligatory Xanterra bear and leaf soap bars and a full complement of visitors' guides and brochures. One particularly inexplicable item of tourism propaganda I happened upon while lazing in the cabin before our cruise extols the lake with an odd TV-matchmaker-show personification: "If Yellowstone Lake were a person, she'd be fun and yet demanding, mysterious and yet revealing, shallow and yet deep, beautiful and yet unsightly, serene and yet tumultuous."

With a parting nod to the Fishing Bridge RV camp, we turn from shore and face into the distances of Yellowstone Lake. The "shallow" and "unsightly" are beyond me, but the "beautiful" and "tumultuous" have never been clearer. The only vessel risking a chop that would merit small-craft warnings on Lake Ontario, the *Queen* gamely breasts the heavy swells, our progress accompanied briefly by the occasional storm-petreling swallow or quick purposeful squad of goldeneyes. Far to the south, the lake's wilderness arms beckon, but our destination is Stevenson Island, the closest to Bridge Bay of a handful of isles scattered across the 132-square-mile surface. Stevenson is rumored to host a pair of bald eagles, and, Captain Lindsay tells us, a few winters back two bison crossed the ice, one staying on for a couple of years. Both captains—in an egalitarian flouting of maritime convention, the entire crew consists of captains—point out Dot Island, where E. C. Waters, an ambitious, egotistical concessionaire (he was labeled "one of Yellowstone National Park's most obnoxious businessmen" by the *Billings Gazette*) once kept a makeshift zoo, its inhumane conditions, among other things, ultimately leading to the proprietor's ouster from the park. The import, plain enough if implied, is that this was how things were done before the enlightened age of Xanterra.

The passage across the open lake has been a noisy affair, Captain Lindsay maintaining a stream of informative banter above the din of crying babies, customers chatting in various languages, and the alarming groans of the steely craft galloping against the unyielding lake. Now, the *Queen* manages a stuttering hover in the somewhat calmer lee of the island, hard by the ribs of the 125-foot-long steamship *E. C. Waters*, named by the ubiquitous entrepreneur for none other than himself. Shortly after its 1905 debut the ship was abandoned—the ersatz skipper had neglected to procure an operating license. Its usable parts long since salvaged, the pitched hulk subsides, reduced in high seas to a reef of angled spikes, though Captain Lindsay assures us that on calmer days the steamer's frame is more obviously still intact.

In the long summer twilight, the *Queen* chugs homeward. The surface smooths to a mild churn at the entrance to Bridge Bay despite the thermal turmoil below, and the jostled passengers also settle a bit, allowing Captain Lindsay to stop shouting and speak in something like a normal voice. Her subject now is lake trout, some forty thousand of which have already been lifted from the water in gillnets this season by elite "troutslayer SWAT teams." First reported in Yellowstone Lake around 1990, lakers, or mackinaws, have a well-deserved reputation as destroyers of smaller salmonids. Since the lakers took hold, Yellowstone Lake cutthroat trout runs—only recently and painstakingly restored after decades of overfishing—have been reduced to a trickle. The loss has serious ecological implications. Spawning cutthroats in the creeks and rivers around Yellowstone Lake provide a key early summer food source for a variety of animals including eagles, ospreys, pelicans, otters, and bears. Lakers spawn in deep water, making them practically inaccessible to land-, sky-, or surface-bound piscavores. Resourceful and opportunistic, bears in search of replacement protein may find new menu items around campgrounds and lodges, a potentially dangerous situation for both bruins and humans.

2

When Yellowstone National Park was established, the lake apparently hosted only two fish species, longnose dace and cutthroat trout. The Yellowstone River above the lake is basically self-contained, and any potential migrants from below would have been checked by the Grand Canyon's powerful waterfalls. Park tourism, however, brought a smattering of piscine newcomers. Small fish—redside shiners, lake chubs, and longnose suckers—may have been dumped by anglers disposing of leftover bait, or perhaps in unsanctioned attempts to increase forage for larger gamefish.

A 2005 chemical study traces the lake trout to nearby Lewis Lake; in the absence of a connecting waterway—Lewis Lake drains to the Snake and the Pacific—no one knows for sure how they got to Yellowstone Lake.

One of the more fanciful theories has airborne firefighters scooping them into huge suspended buckets, inadvertently sloshing them overboard into Yellowstone Lake en route to a wildland fire. It's more tempting to believe that, after a weekend spent circling a pail, the lakers were set free by a young angler's parent: a fish is a fish, after all, and belongs in the water. It would be a relief to chalk up the introduction to simple ignorance, kindness to the captives even, rather than malevolence or greed. As fishery managers have found, however, it isn't easy to establish self-sustaining populations of mackinaws. Yellowstone biologists believe that the rapidity and scope of the lakers' invasion points to a sophisticated program of repeated "ecosabotage," beginning in the 1980s and extending to as late as 1996. Former park supervisor Bob Barbee characterizes this attack on the lake's ecological integrity as "an appalling act of environmental vandalism." So far, no one has been able to cash in on the standing $10,000 reward for information leading to the clandestine ichthyologists' apprehension, but it's likely that the shadowy introduction was intended to "improve on" the limited number of species available to Yellowstone Lake anglers.

Fiddling with the supply and variety of game species is a long-established hook-and-bullet tradition. Some introductions fail outright—thankfully, neither rainbow trout nor Atlantic salmon caught on in Yellowstone Lake. Occasionally, hatchery newcomers find an honored, apparently harmless, place in the local fauna. Who would want to eliminate Yellowstone Park's backcountry-lake enclaves of arctic grayling, which have outlasted extirpated stream populations of an uncommon beauty living at the edge of its natural range? And "fishery-enhancement" projects can boast some undeniable economic successes. In Montana east of Yellowstone, the blue-ribbon trout mill below the Bighorn Canyon dams is almost entirely artificial, the result of adding nonnative brown and rainbow trout to a transformed river. The US Fish and Wildlife Service claims that "the non-native fishery has become a boon not just for anglers but for each [Mountain-Prairie Region] state. Through a web of commerce connected to fishing-related expenditures, an estimated $100 million is generated annually." In the Great Lakes, imported Pacific salmon have revitalized a moribund sport fishing industry. Calculating the monetary value of vast, diverse international Great Lakes fisheries involves complicated multivariable analysis, but a SUNY–Brockport Center for Applied Aquatic Sciences and Aquaculture report estimates that anglers on New York's "North Coast," where exotic salmon, steelhead, and brown trout are among the most sought-after species, contributed $170 million to local communities in 1996 alone.

Such profits often come at a high price, as misguided managerial tinkering can distort established ecological relationships to the point of irrevocably altering entire aquatic ecosystems. Cutthroats have been supplanted by lakers, introduced eastern brook trout, Pacific rainbows, and Old World browns in many western waters, and, where cutthroats themselves have been stocked, genetically distinct strains have sometimes been jumbled promiscuously. Small unharvestable inhabitants of "barren" lakes—in practice lakes without native gamefish—have seldom, at least until recently, blipped the radar screens of fisheries biologists. Even where the fish-and-game departments have exercised restraint, wildcatters have not. A few years before the mackinaw invasion, park biologists successfully curtailed a freelance brook trout introduction in a Yellowstone Lake tributary.

Once established, intruders that make their way into large water bodies can be just about impossible to dislodge. In the Great Lakes, carp, zebra mussels, and round gobies join sea lampreys in an apparently permanent and ever-growing menagerie of exotic undesirables. In Yellowstone Park, whirling disease—a trout disorder associated with "fishing ranches"—and New Zealand mud snails have already arrived, with quagga mussels likely somewhere nearby, maybe clinging to the hull of a cabin cruiser anchored at Bridge Bay marina.

∼

As a child of the Great Lakes, I find it hard to picture lake trout in such a rogue's gallery. Lakers are spectacular fish; members of the char branch of the salmonid family, they are sleek, speckled, and—occasionally approaching one hundred pounds—much larger than the biggest rainbow or brown. Restricted in their native range to cold oligotrophic lakes of North America, the outsize trout became a prize trophy fish in Canada and the northern United States following settlement. Tasty like most of their family, lakers were also popular market fare in the Great Lakes, where their numbers warranted the effort. For my generation, however, Great Lakes mackinaws were little more than legends of a more bountiful past when the water was cleaner, the fishermen fewer, and sea lampreys probably limited to occasional individuals enterprising enough to work their way up the

Saint Lawrence to Lake Ontario. Once the Great Lakes had been flanked by commercial waterways, these opportunistic parasites—their jawless sucker mouths are adapted to extract blood and other fluids from unlucky fish—found the murky waters of the New York State Erie Canal system an easy conduit not only to Lake Ontario but, by way of the Welland Canal, to a whole new inland fishery beyond Niagara Falls. The species prospered, and lampreys were soon breeding throughout the Great Lakes basin. Among their favorite targets were lake trout. Mackinaws, already pressed by overharvesting and pollution—they seem especially susceptible to dioxin—mostly vanished by the 1930s.

Lampreys have been advanced as a possible, if last-ditch, weapon against those same trout introduced into Yellowstone Lake. If, the proposal goes, sterilized lampreys were poured into the West Thumb—headquarters for the trout entrada—would they not prey on and eventually eradicate the lakers? It may sound good at first, but further reflection reveals some serious questions about this potential magic bullet. Even with widespread lamprey spawning and new oceanic recruits, and in waters made inhospitable to lakers by high dioxin levels, some Great Lakes mackinaws survived the assault, so the chances of success under controlled conditions at Yellowstone are dubious at best. And what if a few unsterilized lampreys managed to slip into Yellowstone Lake in the process? Or if the lampreys found the remaining cutthroats to their liking? Finally, there's the uninviting prospect of interfering with lake ecology in such a heavy-handed way. Would the original balance ever be restored, or would such wholesale intervention leave the lake on a kind of managerial life-support? Of course, one might argue that that's exactly the case now. Employing, in addition to some fifteen miles of nets, a sophisticated array of video cameras, LIDAR mapping equipment, electrofishing gear, and transponder-tagged "Judas fish" to pinpoint spawning areas, troutslayers have removed over a million invasive fish thus far.

The jury's still out on whether these actions are having any significant impact. Useful information has been gathered concerning lake trout behavior and concentration patterns. The Greater Yellowstone Science Learning Center cautiously interprets as good news recent declines in the apparent rate of lake trout population growth, and cutthroat numbers show some improvement over the past few years. But there are still hundreds of thousands of mackinaws in Yellowstone Lake. Unless a durable equilibrium is struck between native prey and nonnative predator, the battle will continue indefinitely, with the best that the slayers—and the forty-two species Captain Lindsay says depend on the cutthroats—can hope for is to tread water against impending disaster: the functional extinction of what was once the world's largest lake-dwelling cutthroat population.

The troutslayers' task seems the very definition of a labor of Sisyphus. Many exotics prove uncontainable, eventually becoming so thoroughly established that few people see them as newcomers, much less connect their presence with the disappearance of competing natives. The tide has been turned, however, in a few notable cases. The Great Lakes Fishery Commission reports that, as the result of a concentrated research program, a variety of control methods ranging from highly specific chemical "lampricides" to barriers and sterile male releases have reduced Great Lakes sea lamprey populations by 90 percent. As with Yellowstone's lakers, it's probably impossible to completely eliminate these exotics, but lamprey predation is no longer considered a significant impediment to the reestablishment of lake trout in the Great Lakes.

Great Lakes mackinaws still face formidable obstacles, water quality foremost among them. Though natural spawning has occurred, the population remains dependent on hatchery inputs and managerial interventions, including a repatriation that Moses himself might be proud of. After surveying Yellowstone Park waters at the end of the nineteenth century, ichthyologist David Starr Jordan advanced the introduction of nonnative trout as a remedy for what he lamented as the park's deficient angling resources. Jordan's advice struck a can-do progressive chord among Yellowstone's early managers, and, in 1889, a grueling rail and pack mule journey brought the park's first mackinaws, forebears of the Yellowstone Lake invaders, from Lake Michigan. One hundred years later—amid rumors that a new predator was threatening Yellowstone's cutthroats—Great Lakes WATER Institute biologists dipped nets into Lewis Lake. Chosen for seedstock as the best genetic approximation of Lake Michigan's indigenous lakers, representative descendants of Jordan's hardy transplants, according to the institute's Casey Twanow, "found their way back to their ancestral home."

3

If someone had approached me in 1991 with a plan to string Yellowstone Lake's depths with gillnets, there's no question that I would have recoiled against such a fundamentally "unnatural," downright sacrilegious, imposition. After all, as Aldo Leopold saw it, wilderness provides an ecological template free from human tinkering, a robust network of interactions that changes over time, yes, but that maintains a level of stability we might as well call health. Or, to apply Wallace Stegner's phrase, a "geography of hope." And all we have to do is just leave it alone, right?

Contemporary environmental conundrums such as invasive exotics may require hands-on management way beyond the comfort level of an unrepentant wilderness-loving baby boomer like myself. Such issues blur distinctions between disruptive interference and necessary preservation, and tend to obscure the predictable consequences of any managerial action or inaction. Nonnative organisms sometimes become insinuated into local food chains, augmenting or replacing native species as fare for desired or endangered predators. Long-established Great Lakes invaders, alewives now constitute a major food resource for both exotic and native salmonids. These abundant forage fish, however, represent a boon with a barb, a thiamine-inhibiting enzyme that impacts the predators' reproduction. Fortunately, no such complicated ecological tradeoffs are in play at Yellowstone Lake, at least at this stage in the laker entrada. We know what the lake's ecosystem "should" be, and we know what has to be accomplished to "keep it as it was."

The twenty-first century is fated to be an age of planetary environmental disruptions. Acknowledging human influence on such a scale will require us to sacrifice, or at least modify, our ultimately illusory notion of human separateness in favor of a more integrated awareness that we are an inextricable part of Earth's ecological systems. Despite the good intentions embodied in the 1964 Wilderness Act, there's really no place "where man himself is a visitor who does not remain." If we want wild places like Yellowstone to stay the way they are—or were—the need for wildness will have to remain in our individual and collective hearts and minds, and not just during summer vacations. These days, it seems that environmental groups are always urging us to "save" something—the redwoods, the polar bears, even the planet itself. While assuming the redeemer's mantle reflects a certain glib hubris that, unchecked, could ultimately cause more harm than good, the urgency of these campaigns also marks acceptance that responsibility as planetary stewards is, and will continue to be, thrust upon us and our descendants, willing and able or not.

Yellowstone answers to a special calling. From its 1872 designation as the world's first national park to the daunting challenges—exotics, creeping edge development, climate change—it faces today, the park has served as a reservoir of physical and spiritual well-being and as a barometer measuring the connection between planetary health and cultural responsibility. Yellowstone hasn't failed us, and, by and large, we haven't failed Yellowstone either, at least not yet. In these destructive times, that's saying something. If we can "save Yellowstone," or keep saving it, then maybe there's a chance we can avoid ruining the rest of the planet.

~

I've been exploring Yellowstone for long enough that I consider myself something of a native, but when it comes right down to it I'm really part of the most ubiquitous intrusion of all, the juggernaut of human tourism. In midsummer, even the weekday roads are clogged with the clutter of contemporary humanity. Just swinging through a roadside pulloff draws a crowd, hopeful for a bear, a wolf. A Hayden Valley buffalo jam might back up half a mile on either side, and a moose in a roadside pond will find herself performing for an audience sprawled across both traffic lanes, cameras waving from every window.

The annual tourist migration brings undeniable inconvenience. Concessionaires recommend making dinner reservations weeks or months in advance, and taking in the more famous vistas—Old Faithful, the Lower Falls—involves a bit of jockeying and concomitant irritation. July and August fill the hotels and parking lots and, I suppose, keep Xanterra, and, for that matter, the Park Service, in business. On the bustling walkways at Old Faithful, Lake, Canyon, or Mammoth Hot Springs, it isn't always easy to remember that some 97 percent of Yellowstone is glorious undeveloped backcountry. Locals disparage the ignorant antics of "tourons" as a way to lay claim to a more intimate relationship with the park, and also, undoubtedly, from frustration rooted in tourism-dependent economies. Beneath the bravado, however, is the understanding that National Park crowds—despite recent assertions that the only safe visitor is one with a concealed handgun—are as a rule at least provisionally at peace with the world. A day or two in Yellowstone, even in July in the developed areas, is a recentering, a reminder that life, troubled times and all, can be pretty good.

Emergent where human culture fosters awareness of our planetary context, that good-life atmosphere permeates Lake Village the morning after our cruise. On Lake Lodge's spacious porch, a young man in sixties garb strums a guitar. In the Hotel lobby, church-camp congregants huddled before a window framing Mount Sheridan's glistening snowscape earnestly discuss a passage from the gospel of Saint John. Other, less devout guests doze over novels, settling a hearty Hotel breakfast, as I am, in preparation for a full day exploring the roads and trails. Perhaps a few will board the *Lake Queen II* for a sunset cruise this evening. All alike bask in Yellowstone Lake's generous ambience.

Poet and environmental visionary Gary Snyder once said that the descendants of European explorers "haven't discovered North America yet. People live on it without knowing what it is or where they are. They live on it literally like invaders." The history of our national parks is irremediably tangled with our manifest destiny march across America; in Yellowstone, native people—the Sheepeater Shoshones—were dispossessed for the clientele later associated with E. C. Waters. Some of us like to think we've moved beyond conquest and exploitation in our designs toward the continent, but today's park patrons share responsibility for the ongoing piecemeal chipping away at Greater Yellowstone's wilderness edges. That conceded, perhaps it's not too much to suggest that in places like Yellowstone, we invaders are finally discovering the continent, "what it is" and "where [we] are," and learning to quiet our worst impulses enough to hold something back from the depredations of our invading selves.

Yellowstone Lake's shoreline answers to most definitions of prime real estate; it's no coincidence that the lake is the site of both the park's oldest and newest commercial developments. The relatively recent scar of Grant Village, completed in 1984—it was supposed to replace the Fishing Bridge RV camp, which, thanks to pressure from Cody tourism interests and Wyoming politicians, remains open today—attests to the value of lakefront property. Fodor's credits the Lake Hotel with "priceless views of Lake Yellowstone at sunrise or sunset." *Priceless* is inherently ironic, suggesting that a price, a very high one, could be demanded for such property.

Remote and given to extremes, the lake gains a measure of protection from its formidable blend of submerged and surface turbulence. But preventing Yellowstone Lake from strangling in its own facilities has required vigilance on the part of the federal government, the advocacy of citizens' groups, and the enlightened forbearance of the populace as a whole. Aboard the *Lake Queen II*, Captain Lindsay's script hails the Park Service's noble intention to hold the line on "pillow count" at Yellowstone's concessions. Complacency, however, would be ill advised. Dressing up the good life with a beautiful lake prospect seems almost a part of human nature, the part that, when combined with the invader's treasure-quest mentality, turns wilderness shores into "priceless" waterfront property.

Old photographs show shoulder-to-shoulder anglers lining Fishing Bridge. The park's limited fish supply was not equal to the demand of so many hooks, so a hatchery at Lake Village dutifully provided trout for the taking. Yellowstone Lake cutthroats were scattered in previously fishless waters, both within Yellowstone and elsewhere. The hatchery closed in 1957, and the adoption of more meditative, less consumptive catch-and-release practices allowed cutthroat stocks to recover.

Running the LeHardy Rapids north of the lake in early summer, the cutthroats became something of a minor attraction for wildlife enthusiasts not armed with fly rods, a demographic whose attention is more typically occupied by bears and other megafauna. The fish's progress through the rapids, visible as a leap here, a tail there, was nearly impossible to photograph. Among other early-1990s troutwatchers, we put away cameras and, albeit vicariously, immersed ourselves in the single-minded urge to go upstream. At least that's how it felt.

While the Park Service and Yellowstone anglers take pride in infusing wildlife management science with Izaak Walton philosophy, there are, undoubtedly, representatives of Cody or West Yellowstone "interests," the ecosaboteurs themselves perhaps among them, rubbing their palms together at the prospect of a return to the ethos of less "consciousness-raised" days. Yellowstone's mackinaws tempt anglers with opportunities for pioneer-style excess. You can catch as many as you want, so long as you don't throw any, no matter how small, back in. If, in its enthusiasm to rid the lake of the exotic predators, the Park Service were to encourage the development of a lake trout sport fishery, the unintended result could be to entrench the lakers in the regional economy. It's not hard to imagine a mid-twenty-first-century Yellowstone Lake legendary as a destination for mackinaw enthusiasts, with outfitters lining the streets of gateway communities and a frenzy of hardy cabin cruisers chasing fishfinder blips back and forth across the West Thumb. Some future Yellowstone Mackinaw Fishfest could even offer an E. C. Waters Prize for the biggest laker, or, better yet, the fullest stringer. If such a piscine gold rush were to take hold, lake trout hatcheries would not be far behind.

∼

When Hurons and Iroquois vied for Lake Ontario's shores, landlocked Atlantic salmon—perhaps the world's greatest concentration of the species—and harbor seals joined lake trout in a fauna unique in the Great Lakes, Niagara Falls constituting an insurmountable barrier to the most athletic salmon. It's even possible that small native populations of upper lakes invaders such as sea lampreys and alewives may have been unobtrusively integrated into Ontario's self-contained ecosystem. It must have been quite a place. Today's Lake Ontario is a thoroughly humanized environment. The seals were killed off in the early 1800s, followed into oblivion by the salmon, which fell victim to their own popularity and to forest clearing and subsequent warming of their spawning streams. A network of natural waterways and canals brought packet boats crammed with nineteenth-century immigrants, my ancestors among them, from Europe, and, since the opening of the Saint Lawrence Seaway, giant tankers have plied the deep water, their bilges harboring more incipient entradas than two nations worth of fisheries biologists have been able to inflict. But amid the zebra mussels and Pacific cohos and chinooks, diminished numbers of lake trout, either natural remnants or, more likely, fish-and-wildlife replacements, hang on. And, in a 2009 breakthrough, the first handful of Lake Ontario Atlantic salmon fry in over a century were discovered in, fittingly, the Salmon River at the lake's east end. In truth, Lake Ontario is still quite a place, as I rediscover each time I amble out the Ontario Beach Park pier, which I make a point of doing whenever I find myself in Rochester.

On one summer pilgrimage to the lakefront, we—I was accompanied by Cara, Tom, and Tom's then-fiancé Shilo—stumbled unwittingly into the city's Harborfest. A scatter of rides—the roundup, the Ferris wheel—crowded a parking lot midway. Craft booths displayed T-shirts designed by local artisans. The adolescent redolence of hot dogs and elephant ears beckoned from behind counters decked out in festive Fourth-of-July-style bunting. Gulls raided neglected picnic tables. A regatta, or at least a handsome if coincidental constellation of colorful sailboats, glided toward port in slant late-day sun. Adding to the organ-grinder strains of Ontario Beach Park's Gustav Dentzel carousel, an exact contemporary of the *E. C. Waters* steamship, a community orchestra cranked out oompah versions of popular standards in the park's bandshell. In a hurdy-gurdy Americana kind of way, it was grand.

I honor Lake Ontario, and if it deserves better than the state its people— myself included—have brought it to, it's still one of my most important places. To a large extent, Lake Ontario defined nature for me when I was young. Hemmed in by neighbors' docks, my grandparents' small beach held the unfathomed journeys of winter goldeneyes and migrating shorebirds, and the equally mysterious smaller-scale pathways of crayfish and clams. Strange washed-up skeletons—lampreys, carp, the occasional bass or pike— hinted at lives transpiring where no human could be more than a fleeting guest. A snapshot somewhere in the family collection shows a luminous, overexposed, but unquestionably huge sturgeon against a black background, the straining arm holding the net allegedly belonging to my Uncle Fran.

The lake gave me a horizon, and a vast implied world beyond. I don't think I regret a single minute I've spent along those shores of cobble and shipped-in sand. With so much of contemporary American life contained within indoor "controlled environments," urban and suburban dwellers need the restorative generosity of that good life: a hot dog and a cold beer, a wheeling ring-billed gull, the corny honk of a summer carnival drifting across the sound of the waves.

~

But maybe, at least somewhere, just the waves.

After a sunset cruise on the *Lake Queen II*, if you drive a few miles from Bridge Bay marina to Gull Point, you can clamber down a stony bank and be pretty much alone with Yellowstone Lake. As the lingering afternoon bluster gives way at last to calm, bottomless night, water's rhythmic pulse emerges from beneath the flagging wind. If it's early summer, and you lean out far enough, you can almost feel the deep pull of river in a cutthroat trout's soul.

## A Good Bear

The summer after we moved to Wyoming, we decided Tom was old enough for his, and our, first foray into the Yellowstone backcountry. Studying the visitor center "dayhike sampler" list, we settled on the DeLacy Creek Trail to Shoshone Lake, the largest backcountry lake—not directly accessible by road—in the Lower 48, we were informed. DeLacy turned out to be just about right, an easy three miles along a grass-edged rivulet, the trail meandering between conifer fringe and wildflower meadow. In one opening, two moose browsed, alert, vaguely annoyed, perhaps, but not enough to worry about. On a damp, overcast late June day, it was good to be a moose.

We spent an hour or two at the gravelly shore: a bit of desultory fishing, mostly just being away from roads and the vacationing crowds ten miles away at Old Faithful.

That was some nineteen years ago. Married with a son of his own, Tom now lives far from Yellowstone. A September afternoon finds Cara and me embarking on the same trail to Shoshone Lake. As our path dips gently into lodgepoles, our first reaction is relief—these days, any return to a natural place, especially a Rocky Mountain conifer forest, after long absence is fraught with anxiety. Will the trees still be alive? Or will drought-driven wildfire or heat-loosed beetles have transformed the green woods into another skeletal ruin?

Despite a hint of smoke in the air from distant fires, DeLacy Creek is still a delight. No moose in the meadows today, but a coyote courses along, perhaps scouting for voles. The lakeshore is pretty much as we remember it, a serene oasis in the middle of the roiling park, the even more roiling world. It's not easy to abandon the quiet clear water, the ash-gray volcanic beach, the distant view of Mount Sheridan and the Red Mountains; by the time we begin our return trek, shadows are long, the trail deserted by other hikers.

I first see the grizzly in the middle of a meadow, maybe forty, fifty yards away, across DeLacy Creek, paralleling the trail. As far as I can tell, the bear hasn't picked up our scent, but I lose sight of him, screened by a strand of young lodgepoles. A few yards behind me on the trail, however, Cara knows that the bear has turned, its new trajectory likely to intersect our path in the pines ahead.

The books all counsel that when you come upon a grizzly while hiking you should withdraw, back from where you came, before the bear sees you. But what if you're a dayhiker on the return leg in fading daylight? Then what? We aren't prepared for camping, especially in the bear's neighborhood. For the time being, with nowhere to go either ahead or behind, we stay where we are.

I peek around a tree and there he is, standing on two legs, looking straight at us. As quietly as possible, Cara reminds me that I'm carrying bear spray, which I've only recently purchased and never had cause to unholster before. But by the time I fumble the spray into position—trying to avoid abrupt movements—it's over, the grizzly galloping, all muscle and effortless power, into the trees at the far side of the meadow, heading toward Shoshone Lake.

And that's our bear encounter.

Adrenaline carries us back to the trailhead, through the Old Faithful ranger station—official "bear sighting reports" are used to post trailhead warnings—and at least halfway to Gardiner, where we will stay the night. All's well that ends with a griz loping off. *A good bear, a smart bear,* we say. *It was all up to the bear.* But, if only because nothing occurred to us in those few suspended seconds, certainly no more than a minute or two all told, we managed not to do anything stupid either.

We are left with the golden meadow fading to shadow, the deep green of forest edge, the rich dark fur haloed by low sun; animal and destiny, roving, turning, standing, watching us, there, alive in an autumn moment we will always hold beside our younger selves, an eight-year-old boy jaunting along between us, the tip of his fishing pole bobbing in the damp air of June.

Confluence

And all flows past—
—Theodore Roethke

*There is a road that leads along a river, occasionally crossing bridges, or veering into hills only to return to the stream a few miles ahead. Each curve reveals a cabin, a farm, maybe a town.*

*Or the road continues into the hills, cresting ridges, twisting down wooded ravines, until it reaches another river, which merges with the first where the landscape flattens into a wide valley, clouds spread over meadows, fields. Here are herons poised in roadside marshes, turtles lined on silt-wedged logs, killdeer racing ahead in the shoulder dust, dragging their wings.*

*Or there isn't a road. No farm, no town. Only a rowboat. A Barker panorama unfolding on either side as you float, pulled from below, the bow edging one way and then the other. Sweepers drag against the current. Mired at a shoal, scratched by willow canes, you step into the thick brown drift, grip a gunwale, and shove—toward a larger river, and a larger river, and the sea.*

∼

The Genesee, my first river, was shallow but strong willed at Kishketuck, not many miles above a series of plunges into Letchworth gorge. Once Charlie had to shout awake a placid boatload riding the flow toward the "Grand Canyon of the East." But the current was manageable, if you paid attention and the water wasn't too high, like it must have been the day it gouged out half of Otis Smith Road south of Charlie's unassuming cabin— "Kishketuck House"—meaning in some unspecified indigenous language "house by the river."

From Fillmore, the dirt road named for Smith—no one seemed to know who he was—wound along the Genesee, then clambered over a hill and down past Charlie's brother's place and, later, the modern-day homestead where Don Outterson raised his varnished walls, threatened Thoreau-like to catch and eat the neighborhood woodchuck, and concocted his elaborate homebrews, snaking hops up power poles, mixing in mayapple for "mandrake mead." A wooded ridge—hickory, maple, beech—the haunt of grouse and whitetails, maybe a fisher or two, backed off the valley floor, rising steadily behind the makeshift settlement. Across the river, sycamores screened a cornfield. The bottomland farms were small enough to be unobtrusive, though once in a while the river's voice had to compete with the putt and clang of an unseen tractor or the whine of a distant chainsaw.

On moonlit winter nights, my friends and I hiked through snow to ridgetop railroad tracks, and sometimes on summer weekends we scrambled up tributary waterfalls or just sprawled like Ozark postcard hillbillies in front of the house, watching things happen on the river, an osprey drifting by, say, or swallows of various species zipping back and forth, or someone getting sunburned in a rowboat to the subliminal music of toads. On early summer evenings, mayflies whirled in eddies at the surface as the blue opposite the sunset deepened. Then nighthawks spun patterns here and there across the water, a silent net broken only by their occasional Tuvan buzz.

The same Genesee pawed into Rochester, my hometown, as a heavy trunk stream, passing squatters' cabins at the Ballantine Bridge, then slipping between abandoned mills and dropping through three falls into its second "bonus" gorge, emerging broader, deeper still at its mouth, dredged first for shipping, later for marina traffic. I would zigzag out the Charlotte pier from side to side—now the lake, now the river, finally the foghorn, where the river's journey ends, or where it joins the bigger, slower drift that tends northeast toward the Saint Lawrence.

～

When we spilled out of the tightly twisting valley of Témiscuata or the parallel cleft occupied by Lake Pohenegamook, home to a legendary monster, the Saint Lawrence lowland was sudden and spacious, filled with a diffuse northern light. At Rivière-du-loup, translated as "river of seals" or "the place where *The Wolf* was wrecked," the banks had already begun to break apart, the river taking on the nature of *la mer*. Scraps of sponge and kelp fringed coves, and barnacles marked the waterline of piers, but despite the marine life, the *Bas-Saint-Laurent* was an inland waterway; there was still another side, the mountainous horizon of the Saguenay.

Tom was in middle school when we lived for a few years in the "crown" of northernmost Maine. Each summer we crossed the New Brunswick Panhandle into *La Belle Province* and made our way to Rivière-du-loup for whale watching in Quebec's Saguenay–Saint Lawrence Marine Park. Nervously granting a wide berth to the hundred-car ferry with which it shared harbor space, the intimately small *Cavalier des mers* would bump across the waves toward the center of the estuary. Sometimes a parasitic jaeger terrorized the gulls accompanying the vessel, or a pair of razorbills buzzed across the bow headed for one of the rocky Pèlerins scattered over the river. It was a lucky cruise that brought a pod of belugas close to the boat. The ship's naturalist would explain, first in French and then, if necessary, in uncomfortable but efficient English, that whale-watchers were bound ethically and legally not to approach these "sea canaries," endangered by genetic isolation and chemical pollutants; of course, no human rules could prevent belugas from investigating us. As we drew closer to the Saguenay side, the dunes around Tadoussac gleamed white against indigo Laurentian cliffs. In the deep water the big whales rose—minkes and fins, once in a while, it was said, a blue. When fog lowered we heard them blow, close by, though we couldn't see the slow rise of their backs, the "footprint" gradually dissipating as if a pool of light oil had been dolloped on the surface.

Despite his susceptibility to seasickness, Tom sometimes went out twice, we adults taking turns ashore with Rita the dog. While Cara and Tom were whale-watching, I'd head downstream a short distance to Cacouna, sanctuary for a contemplative community at *le cénacle* and apparently for wildlife far from home—a southern snowy egret working a shallow channel, an even more surprising bevy of Old World whooper swans preening in the marshes. Sunsets from the headland at Cacouna were a red blare crossed by sharp silhouettes of eiders and gannets. Belugas sometimes hung near enough to shore that you could see the white spyhumps gradually blacken in the declining light. On an August evening when the Saint Lawrence was already slipping into autumn, I watched a minke surface several times, momentarily following Champlain's ships west into the continent.

Four hundred miles upstream, the Saint Lawrence is fresh but just as broad, the gouged channel of the Seaway weaving a path through islands— here Canada, there New York State. The archipelago is both spacious and enclosed, big river vistas tucked paradoxically between freshwater skerries, a rock and two trees enough to define an isle. Long before I ever saw Rivière-du-loup, my Rochester friend Dave owned a cottage, complete with Victorian gingerbread flourishes, at Thousand Islands Park. During the 1970s, Abbie Hoffman, on the lam from drug charges, found the islands an ideal out-of-the-way hideout where a stranger was just another tourist and countless waterways led to Canada. One of my friends swore he saw Hoffman, aka Barry Freed, nodding knowingly from a pier. It could be. The islands did harbor secrets. One summer night, spiders quivering in floodlit boathouse corners, a distant song grew into a skiff. When he tied up at the TIP dock, we asked the lone boatman about the tune, which he said was "something we sing around here," a distinct folk music of the islands.

Aside from solemn tankers and freighters going about their humorless business, most Thousand Islands boats were pleasure craft—old varnish-grained woodies, cabin cruisers. We used red fiberglass canoes, light but broad enough to float relatively stable in the big river, even when rushed by thrill-dispensing speedboats. It was such a canoe that carried me, with Dave and his brother-in-law, to Boldt Castle one October when the fall colors were so high the wooded islands seemed almost inaccessible to normal human sight. The castle was constructed as a Valentine's Day gift from hotel mogul George Boldt to his wife, Louise, whose sudden death had left the structure unfinished. Heartbroken, Boldt abandoned his summer palace to a tourist-trap future only marginally less tragic than its past, the family's tale of loss recited countless times each summer for paying customers, including, ironically, wedding parties. That October, the "attraction" closed for the season, we ate leftover chicken while a late phoebe claimed the parapets and the Saint Lawrence swept seaward everything that could no longer fit in the Great Lakes.

～

Our first September in Fort Kent, Maine, a winding hour south of Rivière-du-loup, we stayed in a faded yellow farmhouse a few miles out the Saint John River road from town. The place had the neglected pastoral appeal of old farmsteads, an effect augmented by picturesque ramshackle outbuildings filled with mysterious anachronistic tools. Tom soon discovered that the small swamp between the house and barn held frogs and salamanders. A flooded snag served as hunting station for the resident merlin. Some mornings, fresh moose tracks etched the adjacent potato field's crusty mud. Behind the barn, a deer path led up the valley flank through Acadian forest—spruce-fir with a generous helping of broad-leaf fall-color trees. From the ridgetop, old logging scars revealed the river bends, the narrow French-style farms laid out for both wood and water.

The road in front of the house bordered the Saint John; boulder-strewn, mercury-colored in the subdued glare, it reminded me of the steely Black River I'd often passed at Watertown—a kind of north country initiation en route from Rochester to the Thousand Islands. As at the Islands, across the water was Canada; the Saint John Valley, however, was enclosed, insular, devoid of broad prospects. There wasn't much walking room between the river and the sparse but formidable traffic of potato-laden farm vehicles and even more dangerous logging trucks. But moonlight on the river was worth clambering across the guardrail for. One night shortly after we arrived, a low aurora pulsed eerily over the New Brunswick side of the Valley. It wasn't hard to imagine wary Acadian explorers paddling birchbark canoes.

Those pioneers marked their landing with a Catholic cross in 1785, staking the Saint John Valley a foundation myth retold to this day in a harmonious, perhaps slowly fading French and English idiom by Bouchards and Pelletiers, Cyrs and Plourdes. Remnants of the exiled French Canadians of *Evangeline* fame, perhaps after stints in Louisiana or the Motherland itself, reclaimed their central New Brunswick farms, far downstream from the Valley, only to be displaced again by English-speaking settlers, especially Tories fleeing the American Revolution. Forced to relocate once more, the Acadians found refuge at last in the remote upper reaches of the Saint John beyond the Grand Falls. Some years ago, University of Ottawa scholar Beatrice Craig ruffled a lot of feathers by claiming, with research and documentation, that most of the French families in the Valley were descended not from Acadian war refugees but from more prosaic Québécois farmers in search of fresh soil. Though her articles, in both French and English, appeared in *The River Review/La revue rivière*, which I edited, and papers from her exhaustive twenty-year study of the Valley were housed in Fort

Kent's Acadian Archives, Craig's revisionism left Valley raconteurs wishing she'd kept her findings to herself.

The college (or university, as it called itself) at Fort Kent made do with a full-time faculty of about thirty disgruntled professors whose careers had stalled. Valley natives were friendly enough, but they knew us—the university transients—as "people from away" who would likely soon go somewhere else. The first time I met my department chair, he told me, "I love it here. Unfortunately, my wife hates it." They left for good a year or two later. It was a typical turn of events. The upper Saint John belonged to the Valley French, along with a handful of heirs to a nineteenth-century Scandinavian "immigrant colony," centered, appropriately, in towns called Stockholm and New Sweden, and a few tough souls who managed to insinuate themselves through marriage or just a determined willingness to stay on the place's own terms. Those terms assumed a shared history: Tom learned some French in middle school, and was even presented with a certificate testifying to his understanding of "his heritage" upon completing an Acadian culture program. Perhaps this is how it should be. It's rare today to find a true homeland with its population more-or-less intact, and the Saint John Valley guards what may be as indigenous a sense of belonging as descendants of Europeans on this continent can have. It's not an easy place to inhabit, though, unless you were born to snow and the grudging Valley light, the dingy towns, the threadbare fourth-growth woods, the ghosts of the dispossessed.

Straggling for a few blocks along the Saint John, downtown Fort Kent held off ice-out floods with a rock-armored levee. Weather and black flies permitting, I sometimes scrambled up a dirt path worn by use into the grassy townward slope for a workday lunch above the water. The view centered on a steel bridge linking the village and Clair, New Brunswick, across a boundary fixed in 1842 by a treaty tangential, at most, to the Valley's daily life. Beset by economic and technological pressures emanating "from away," the Valley's people held on to their upper river as a refuge far enough away itself, they hoped, to make an inconspicuous hideout where they could cherish the legend of their historical defeat because it made the river theirs. Take that, Beatrice Craig!

∼

Those years in Fort Kent weren't my first exposure to American Acadia. In 1982, having pretty much used up the life I'd been living, along with several Brockport friends I accepted a poster invitation to study creative writing at McNeese State University, amid the French cuisine (boudin sausage, as it turned out), exotic water birds, and jazz music of "Cajun Fun Country," Louisiana. What could be better? Besides, wasn't Lake Charles—"Straight down the Mississippi River / To the Gulf of Mexico"—Levon Helm's dream destination in "Up on Cripple Creek"? A handful of classes amid mostly empty library shelves in the suburbs of a gritty refinery town was not exactly what I had envisioned. My friends and I, as we soon discovered, had been recruited to bolster institutional support for the new MFA. Just look at all that national interest! International even: one of our Upstate entourage was billed as a Canadian because he had spent the previous year in the border town of Windsor, Ontario. Once the program was firmly entrenched, McNeese showed little interest in keeping us Yankees around, and we had all headed elsewhere by the next round of summer heat.

I didn't own a car that year, but sometimes I was able to escape for a while on a borrowed bicycle. From Bord-du-Lac Park, a downtown green with a few ragged palms and a framing view of the I-10 bridge, I'd gingerly make my way past a narrow industrial no-man's-land of mysterious warehouses and barbed wire fencetops. Town petered out pretty quickly to the north; the dirt road tracking the Calcasieu River was traveled mostly by fishermen en route to familiar spots shaded by cypress and Spanish moss, catfish holes spiced with toothy gars, bowfins, the occasional alligator. Cormorants flapped and grumbled in skeletal flooded trees. After a storm, I watched a small marine crab steering itself along the flow, farther inland than the tide I would have thought, purposefully sculling toward the Gulf of Mexico.

The bike I borrowed belonged to Cara, a Salt Lake City native who had fallen for one of those McNeese ads posted at the University of Utah. We met on the hot sidewalks between classes and a nondescript tract enjoying a brief prosperity as ad hoc housing for all those "national interest" MFA students. Late that fall, we drove a weekend rental car down the Creole Nature Trail, passing through an expanse of swaying, light-gathering cordgrass. Gulfbound, we followed the Calcasieu as it widened into Calcasieu Lake—Big Lake to locals—and spilled through Sabine National Wildlife

Refuge, a watery plain harboring spoonbills, snow geese, and one of the country's densest gator populations; I can still picture the first one I saw, effortlessly sweeping its powerful tail down a slough. Nutrias nosed like oversized muskrats in roadside canals. A spontaneous detour brought us sunset under the swirling seabirds of Rutherford Beach.

Lake Charles introduced me to life away from the Northeast, and the Calcasieu was my first "foreign" river. Until then, the Great Lakes Basin must have been the source of the however-large percentage of water that constituted most of my own particular installation of the human body. I suppose that my boarding the Greyhound in Rochester sparked a gradual exchange of internal water as well as a more obvious shift in where the raindrops on my roof were headed. I'd already spent a full day on the road, and wasn't thinking of under-the-skin geography, but I remember shifting awake as the bus crossed the Ohio River at dawn, replica paddlewheelers lined up at Louisville docks, in a new place. Like the river below the wheels, I had left my northern origin behind.

Past Louisville, the bus went on through Nashville, then Huntsville, Alabama, where regionally attuned riders assessed the season's cotton crop. White wading birds and Spanish moss showed up somewhere south of Birmingham; kudzu draped Tuscaloosa into a topiary town. I stretched my legs in Meridian, Mississippi, a name I knew from my father's World War II stories, the South nearly as exotic to him as later posts in Italy and Egypt. I spent that second Greyhound night in New Orleans, boarding one last time at dawn for the egret-dotted prairies of the Calcasieu.

∼

The honorific title "Source of the Everglades" is applied to places as far north as the SUMICA Reserve in Polk County, one hundred miles, give or take, above Lake Okeechobee and about an hour's drive from Lakeland, where we lived for the seven years I spent teaching at Florida Southern College. Convinced that the Saint John Valley would never really be our home, I had reluctantly turned down tenure at Fort Kent, another job search landing us across the Gulf of Mexico from Lake Charles's Cajun Fun Country, where Cara and I had met almost two decades before.

As a kindergartner, Tom had pored over the United States atlas, invariably settling on the map of Florida, which he'd examine, for some reason, with surprising intensity. The hold of the real place, however, didn't survive high school; after he left for Pasadena, Cara and I hiked mostly by ourselves. In summer, Gulf or Atlantic beaches were the only viable outdoor destinations; the dry season, Florida's winter, was time for the interior. Designated as open space or, officially, "Environmental Lands," places like SUMICA (an acronym derived from the name of an abandoned turpentine camp) offered sandy trails that led for many blessed lonely miles away from the booming sprawl in which most of our days were spent. Inland Florida was prickly country; palmettos hid karst bedrock known to break unwary ankles, and there were enough ticks and chiggers in the grass, coral snakes and diamondbacks holed up below the scrub, to keep the crowds at bay. We encountered few hikers.

Between Lakeland and SUMICA the landscape sometimes broke into surprising vistas: ranches, soaked or parched in season, where sandhill cranes and egrets roamed with scrawny sharp-horned cattle; cabbage palm groves; sudden rivers, all under the ubiquitous tilt of vultures in the unforgiving sun. SUMICA occupied a flat expanse of sandy scrub, staggerbush tangles, and dense palmetto flats, relieved by live oak shade. Spanish moss wisped in any hint of breeze at an oak hammock's edge. Under the canopy a humid stillness might reveal a seep or muffled slough. That splash could be a turtle or a small gator, and in the deeper pools gars and mudfish—bowfins—lurked. The vegetation-stained "black water" seemed not to move at all, but a current was revealed by tiny clumps of moss and pollen working their way deliberately around fallen branches, then hanging in a leafmat, wedged tightly enough, perhaps, to live as land until the next storm shook them back into the incipient southward current.

The SUMICA trail skirted the trees edging Walk-in-Water Lake; if we wanted to get closer and weren't afraid of muddy shoes, we could slog our way down spongy wild hog scars to the lake, which drains into a network of trickles and sloughs—in Louisiana they'd be called bayous—that feed the Kissimmee River, which in turn spills through Lake Okeechobee into the glades proper. At least that's what's supposed to happen. The Kissimmee was "straightened" in the 1960s for flood control, a mistake, it turns out, leaving wetlands shriveled and Florida's biggest lake so badly polluted that the channelization is currently being at least partially reversed.

Northeast of SUMICA, where the young Kissimmee River sprawls through a series of shallow depressions, another sandy trail led toward Lake Kissimmee past spoil banks left by bulldozers, perhaps enlisted in that ambitious restoration. Armadillos and gopher tortoises rooted in palmettos and tiny Florida raccoons pried at oak roots. The sky was filled with large primordial birds. In addition to the ever-present vultures and herons, caracaras pestered petulant bald eagles, which in turn pestered equally petulant ospreys. Devoid of a stable shoreline, Lake Kissimmee marked the trail's end with an indistinct rack line composed mostly of the round greenish shells of apple snails. The distant airboat whine and hovering snail kites testified to the lake's Everglades connection, more direct and obvious than SUMICA's subtle drift.

A Christmas break camping trip found Cara, Tom, and me traversing the Everglades Park road over imperceptible single-digit "passes." The road dropped no more than a few feet between our tentsite at Long Pine Key and land's end at Flamingo, but that was enough to spill the river of grass into mangrove forest. At West Lake, really a tidal inlet, the lunar pulse filtered through a maze of sinuous branches, bowed prop roots, and the bizarre tree-snorkels called pneumatophores. Neither land nor sea, the mangrove forest confronted human eyes with bewildering Escher intricacy, but the seaforest made a familiar homeworld for small blackish climbing crabs, skulking cuckoos, fry of snook and drum, rare American crocodiles.

Broken by Calusa shell mounds, boat landings, and tropical-paradise mansions, the mangrove fringe guards the coast from the Everglades north to Tampa Bay. A determined walker at the right tide could pick through that barrier, all warm muck and oyster bed, to rootbound hollows where yellow-crowned night herons stalked their secret way. We'd come across openings, hidden from land, but not from the tidal channels; caution signs warned boaters to slow down: manatees, their ears untuned to outboard buzz, grazed in the brackish lagoons. Bull sharks also plied those waterways, occasionally weaving past the mangroves into upscale tracts, an unsubtle reminder that the trim docks and oleander hedges were only provisionally borrowed from the rising sea.

～

In 1986, a few years after leaving Lake Charles, I returned to graduate school, taking up the study of American Literature at Purdue University's

West Lafayette campus. I thought I'd benefit from a systematic exposure to my country's writers, and, with Tom a preschooler, we needed a more settled family life than anything portended by the vagabond years since that morning my bus crossed the Ohio River bridge at Louisville. So we found ourselves along the "Banks of the Wabash," celebrated in Indiana's official state song.

Slow but powerful, deep and silty, the Wabash pours like glycerin through the plains of Tippecanoe County. A fair portion of that silt consists of hyperfertilized topsoil either blowing or running into the water from "fencerow to fencerow" corn and soybean fields. Still, it's not easy to tell exactly what the river, sprawling across the deep soils of the continental interior, would have looked like, say, to Tecumseh; it stands to reason that it should be a bit on the brown side.

The Wabash Heritage Trail began at the Tippecanoe Battlefield, where the absent Tecumseh's confederacy had been broken up by William Henry Harrison's territorial militia in 1811. Rockhopping several times across the reclusive trickle of Burnett's Creek, I burrowed through beeches and hickories until the path crossed an old iron bridge, reduced to foot traffic, over the Wabash. From there, the trail continued downstream toward Lafayette, making the whole route from Battle Ground to my usual endpoint in sight of the Sagamore Parkway bridge about six miles one way. I rarely saw anyone walking the trail, despite the popularity of the battlefield museum and nature center, and the boat ramp, mostly for fishermen, beside the footbridge.

The fields bordering the Wabash were obscured from view by a dense if narrow screen of underbrush, willows, river birches, and larger hardwoods. Where Heron Island divided the flow, all that was not the river disappeared. Green herons tightroped out undermined snags, leaning with circus grace to stab at minnows. Orange pentecostal flames when coaxed into the open by sun-loving bugs, prothonotary warblers more often remained hidden, their loud, simple phrases ringing from leafshadow. The steady current molded around logs, trailed from drooping branches. Mud sucked at my shoes when I had to step offtrail around sycamore roots.

For some reason, I always walked the Heritage Trail in midsummer, and usually by myself. Typically, I'd get a not-quite-early-enough start; Indiana summers are a misery of humidity, and even the hardiest catfish-seeker knew to abandon the river before I'd begun retracing my steps back toward Battle Ground, my shirt soaked against my back. Despite the heat, I walked purposefully through the volatile midwestern afternoon, watching for signs that the haze had begun to congeal into cooling but dangerous thundershowers. Occasionally, those afternoon storms scudded against a meteorological boundary, the sky taking on an ominous green tinge.

That warning color holds the alchemy of continental winds and Gulf moisture colliding in the American interior, the most tornado-prone area on Earth. Purdue's Married Student Housing fended off twisters with siren banks and cell-block construction, relatively safe if not exactly welcoming for students from all over the world. Each warm-weather Saturday without a home football game, lunch was interrupted by the startling blast of the tornado horns being tested. Coming home late one evening, we found an international assemblage of neighbors in our storm-shelter stairwell; unbeknownst to us, the sirens had announced a menacing funnel a short time before. In Indiana, even a tornado watch is serious, if routine, business; every so often a shed, a farm, or an entire village is shattered to debris strewn across fields or swirled down a swollen river.

On a recent visit to Purdue—my first since defending my dissertation—Cara and I found the Wabash Heritage Trail in the process of being extended downriver through Lafayette to Fort Ouiatenon, a county park commemorating a nearby eighteenth-century French trading post. Each November, at the Feast of the Hunter's Moon, more-or-less authentic period wall tents sprawl around the fort's replica blockhouse, and costumed "voyageurs" race canoes, sell T-shirts and folk crafts, and pose for photos; in a 1980s snapshot, my toddler son leans somewhat apprehensively away from a grizzled ersatz veteran of the fur trade. When the trappers are elsewhere, making the rounds of folk festivals and historic reenactments, Fort Ouiatenon is a quiet place to watch the moon rise: great blue herons etched on gravel bars, horned owls calling from the dusky woods.

～

Compared to the Wabash, the Shoshone isn't much of a river, even at rare times when it's running full, but without it there would be no Powell, Wyoming; no Northwest College, where, fresh from Purdue, I landed my first teaching job; no Avenue B, where we lived; and no Westside Elementary, where Tom spent his grade school years. The Bighorn Basin is a dry, rough country of badlands and greasewood flats, through which the Shoshone, a Bighorn tributary, runs as a minor miracle, bringing sparse but dependable supplies of fresh Absaroka Mountain snowmelt across the rainshadow desert. Enough water, even, for a hardscrabble agriculture of beans, barley, and sugar beets; determined or resigned faces of "sucker wagon" sodbusters—perhaps my students' forebears—gazed in sepia from the walls of libraries and pioneer museums. Whatever big cottonwoods had rooted themselves along the Shoshone's dust and gumbo banks had been fed to frontier stoves or hammered into homesteads, leaving willow scraggles and a smattering of exotics—Russian olive, tamarisk, tumbleweed—added to the mix so long ago they seemed as naturalized as cowpies, shell casings, the occasional rusted something that used to be a washing machine or television.

No one made much use of the gravel parking lot and riverside path at the southern edge of Powell, where the Shoshone had carved a shallow gorge, complete with a small side waterfall, into friable shale and gluey bentonite. We knew the river more from where it curved below the highway outside Cody, and from west of the basin where the Shoshone's forks—North and South—poured from the Absarokas; the North Fork road led from Cody to Yellowstone, the young river slipping modestly away at the park's east entrance like a guide whose work was done. Most Powellites seemed to ignore their own stretch of waterfront, its obscurity amplified for Northwest College faculty swept by the vagaries of the "national search" into a forgotten pocket of a world-famous region. But even we newcomers knew that Shoshone water, fed into irrigation ditches by the Willwood Diversion Dam, had transformed the cold desert into the "Powell Valley," a bleak stand-in for the kind of small self-sufficient agrarian community envisioned by namesake Major John Wesley Powell, an oasis of sorts between the brittle escarpment of Polecat Bench and the equally crumbly badlands of the McCullough Peaks. From the bench, an old river terrace rising about a thousand feet above the beetfields north of town, the irrigation "project" was an almost garish patch of summer green amid a landscape of seared tans, grays, and reds. Winter brought a snowcrusted midwestern brown; when inversion fog closed off the mountains, Powell could have been a farm supply town in Indiana.

Rita was a puppy then, and Tom was young enough that a short walk in the McCullough badlands or on Polecat Bench was just about right for a winter day. Despite sweeping views of distant mountains, the bench was close-to-the-ground country, etched with dry gullies perfect for exploring with a small child and a young dog. Meager snow sifted against cracks in jagged upturned shale, crystal white contrasting with the gift of bright orange lichen. Clumped under brush, comma-shaped sage grouse droppings were easier found than the big canny birds themselves. Stone circles marked centuries of Indian camps, probably, but not necessarily, Crow. Bone fragments were everywhere. Still-older petrified wood chips told tales of wetter times. The Bighorn Basin held fossil treasures: we collected our share of ancient oyster shells, dinosaur gizzard stones, a tiny mammalian leg joint smoothed by floods and blowing sand. But wind and BB snow would drive us home before long, to the sparse shelter of the Shoshone River flats.

Stashed in a coffee can, our Bighorn Basin fossil collection accompanied us to Maine, then Florida. A few of the most unusual, like that leg joint, are still with us in Montana, not too far from where they started—their cross-country journeying, like their time spent as living beings, an ephemeral interlude in an eons-long history of stone.

~

One hundred miles north of Powell and more than a decade later, abutments of the low bridge that escorts South Billings Boulevard across the Yellowstone River carry generations of suggestive but corny high school graffiti—"butter my muffin"—splattered against chipped concrete. The trail from Riverfront Park to Norm Schoenthal's Island ducks under the bridge, emerging into plains cottonwoods starkly etched against gray winter sky.

Goldeneyes scull along ice edges, then take off upstream to ride again down to island bars where bunches of Canadas and a few mergansers laze. A young bald eagle makes a dark splotch in the leafless cottonwoods. Where the path hooks along the stray braid of river that defines Norm's Island, a goldeneye, perhaps tired of playing the river, floats serenely in an ice-free bend. The most obvious feature here is a cacophony of crows, some gathered in the trees, others huddled in enclaves among the Canadas, which are twice as big and equally assertive as the corvids.

Norm's Island is part of a network of county and city parks, popular recreation spots and flood basins during high runoff. The distant Beartooths loom on clear days, but the deciduous woods and lush beaver troughs give the river bottomland a vaguely midcontinental feel, with small herds of white-tailed deer, the exuberant flash of redstarts, the relentless summer buzz of cicadas. One cloudy spring day a few sandhill cranes joined the gulls and geese on a gravel bar. It could have been Nebraska. But what it really is is River, a country of its own wedged between prairie, mountain, and badland, a place of tall trees shielding mysterious cabins on tenuous islands, fugitive holdfasts drawn inevitably downstream, only marginally less provisional than those shacks below the Ballantine Bridge in Rochester.

Catching a quick respite in a Billings city park, it's easy to forget that the Yellowstone is the last undammed major river in the Lower 48. *Undammed* is a relative term, with irrigation canals borrowing water for fields and towns strung along the valley—one of those ditches slinks through my neighborhood, fringed with a tangle of summer green like a misplaced bayou; empty and forlorn in winter, a few mallards waiting patiently in persistent mud. Downstream from Billings, diversion structures stymie migrating pallid sturgeons, but their effect on the overall flow is limited, and the Yellowstone is spared the evaporating reservoirs and resulting stranded, senescent cottonwood groves that plague other western rivers.

Having already picked up Clark's Fork, with the Bighorn, Tongue, and Powder Rivers to join downstream, the Yellowstone at Billings flashes the vigor of early middle age. Trout make room for channel cats; by Miles City, there will be paddlefish, ancient denizens of the continent's deep, inexorable center. Freighted with the wilderness legends and city stories of Plains tribes, explorers, trappers, ranchers, outlaws, sodbusters, miners, shopkeepers, empire builders, even college professors, the Yellowstone joins the Missouri just across the North Dakota line. On a map of North America, Big Muddy arcs gracefully across the continent like the grandest bough in the Mississippi's live oak crown.

~

The Mississippi. Old Man River. Father of Waters. Traveling the Great River Road toward Indiana after an inconclusive Twin Cities job interview, Cara, Tom, and I passed through river towns like Red Wing, Minnesota; La Crosse, Wisconsin; and Guttenberg, Iowa, where a small aquarium displayed gars, paddlefish, and other aquatic fauna of the big river. At Effigy Mounds National Monument, we walked among earthworks modeled into shapes of falcons and bears a millennium ago by Woodland period people whose motivations, despite centuries of speculation, remain unfathomed.

Leaving the mounds, we reached Dubuque's surprisingly monumental Victorian architecture, in part a legacy of river commerce, near sunset. It was dark when we passed over the Mississippi on the Gateway Suspension Bridge linking Clinton, Iowa, and East Clinton, Illinois. For me, the Father of Waters has always been a river of bridges: the Burlington Rail Bridge the California Zephyr crossed carrying me from Indiana to Salt Lake City; the cantilevered span at Caruthersville, Missouri, my family and I traversed en route from Utah to the Civil War battlefield at Shiloh; bridges at the Quad Cities, at Memphis and Saint Louis. Maybe because so many of my crossings have marked the midpoint of continental-scale journeys, the Mississippi makes for me the natural boundary between emigration and immigration, between leaving someplace and arriving somewhere else.

My first Mississippi bridge crossing was the I-10 span at Baton Rouge that 1982 morning on the bus from New Orleans to Lake Charles. A few months later, Cara and I traveled the delta to Grand Isle, the setting for Edna Pontellier's "awakening" in Kate Chopin's novel. Delayed at a drawbridge, we stood by the car at Galliano, watching a wheel of pelicans—now eclipsed, now a gleam of white as they banked—tilting in the sun above Bayou Lafourche shrimpboats. But we had to turn north to reach the Mississippi. Its outlet into the bayou cut off by a dam built in Chopin's day, the river no longer replenishes the stagnant channel and its starving wetlands; without the Mississippi's sustaining flow, the marshes south of New Orleans succumb to the encroaching sea.

I didn't know much local history at the time; nor was I aware of the Gulf dead zone sprawling like a sinister nudibranch off the Louisiana coast. Just where the life-sustaining river meets the life-generating sea, the egret and gator-haunted marsh giving way to the dolphin fields of the warm Gulf, the ocean runs out of oxygen. Topsoil, laden not only with the concentrated byproducts of industrialized farming but with waste from suburban landscaping and overloaded city sewer systems as well, chokes inshore shallows—the Chesapeake, Florida Bay—all along the American coasts. On a smaller scale, the Genesee pours a murky submerged delta into Lake Ontario. Our rivers, for better or worse, take us with them.

In "What the River Carries," the title piece in her 2012 essay collection, Lisa Knopp freights the Mississippi with cargo ranging from dissolved oxygen to the bodies of murder victims to philosophical principles. As they did for Sam Clemens, the great waterways of the American interior also carry for Knopp the personal sediment of memory and family history. The rivers of my own experience lead inexorably back to the Genesee. A canoe would be best; tracking upstream past the homes and graves of my parents and grandparents, portaging around the waterfalls at Rochester and Letchworth Park, would bring me to Kishketuck. With luck I'd get there in June, the month of my birth, just as evening hangs a net of nighthawks across the shallow, determined water.

～

*After the hills, the falls, the valley farms and brick warehouses, even the harbor foghorn's hollow pulse is swept into the sea. The road ends in a gravel lot. The boat pulls through a screen of alder or mangrove, the last attempt to hold back clamshells, plastic bags, anything that has been borrowed by the land. In front of you now is a wide bay, and in front of that is everywhere on Earth that you have not passed so far.*

# Coda

## Billings, Montana

Like Sitting Bull and frontiersman Luther Kelly, today's Yellowstone Valley inhabitants like the view. We like to watch ravens coast the updrafts. We like to trace mule deer paths through brushy ravines, to glimpse the quick scurry of a sagebrush lizard, to sniff out rumors of bobcats and lions.

From Kelly's grave atop the Rimrock cliffs, the prairie swells northward, past Billings Heights housing tracts, to the burned-over Bull Mountains. South, across the river, rise the humpbacked Pryors, and, to the southwest, the massive granite blocks that make up the Beartooths; crossing those shattered plateaus will get you to Yellowstone Park. Nearer at hand, muscled by refinery stacks and storage tanks, downtown Billings tucks into a river bend.

Going to the river is like traveling hundreds of miles east. Down there, the deer are whitetails, not mulies. Eagles and songbirds nest in healthy cottonwoods, compliments of the free-flowing Yellowstone. Eyed by great blue herons, softshell turtles patter between gravel bars.

One Christmas Bird Count, I tallied ducks from a riverfront siding while chickadees nabbed spilled grain around parked boxcars. The jackpot proved not so lucky for a certain raccoon. He must have been feasting when the BNSF freight—carrying wheat perhaps, more likely coal—rounded the bend. Coal, oil, and gas comprise eastern Montana's version of the bounty signaled by the Treasure State's motto, *oro y plata*. Maybe that explains why local politicians so eagerly fawned when a Denver entrepreneur announced plans to turn the Beartooth front into the next Bakken play. Boom and bust. Ask that raccoon.

People around here say spring greenup makes the prairie "look like Ireland." Not really. But the snow-streaked mountains, the outlandish yellow-orange blooms of prickly pear, canyon wren songs tripping down sandstone, are more than enough. Walking the rimtop path between winter's ice and summer's fires, we dream of mountain hikes, worry about bark beetles, about fracking and coal, and cling to one more year on this last best edge.

# Bibliography

Listed below are sources from which significant scientific, historical, and otherwise factual material included in the essays has been derived. Familiar literary and popular works, references made in passing, and, in a few cases, online sources no longer easily accessed by likely readers of this book, are simply identified in text at the point of reference.

*Part I*

**"Peregrines"**
Olear, M. "The Return of the Wanderer." *Zoogoer,* November–December, 2002.

**"Canadas"**
Bass, Rick. "Flights of Spring." *Audubon,* March 2004.

Drake, David and Joseph Paulin. "A Goose is a Goose? Identifying Differences Between Migratory and Resident Canada Geese." Fact Sheet, Rutgers Cooperative Extension, 2003.

"Galway Kinnell." In *Contemporary American Poetry,* Eighth Edition, edited by A. Poulin, Jr., and Michael Waters. 626–7. Boston: Houghton-Mifflin Company, 2006.

Grandy, J. W. and John Hadidian. "Making Peace with Canada Geese." *HSUS News,* Spring 1997.

Hestbeck, J. B. "Canada Geese in the Atlantic Flyway." In *Our Living Resources: A Report to the Nation on the Distribution, Abundance, and Health of U.S. Plants, Animals, and Ecosystems.* United States Department of the Interior, National Biological Service, 1995.

Leopold, Aldo. *A Sand County Almanac*. Oxford: Oxford University Press, 1949.

"1998–9 Canada Goose Hunting Season Announced." Press Release, New York State Department of Environmental Conservation. August 17, 1998.

Plum, Sydney Landon. *Solitary Goose*. Athens: University of Georgia Press, 2007.

Rising, Gerry. "On 'Subspecies' of the Canada Goose." *The Kingbird*, June, 2004.

Waytiuk, Judy. "Honk if You Love Canada Geese." *E Magazine*, November–December, 1996.

"When Geese Become a Problem." Fact Sheet, New York State Department of Environmental Conservation, Division of Fish, Wildlife, and Marine Resources and the US Department of Agriculture Animal and Plant Health Inspection Service, May, 2007.


**"Summertime"**

Mitchell, John G. "Down the Drain." *National Geographic*, September, 2002.

"Native Fish Found in U. S. Lake Ontario for First Time in 50 Years." Public Release, United States Geological Survey, 1998.

Petrie, Scott and Michael W. Schumer. "Waterfowl Responses to Zebra Mussels on the Lower Great Lakes." *Birding*, August, 2002.

Weseloh, D. V. and B. Collier. "The Rise of the Double-Crested Cormorant on the Great Lakes: Winning the War Against Contaminants." Fact Sheet, *Environment Canada*, 1995.


**"Thing in the Woods"**

"Five Young Black Bears May Be Prowling Region." *Democrat and Chronicle* (Rochester, NY), July 11, 2007.

Gallagher, Tim. *The Grail Bird*. Boston and New York: Houghton Mifflin, 2005.

Hoagland, Edward. "Up the Black to Chalkyitsik." In *Hoagland on Nature*. 237–94. Guilford, CT: Lyons Press, 2003.

Jackson, Jerome. "Perspectives in Ornithology." *The Auk* 123, no. 1 (January, 2006): 1–15.

Ortiz, Simon. "Comprehension." *Poetry East* 121 (Fall, 1986).

Schmid, Randolph E. "Experts Debate Sighting of the Ivory-Billed Woodpecker." *Star-Banner* (Ocala, FL), March 17, 2006.

Scherer, Glenn. "George Bush's War on Nature." *Salon*, January 6, 2003.

Souder, William. *Under a Wild Sky.* Minneapolis: Milkweed Editions, 2014.


*Part II*


"Travelers"

Barnard, Jeff and Jason Dearen. "Wayward Whale Delighted Observers Before Her Death." *Native American Times*, August 18, 2011.

Berry, Wendell. *The Unsettling of America.* San Francisco: Sierra Club Books, 1977.

Dasmann, Raymond. "Notice: Unaware Citizens of Biogeographical Provinces." *CoEvolution Quarterly*, Fall, 1976.

Goff, Andrew and Heidi Waters. "Whales. In A River." *North Coast Journal*, July 28, 2011.

Leskiw, Tom. "The Discovery of the Hawaiian Islands: A Case of Human-Bird Mutualism." In *The Watery World: Humans and the Sea.* Edited by V. Messier and N. Batra. 147–56. Newcastle-upon-Tyne, UK: Cambridge Scholars Press, 2010.

Powell, Hugh. "Scrubland Survivors: The Florida Scrub Jay." *All About Birds*, Cornell Laboratory of Ornithology, Autumn, 2008.

Sachs, Aaron. *The Humboldt Current.* New York: Viking, 2006.

Sherony, Dominic E. "The Fall Jaeger Migration on Lake Ontario." *Journal of Field Ornithology* 70, no. 1 (1997): 33–41.


"In Wonderland"

Allen, Kurt S. and Daniel F. Long. "Evaluation of the Douglas-Fir Beetle on the Shoshone National Forest, Wyoming." United States Forest Service, 2003.

Benson, Megan. "The Fight for the Crow Water: Part II." *Montana: The Magazine of Western History*, Spring 2008.

Cerulean, Susan. *Tracking Desire: A Journey after Swallow-Tailed Kites.* Athens and London: University of Georgia Press, 2005.

Graetz, Rick and Susie Graetz. *Crow Country: Montana's Crow Tribe of Indians.* Billings, MT: Northern Rockies Publishing Company, 2000.

Schullery, Paul. *Searching for Yellowstone.* Helena: Montana Historical Society Press, 2004.

Stark, Mike. "Bark Beetles Killing More Douglas Fir." *Billings Gazette,* July 16, 2002.

Westerling, Anthony, Hugo Hidalgo, Dan Cayan, and Tom Swetnam. "Warming and Earlier Spring Increase Western U.S. Forest Wildfire Activity." *Science* 313, no. 5789 (2006): 940–3.

**"The Woods are Burning"**

Advisory Board on Wildlife Management, A. Starker Leopold, chair. "Wildlife Management in the National Parks." *National Park Service,* 1963.

"The Age of Megafires." *60 Minutes,* CBSN, December 30, 2007.

Calloway, Colin. *One Long Winter Count.* Lincoln: University of Nebraska Press, 2003.

Leatherman, D. A., I. Aguayo, and T. M. Mehall. "Mountain Pine Beetle." Fact Sheet, Colorado State University's Extension, April 2007.

McKibben, Bill. "Climate Change and the Unraveling of Creation." *The Christian Century,* December 8, 1999.

Pyne, Stephen. "Passing the Torch." *The American Scholar* 77, no. 2 (Spring 2008): 22–3.

Schullery, Paul. *Mountain Time.* Albuquerque: University of New Mexico Press, 2008.

Smith, Jeremy. "Red Scare." *Montana,* September/October 2008.

Tyre, Daniel B. "Moose Population History on the Northern Yellowstone Winter Range." *Alces* 42, 2006: 133–49.

"Vast Yellowstone Fire Now Seen as Unstoppable Natural Cataclysm." *New York Times,* December 12, 1989.

Ward, Peter D. *Out of Thin Air.* Washington, DC: Joseph Henry Press, 2006.

Westerling, Anthony, Hugo Hidalgo, Dan Cayan, and Tom Swetnam. "Warming and Earlier Spring Increase Western U.S. Forest Wildfire Activity." *Science* 313, no. 5789 (2006): 940–3.

Wuerthner, George. "Land Use Planning Must Address Wildfire Plain." *New West Network,* June 18, 2007.

"The Yellowstone Fires of 1988." *Yellowstone Today,* Summer 2008.

"Red Summer"

"Climate Change." *Yellowstone Today*, Summer 2010.

"Forest Insect Pests." *Greater Yellowstone Science Learning Center*, April 14, 2012.

Kurz, W. A., et al. "Mountain Pine Beetle and Forest Carbon Feedback to Climate Change." *Nature* 452 (April, 2008): 987–90.

Logan, Jesse A., William W. MacFarlane, and Louisa Willcox. "Whitebark Pine Vulnerability to Climate-Driven Mountain Pine Beetle Disturbance in the Greater Yellowstone Ecosystem." *Ecological Applications* 20 no. 4 (June, 2010): 895–902.

Marschall, Mark and Joy Sellers Marschall. *Yellowstone Trails.* Tenth Edition. Yellowstone National Park/Yellowstone Association, 2013.

*Mountain Pine Beetle on the Front Range: What to Know.* Brochure. United States Forest Service, 2009.

"Pine Beetles Infest 2.7M Acres of Montana Forest." *Billings Gazette*, January 21, 2010.

"Pine Beetle Runs Out of Food, B.C. Mills to Run Out of Wood." *Vancouver Sun*, September 22, 2009.

Romme, W. H, et al. "Recent Insect Outbreaks and Fire Risk in Colorado Forests: A Brief Synthesis of Relevant Research." White Paper, Colorado Forest Restoration Institute, 2006.

Stark, Mike. "Insects Take Over Thousands of Yellowstone Acres." *Billings Gazette*, August 10, 2005.

Stephenson, Shauna. "Grizzlies Only Scratch the Surface of What It Will Mean to Lose the Whitebark Pine." *NewWest Network*, August 31, 2010.

Turner, Jack. *Travels in the Greater Yellowstone*, Thomas Dunne Books, 2008.

Viegas, Jennifer. "Heavy Metal Music, Other Sounds, Aimed at Beetle Pests." *Discovery News*, February 10, 2010.

"Whitebark Pine to be Designated a Candidate for Endangered Species Protection." Press Release, United States Forest Service, July 18, 2011.

"White Pine Blister Rust." *High Elevation White Pines.* United States Forest Service, no date.

Willcox, Luisa A. "Whitebark Pine: Functionally Gone in Much of the Greater Yellowstone." *Huffington Post*, May 25, 2011.

Wohl, Ellen. *Of Rock and Rivers.* Berkeley: University of California Press, 2009.

Wuerthner, George. "Beetle Hysteria Again." *NewWest Network*, June 30, 2009.

**"Invaders"**

Achenbach, Joel. "When Yellowstone Explodes." *National Geographic*, August 2009.

*"E. C. Waters* Left to Rot in Yellowstone National Park." *Billings Gazette*, July 16, 2007.

Gresswell, Robert. "Scientific Review Panel Evaluation of the National Park Service Lake Trout Suppression Program in Yellowstone Lake." *United States Geological Survey, Northern Rocky Mountain Science Center*, 2009.

Makerawicz, Joseph A. T. "New York's North Coast: A Troubled Coastline." Technical Report, Water Resource Board, Finger Lakes–Lake Ontario Watershed Protection Alliance, 2000.

Munro, Andrew R., Thomas E. McMahon and James Ruzycki. "Natural Chemical Markers Identify Source and Date of Introduction of an Exotic Species: Lake Trout (*Salvalimus namaycush*) in Yellowstone Lake." *Canadian Journal of Fisheries and Aquatic Sciences* 62, no. 1 (2005): 79–87.

"Native vs. Non-native Fish: A Difficult Issue." *Feature Series* 2, no. 1, United States. Fish and Wildlife Service Mountain Prairie Region, no date.

"Sea Lamprey Control in the Great Lakes." *Great Lakes Fishery Commission*, no date.

Varley, John and Paul Schullery. *Yellowstone Fishes: Ecology, History and Angling in the Park.* Mechanicsburg, PA: Stackpole Books, 1998.

"Wild Atlantic Salmon Found in New York's Salmon River." Press Release, United States Geological Survey, August 19, 2009.

**"Confluence"**

Knopp, Lisa. *What the River Carries.* Columbia: University of Missouri Press, 2012.